THE NEW DAY
POWER OF POSITIVITY

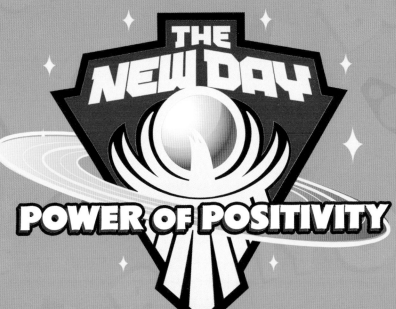

BOOM! STUDIOS

ASSISTANT EDITOR
KENZIE RZONCA

SERIES DESIGNER
GRACE PARK

EDITORS
AMANDA LaFRANCO AND
ELIZABETH BREI

COLLECTION DESIGNER
MICHELLE ANKLEY

SENIOR EDITOR
ERIC HARBURN

WWE: The New Day, August 2022. Published by BOOM! Studios, a division of Boom Entertainment, Inc. WWE is ™ & © 2022 WWE. All WWE programming, talent names, images, likenesses, slogans, wrestling moves, trademarks, logos and copyrights are the exclusive property of WWE and its subsidiaries. All other trademarks, logos and copyrights are the property of their respective owners. © 2022 WWE. All rights reserved. BOOM! Studios™ and the BOOM! Studios logo are trademarks of Boom Entertainment, Inc., registered in various countries and categories. All characters, events, and institutions depicted herein are fictional. Any similarity between any of the names, characters, persons, events, and/or institutions in this publication to actual names, characters, and persons, whether living or dead, events, and/ or institutions is unintended and purely coincidental. BOOM! Studios does not read or accept unsolicited submissions of ideas, stories, or artwork.

BOOM! Studios, 5670 Wilshire Boulevard, Suite 400, Los Angeles, CA 90036-5679. Printed in China. First Printing.

ISBN: 978-1-68415-636-8, eISBN: 978-1-64668-051-1

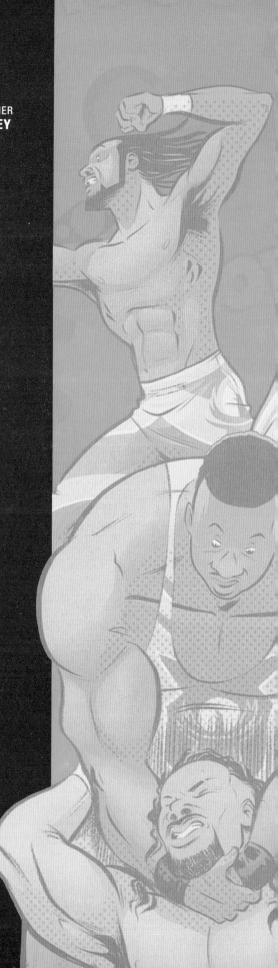

THE NEW DAY
POWER of POSITIVITY

WRITTEN BY
EVAN NARCISSE &
AUSTIN WALKER

ILLUSTRATED BY
DANIEL BAYLISS

LETTERED BY
DC HOPKINS

COVER BY
DANIEL BAYLISS

SPECIAL THANKS TO **CHRIS ROSA, STEVE PANTALEO,
CHAD BARBASH, BEN MAYER, JOHN JONES,
STAN STANSKI, LAUREN DIENES-MIDDLEN,**
AND EVERYONE AT WWE.

CHAPTER
ONE

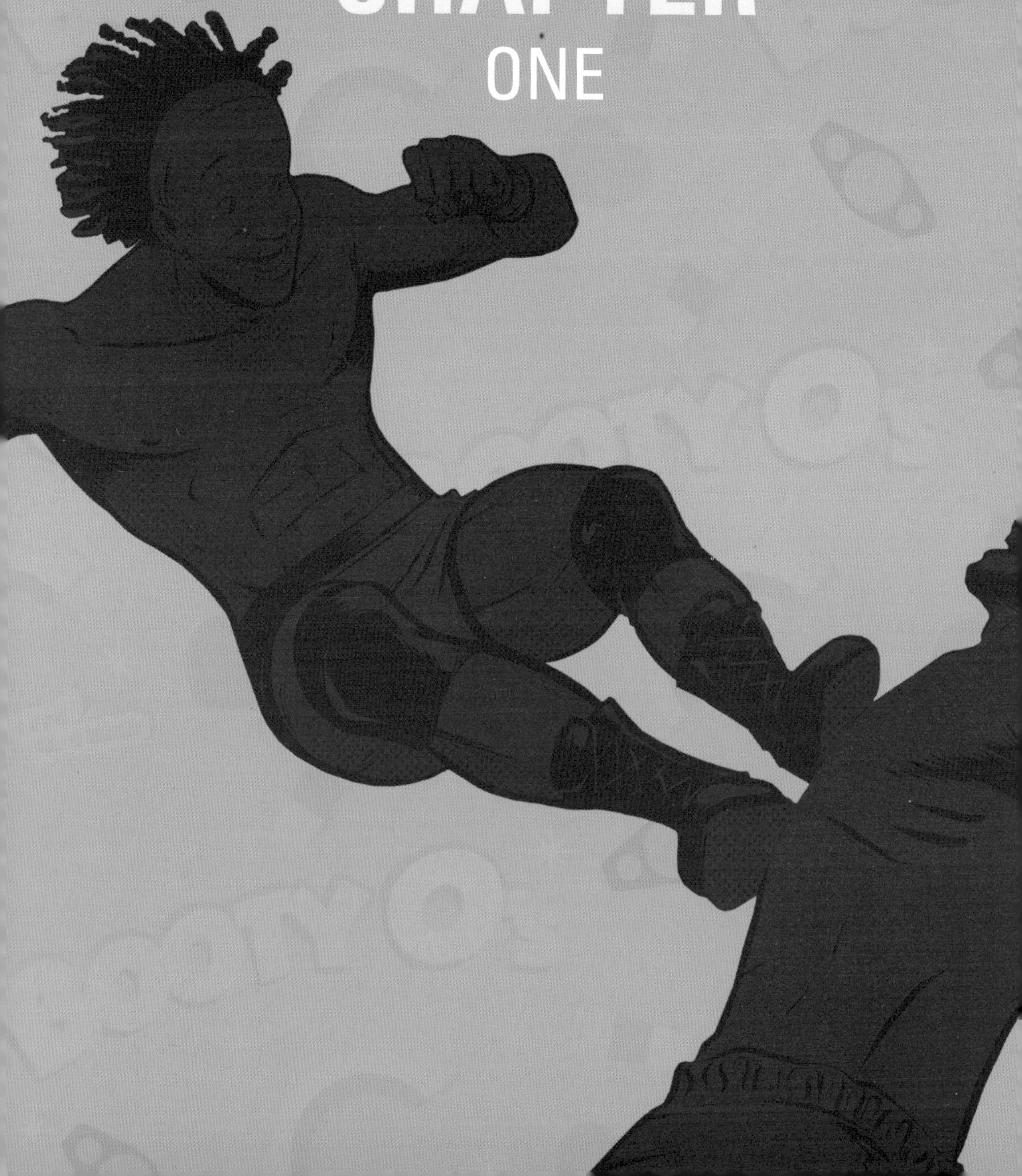

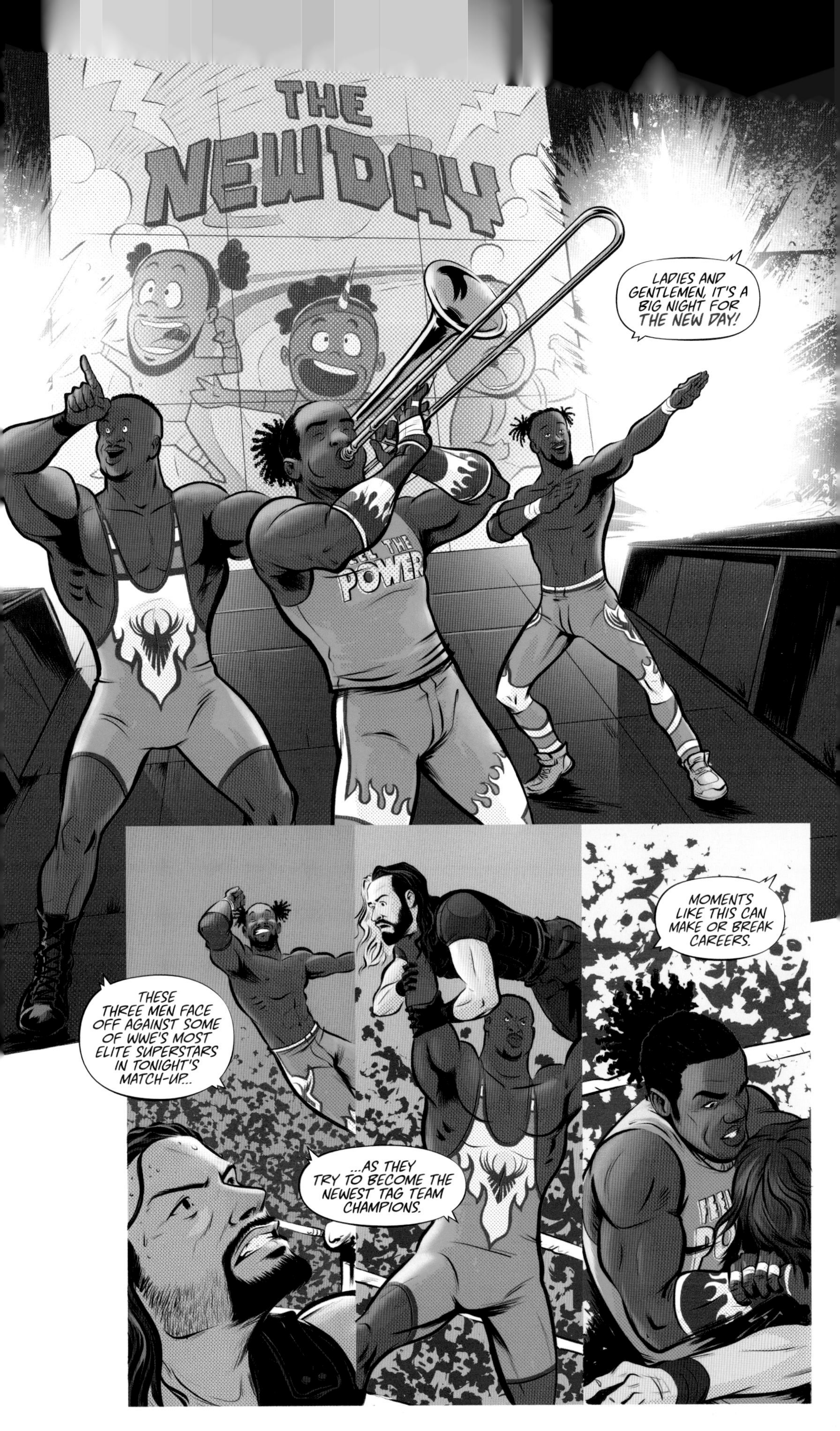
THE NEW DAY
LADIES AND GENTLEMEN, IT'S A BIG NIGHT FOR THE NEW DAY!
THESE THREE MEN FACE OFF AGAINST SOME OF WWE'S MOST ELITE SUPERSTARS IN TONIGHT'S MATCH-UP...
...AS THEY TRY TO BECOME THE NEWEST TAG TEAM CHAMPIONS.
MOMENTS LIKE THIS CAN MAKE OR BREAK CAREERS.

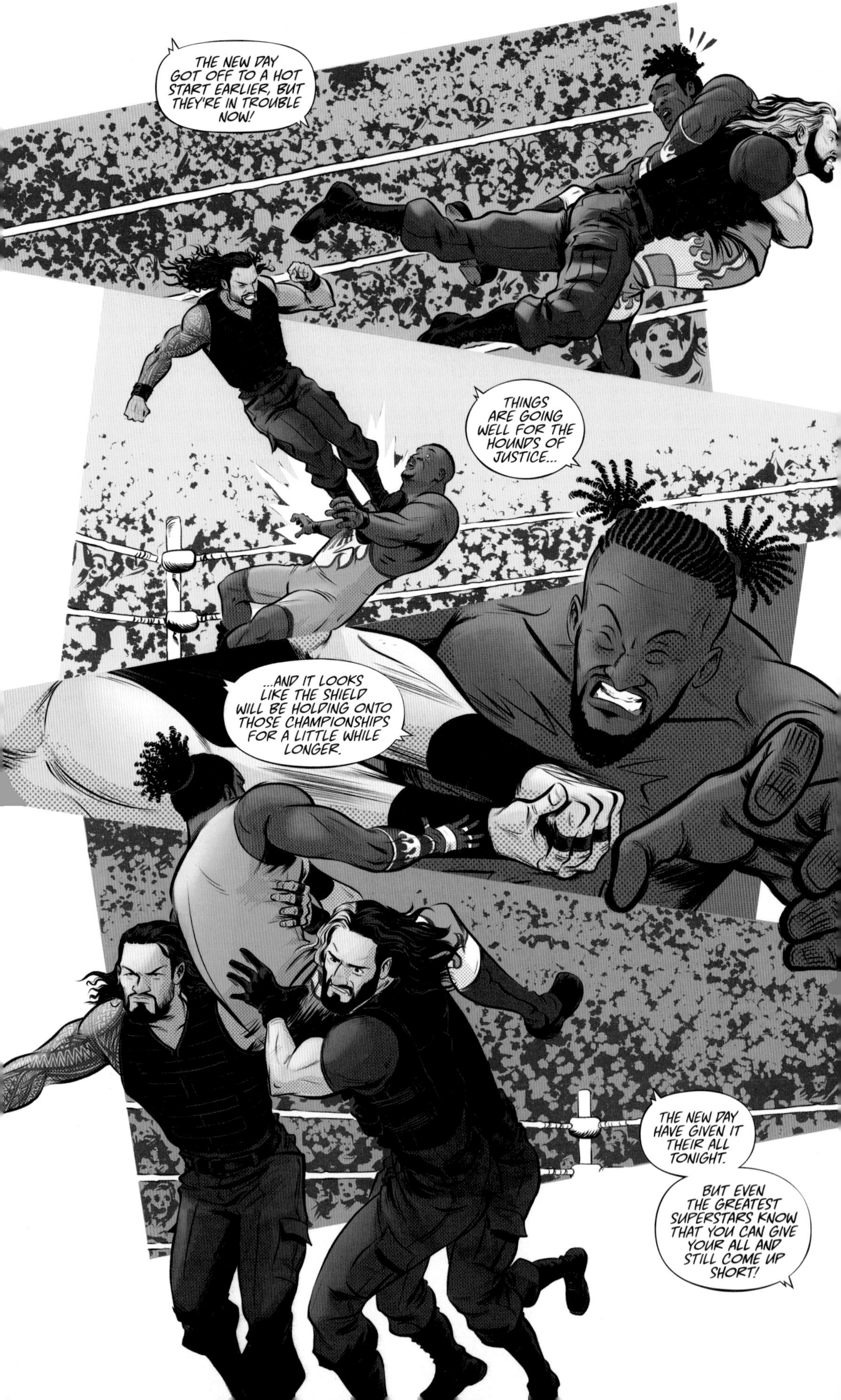
THE NEW DAY GOT OFF TO A HOT START EARLIER, BUT THEY'RE IN TROUBLE NOW!
THINGS ARE GOING WELL FOR THE HOUNDS OF JUSTICE...
...AND IT LOOKS LIKE THE SHIELD WILL BE HOLDING ONTO THOSE CHAMPIONSHIPS FOR A LITTLE WHILE LONGER.
THE NEW DAY HAVE GIVEN IT THEIR ALL TONIGHT.
BUT EVEN THE GREATEST SUPERSTARS KNOW THAT YOU CAN GIVE YOUR ALL AND STILL COME UP SHORT!

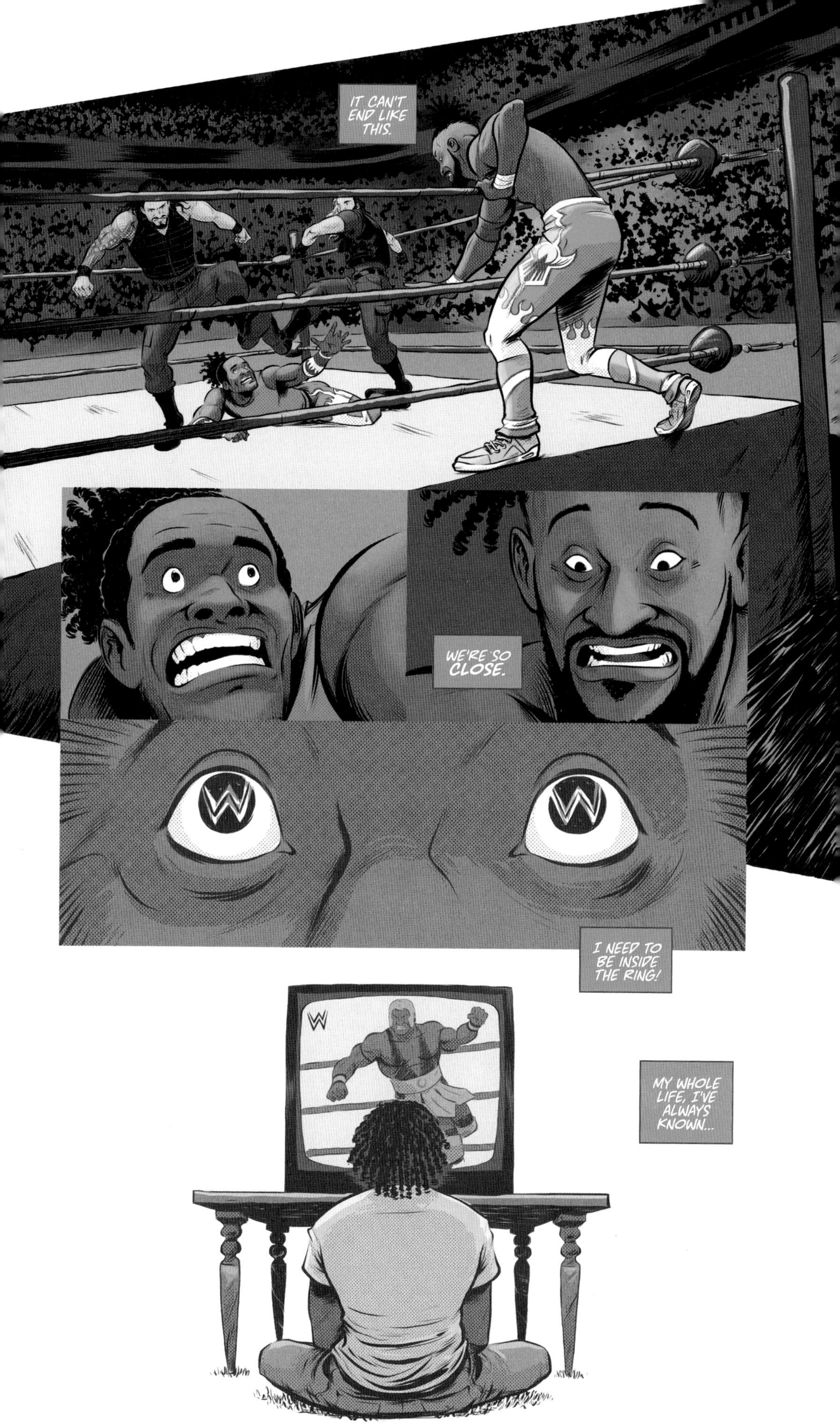
IT CAN'T END LIKE THIS.
WE'RE SO CLOSE.
I NEED TO BE INSIDE THE RING!
MY WHOLE LIFE, I'VE ALWAYS KNOWN...

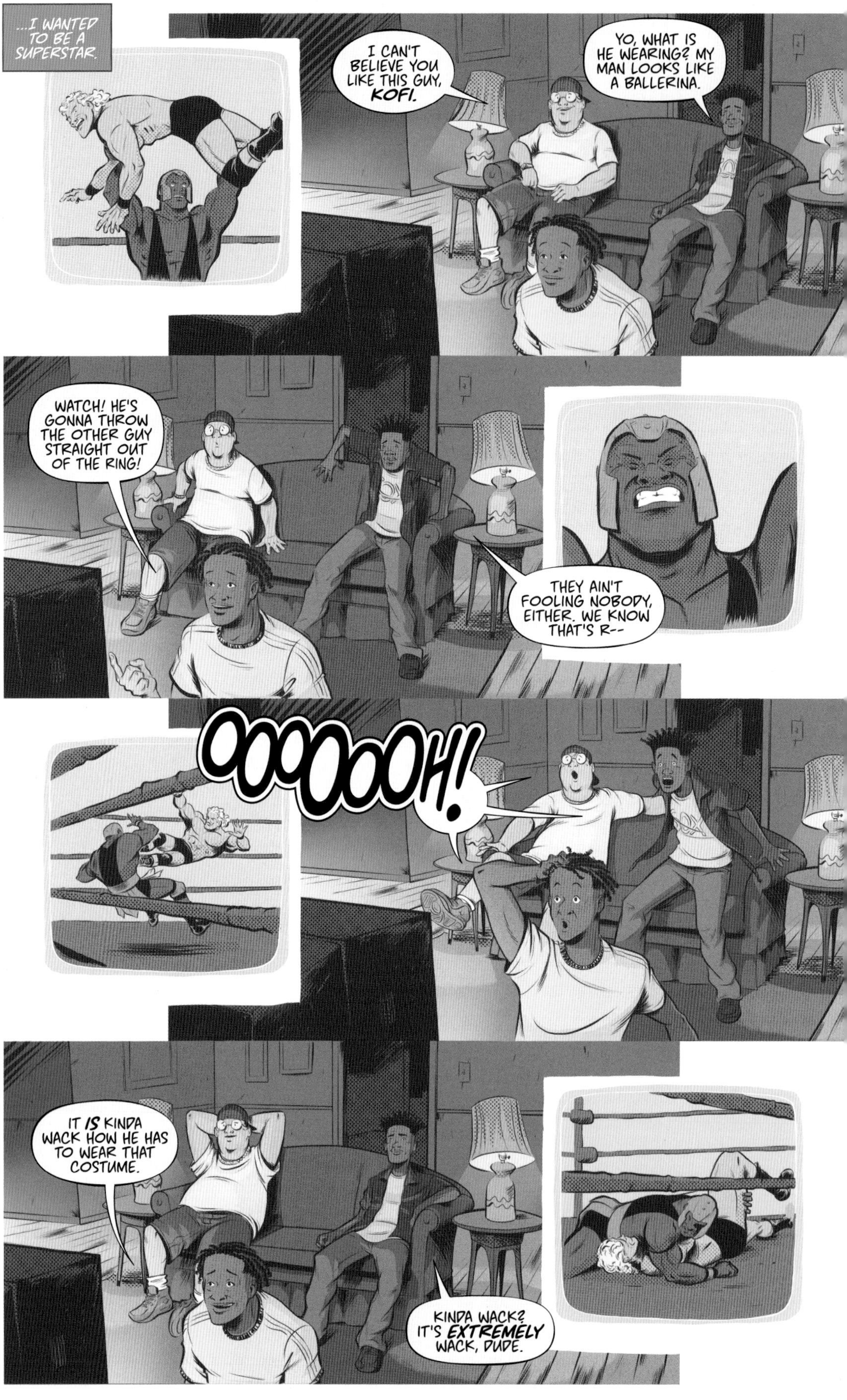
...I WANTED TO BE A SUPERSTAR.
I CAN'T BELIEVE YOU LIKE THIS GUY, KOFI.
YO, WHAT IS HE WEARING? MY MAN LOOKS LIKE A BALLERINA.
WATCH! HE'S GONNA THROW THE OTHER GUY STRAIGHT OUT OF THE RING!
THEY AIN'T FOOLING NOBODY, EITHER. WE KNOW THAT'S R--
OOOOOOOH!
IT IS KINDA WACK HOW HE HAS TO WEAR THAT COSTUME.
KINDA WACK? IT'S EXTREMELY WACK, DUDE.

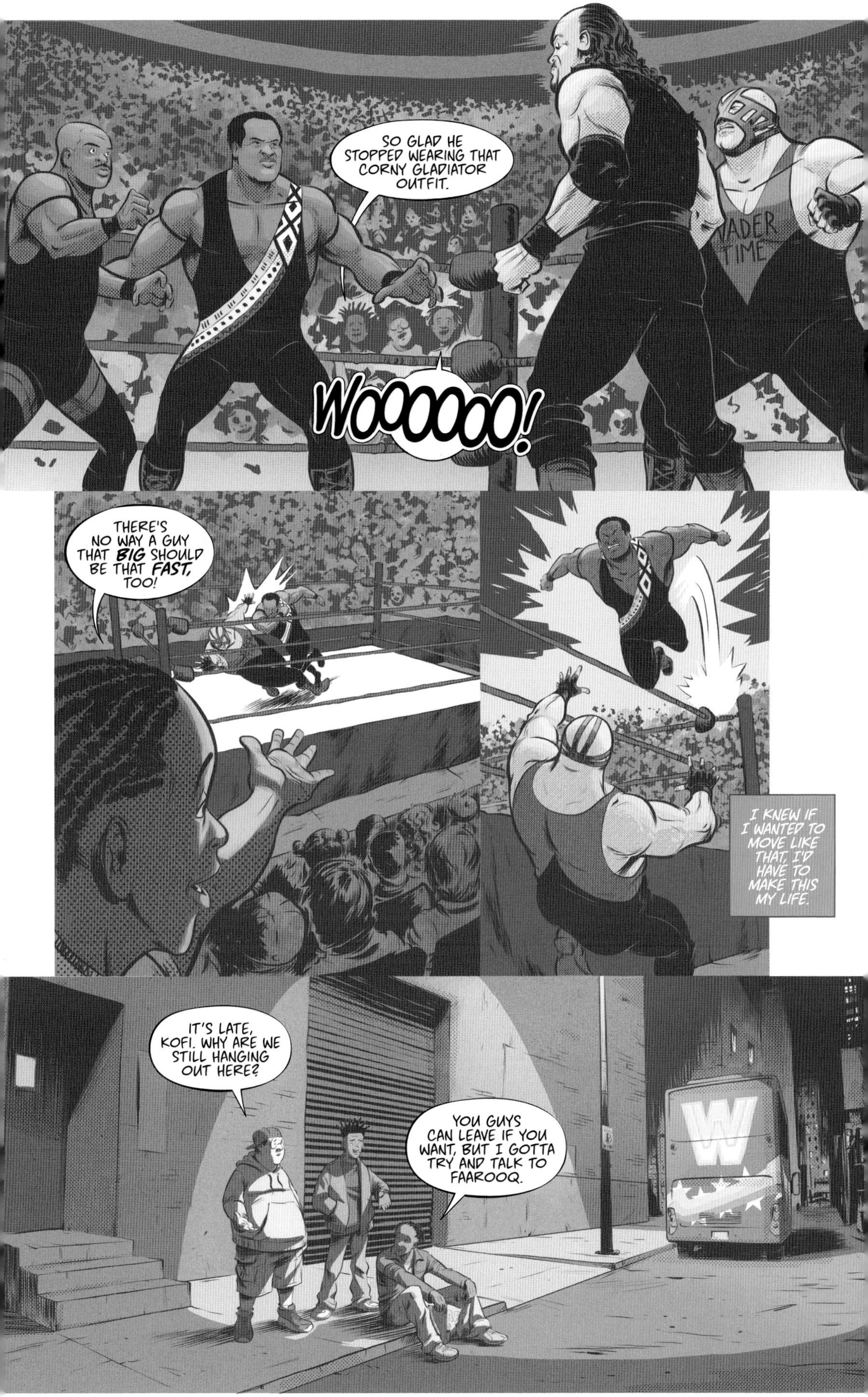

SO GLAD HE STOPPED WEARING THAT CORNY GLADIATOR OUTFIT.
VADER TIME
WOOOOOO!
THERE'S NO WAY A GUY THAT BIG SHOULD BE THAT FAST, TOO!
I KNEW IF I WANTED TO MOVE LIKE THAT, I'D HAVE TO MAKE THIS MY LIFE.
IT'S LATE, KOFI. WHY ARE WE STILL HANGING OUT HERE?
YOU GUYS CAN LEAVE IF YOU WANT, BUT I GOTTA TRY AND TALK TO FAAROOQ.

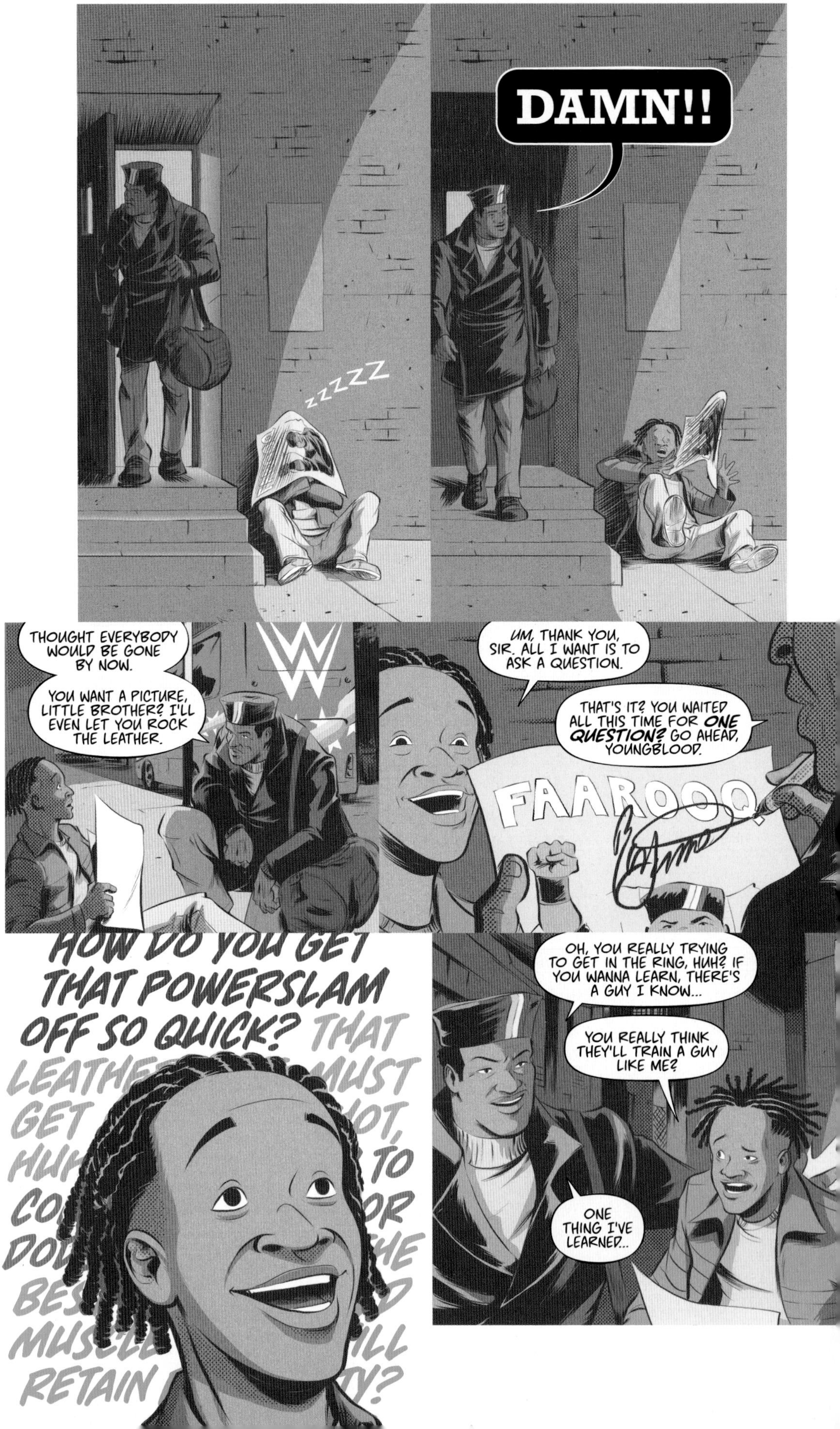
ZZZZZ
DAMN!!
THOUGHT EVERYBODY WOULD BE GONE BY NOW.
YOU WANT A PICTURE, LITTLE BROTHER? I'LL EVEN LET YOU ROCK THE LEATHER.
UM, THANK YOU, SIR. ALL I WANT IS TO ASK A QUESTION.
THAT'S IT? YOU WAITED ALL THIS TIME FOR ONE QUESTION? GO AHEAD, YOUNGBLOOD.
FAAROOQ
HOW DO YOU GET THAT POWERSLAM OFF SO QUICK? THAT
OH, YOU REALLY TRYING TO GET IN THE RING, HUH? IF YOU WANNA LEARN, THERE'S A GUY I KNOW...
YOU REALLY THINK THEY'LL TRAIN A GUY LIKE ME?
ONE THING I'VE LEARNED...

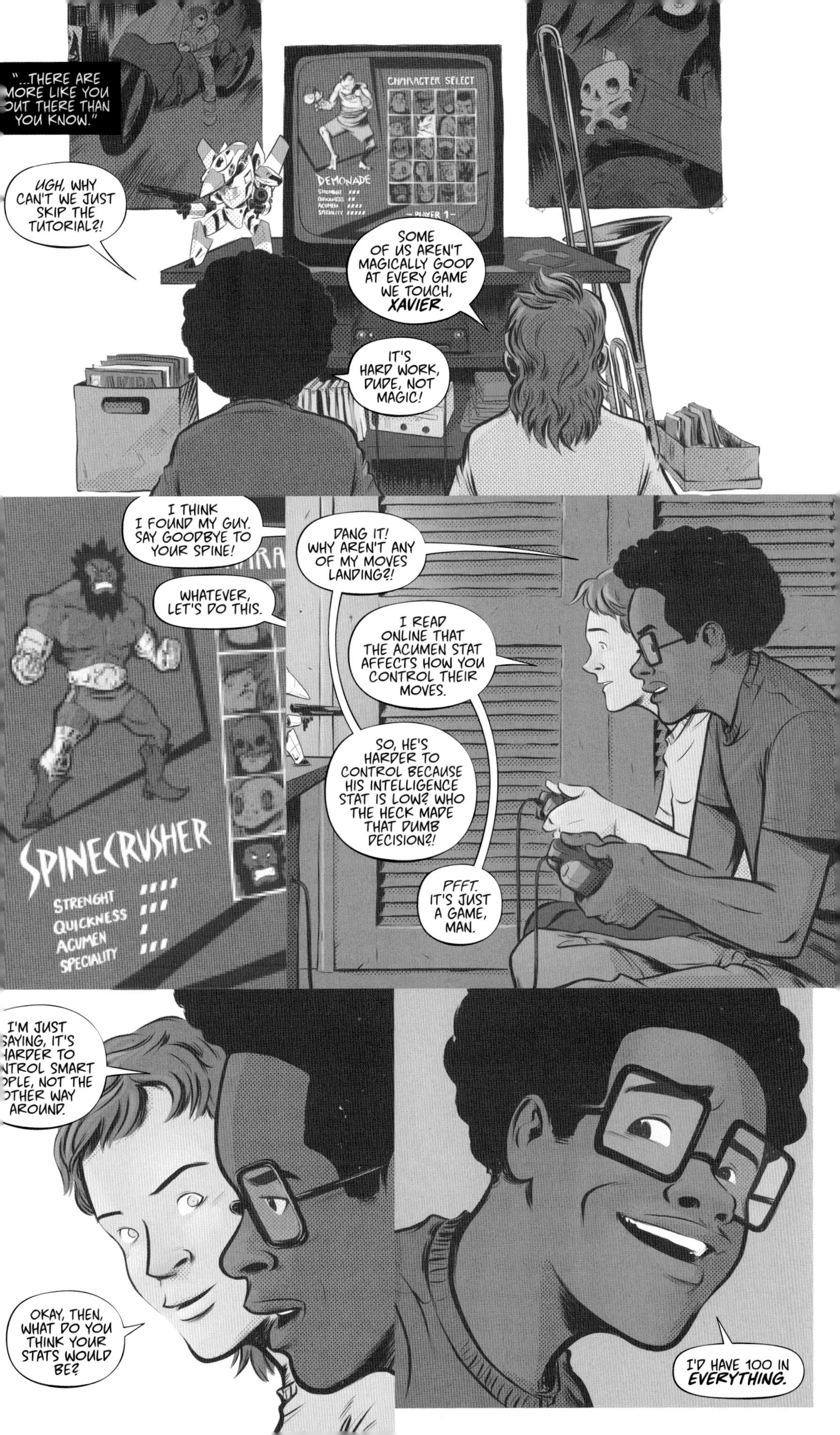
"...THERE ARE MORE LIKE YOU OUT THERE THAN YOU KNOW."
CHARACTER SELECT
DEMONADE
STRENGHT
QUICKNESS
ACUMEN
SPECIALITY
— PLAYER 1 —
UGH, WHY CAN'T WE JUST SKIP THE TUTORIAL?!
SOME OF US AREN'T MAGICALLY GOOD AT EVERY GAME WE TOUCH, XAVIER.
IT'S HARD WORK, DUDE, NOT MAGIC!
I THINK I FOUND MY GUY. SAY GOODBYE TO YOUR SPINE!
WHATEVER, LET'S DO THIS.
DANG IT! WHY AREN'T ANY OF MY MOVES LANDING?!
I READ ONLINE THAT THE ACUMEN STAT AFFECTS HOW YOU CONTROL THEIR MOVES.
SO, HE'S HARDER TO CONTROL BECAUSE HIS INTELLIGENCE STAT IS LOW? WHO THE HECK MADE THAT DUMB DECISION?!
PFFT. IT'S JUST A GAME, MAN.
SPINECRUSHER
STRENGHT
QUICKNESS
ACUMEN
SPECIALITY
I'M JUST SAYING, IT'S HARDER TO NTROL SMART OPLE, NOT THE OTHER WAY AROUND.
OKAY, THEN, WHAT DO YOU THINK YOUR STATS WOULD BE?
I'D HAVE 100 IN EVERYTHING.

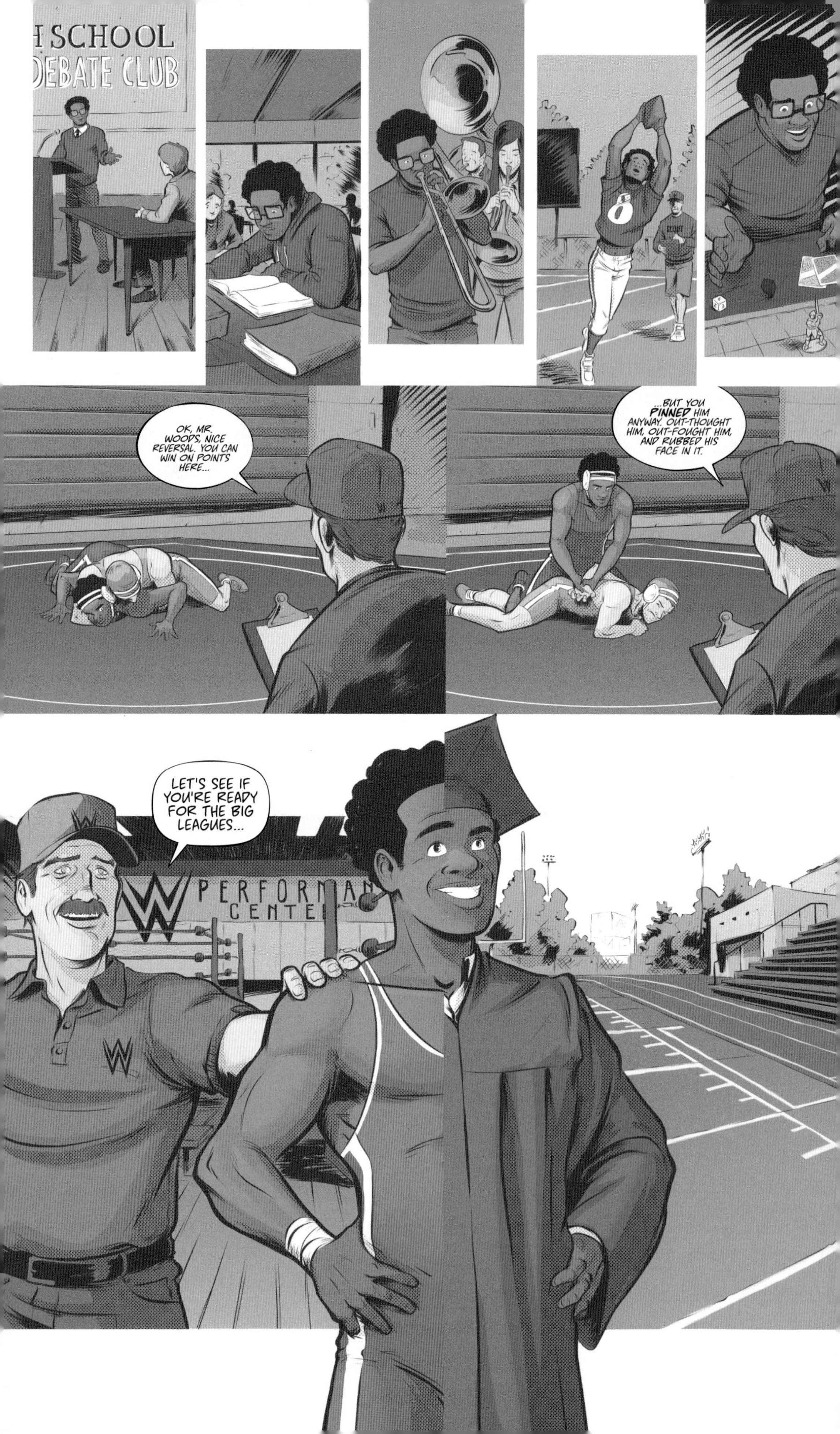
H SCHOOL
DEBATE CLUB
OK, MR. WOODS, NICE REVERSAL. YOU CAN WIN ON POINTS HERE...
...BUT YOU PINNED HIM ANYWAY. OUT-THOUGHT HIM, OUT-FOUGHT HIM, AND RUBBED HIS FACE IN IT.
LET'S SEE IF YOU'RE READY FOR THE BIG LEAGUES...
PERFORMAN
CENTE

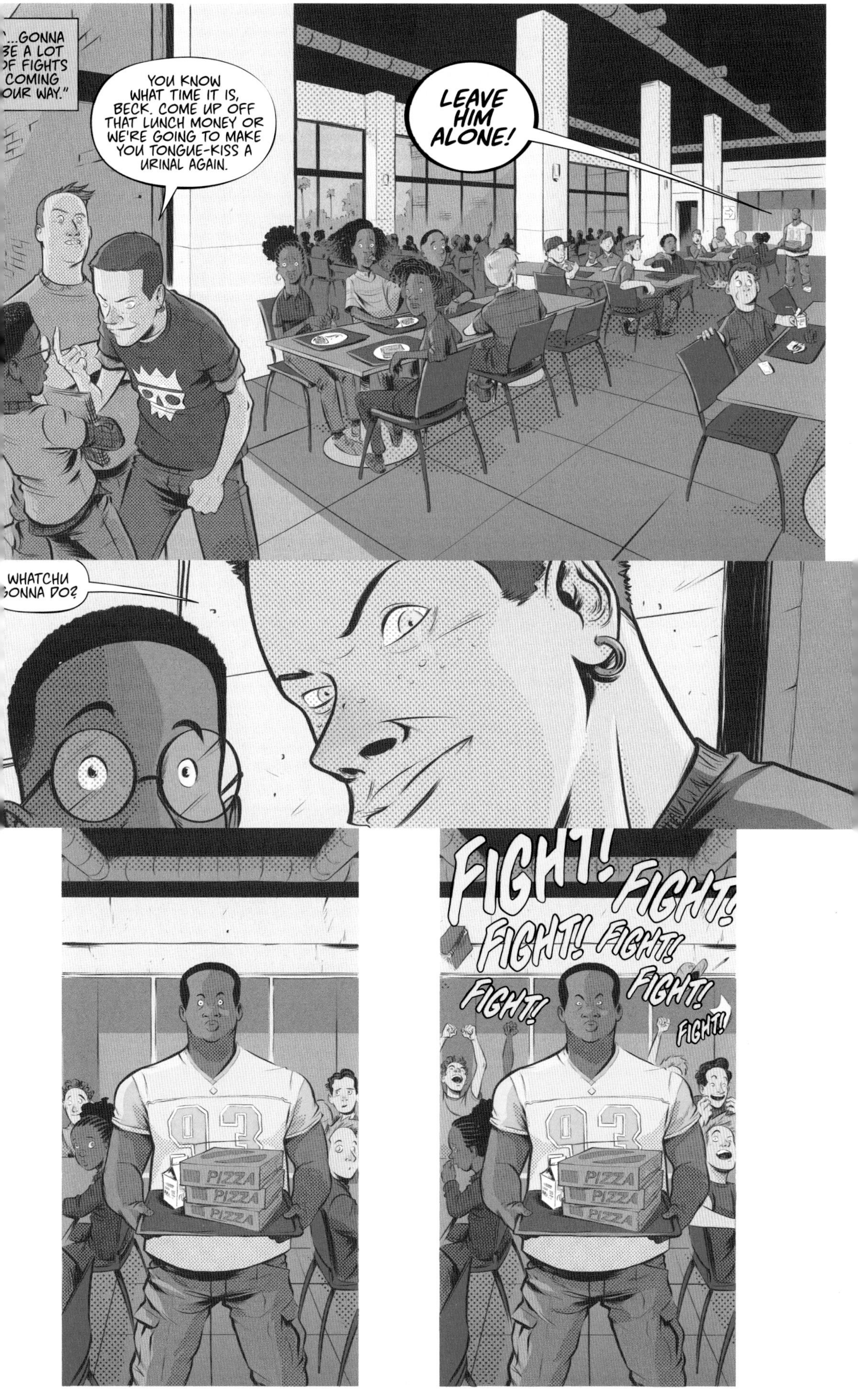
"...GONNA BE A LOT OF FIGHTS COMING OUR WAY."
YOU KNOW WHAT TIME IT IS, BECK. COME UP OFF THAT LUNCH MONEY OR WE'RE GOING TO MAKE YOU TONGUE-KISS A URINAL AGAIN.
LEAVE HIM ALONE!
WHATCHU GONNA DO?
PIZZA
PIZZA
PIZZA
FIGHT! FIGHT! FIGHT! FIGHT! FIGHT! FIGHT! FIGHT!

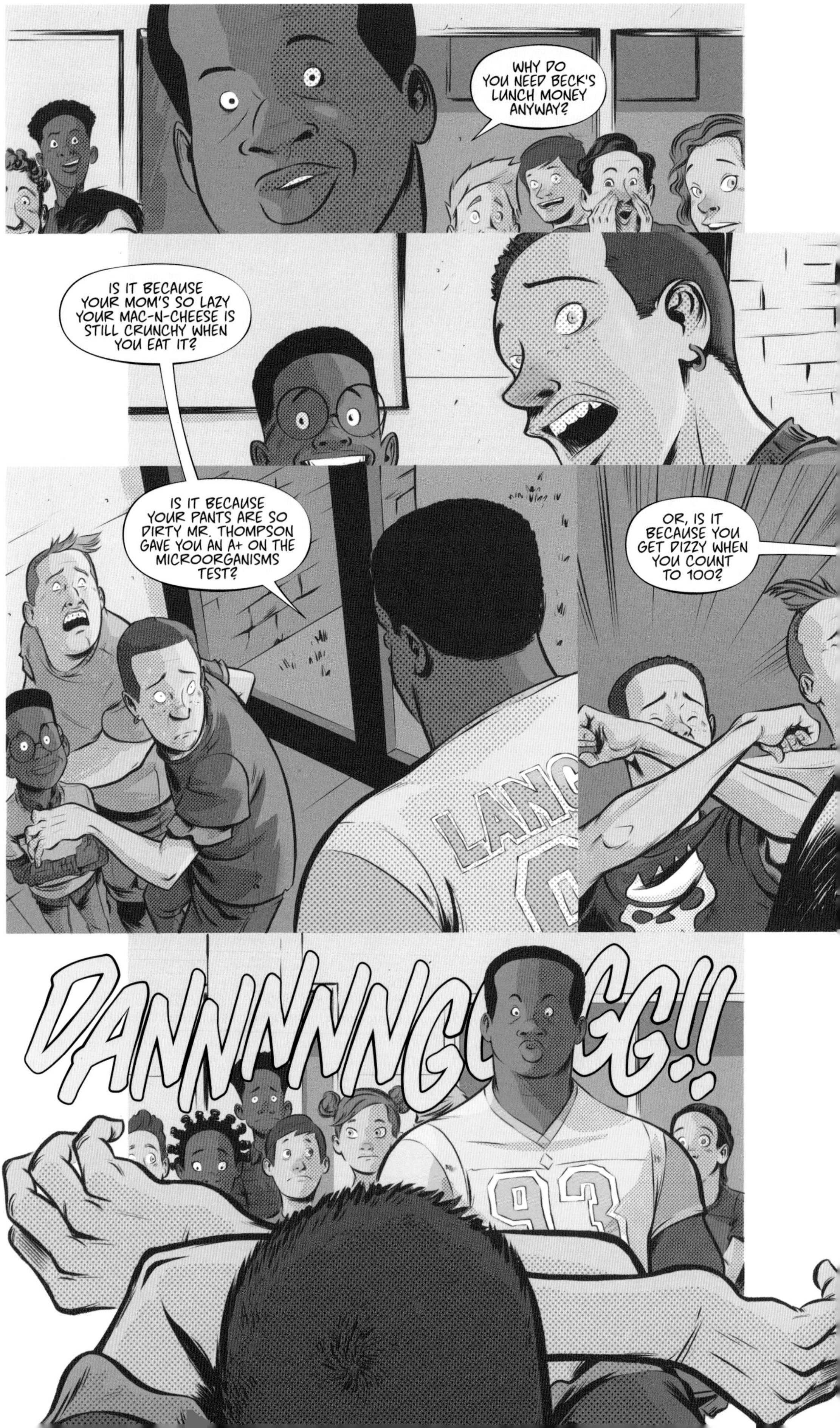
WHY DO YOU NEED BECK'S LUNCH MONEY ANYWAY?
IS IT BECAUSE YOUR MOM'S SO LAZY YOUR MAC-N-CHEESE IS STILL CRUNCHY WHEN YOU EAT IT?
IS IT BECAUSE YOUR PANTS ARE SO DIRTY MR. THOMPSON GAVE YOU AN A+ ON THE MICROORGANISMS TEST?
OR, IS IT BECAUSE YOU GET DIZZY WHEN YOU COUNT TO 100?
DANNNNNGGGGG!!
93

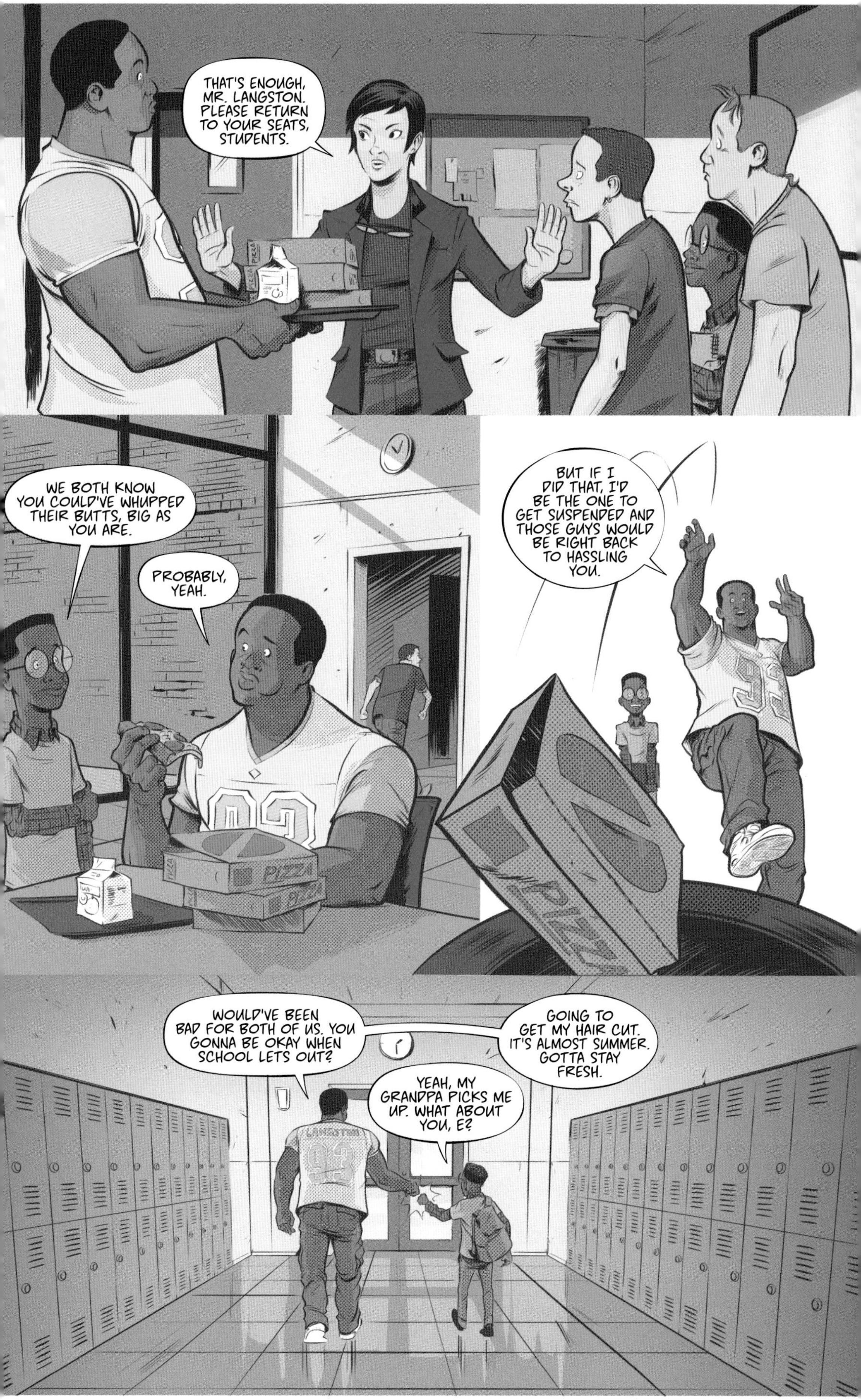
THAT'S ENOUGH, MR. LANGSTON. PLEASE RETURN TO YOUR SEATS, STUDENTS.
WE BOTH KNOW YOU COULD'VE WHUPPED THEIR BUTTS, BIG AS YOU ARE.
PROBABLY, YEAH.
BUT IF I DID THAT, I'D BE THE ONE TO GET SUSPENDED AND THOSE GUYS WOULD BE RIGHT BACK TO HASSLING YOU.
WOULD'VE BEEN BAD FOR BOTH OF US. YOU GONNA BE OKAY WHEN SCHOOL LETS OUT?
YEAH, MY GRANDPA PICKS ME UP. WHAT ABOUT YOU, E?
GOING TO GET MY HAIR CUT. IT'S ALMOST SUMMER. GOTTA STAY FRESH.

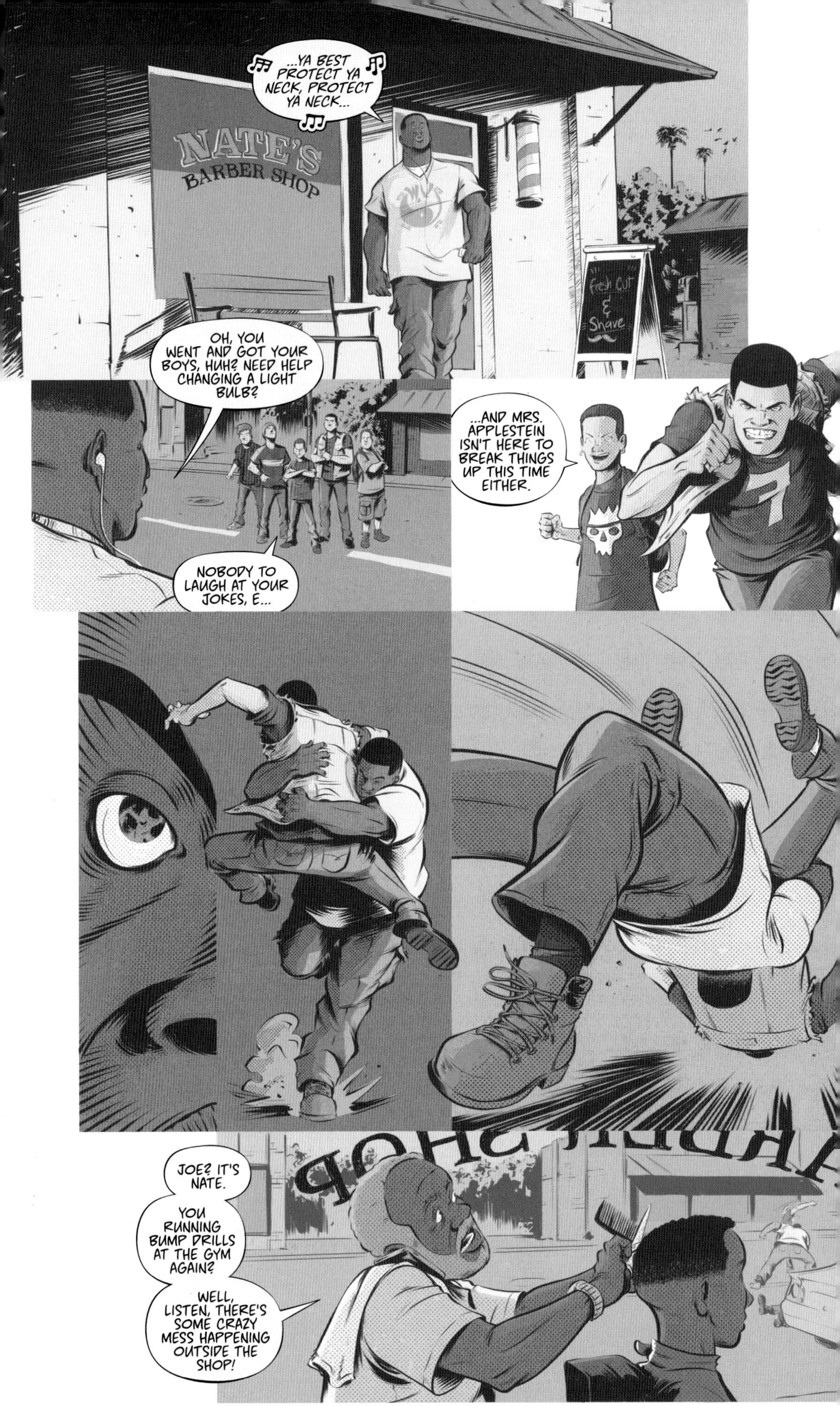
...YA BEST PROTECT YA NECK, PROTECT YA NECK...
NATE'S BARBER SHOP
Fresh Cut & Shave
OH, YOU WENT AND GOT YOUR BOYS, HUH? NEED HELP CHANGING A LIGHT BULB?
NOBODY TO LAUGH AT YOUR JOKES, E...
...AND MRS. APPLESTEIN ISN'T HERE TO BREAK THINGS UP THIS TIME EITHER.
JOE? IT'S NATE.
YOU RUNNING BUMP DRILLS AT THE GYM AGAIN?
WELL, LISTEN, THERE'S SOME CRAZY MESS HAPPENING OUTSIDE THE SHOP!

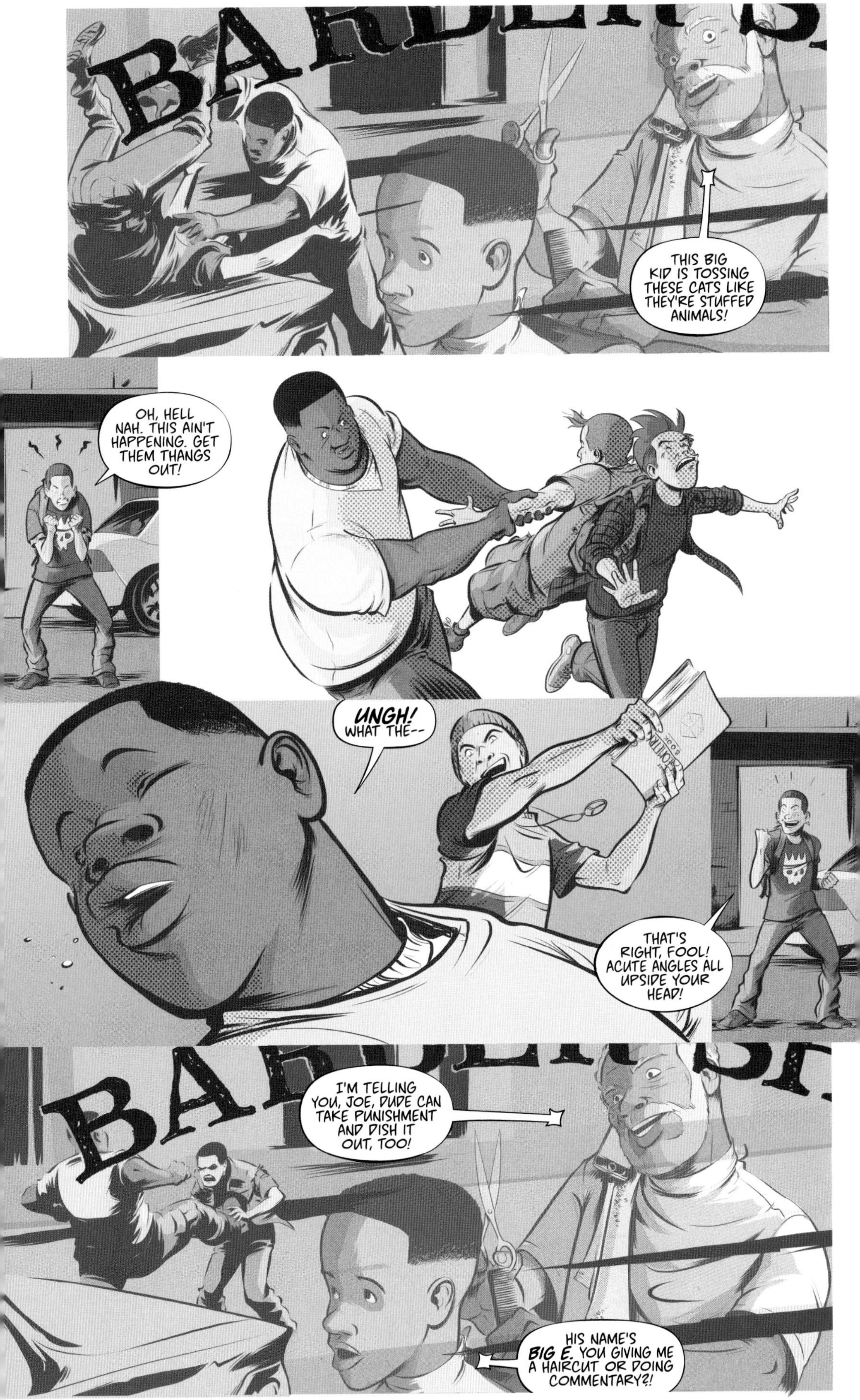
THIS BIG KID IS TOSSING THESE CATS LIKE THEY'RE STUFFED ANIMALS!
OH, HELL NAH. THIS AIN'T HAPPENING. GET THEM THANGS OUT!
UNGH! WHAT THE--
THAT'S RIGHT, FOOL! ACUTE ANGLES ALL UPSIDE YOUR HEAD!
I'M TELLING YOU, JOE, DUDE CAN TAKE PUNISHMENT AND DISH IT OUT, TOO!
HIS NAME'S BIG E. YOU GIVING ME A HAIRCUT OR DOING COMMENTARY?!

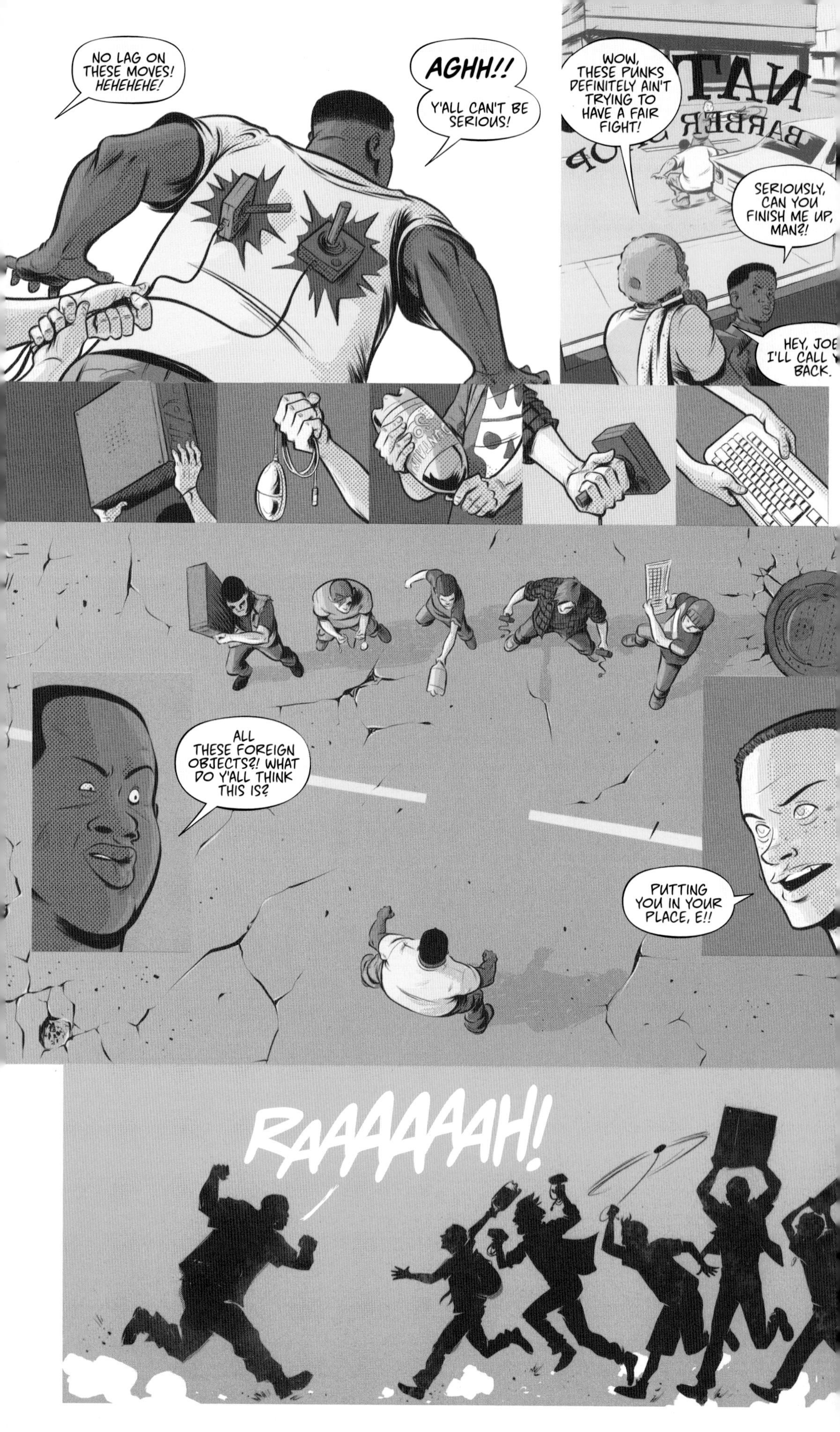
NO LAG ON THESE MOVES! HEHEHEHE!
AGHH!!
Y'ALL CAN'T BE SERIOUS!
NAT
BARBER SHOP
WOW, THESE PUNKS DEFINITELY AIN'T TRYING TO HAVE A FAIR FIGHT!
SERIOUSLY, CAN YOU FINISH ME UP, MAN?!
HEY, JOE I'LL CALL BACK.
ALL THESE FOREIGN OBJECTS?! WHAT DO Y'ALL THINK THIS IS?
PUTTING YOU IN YOUR PLACE, E!!
RAAAAAAH!

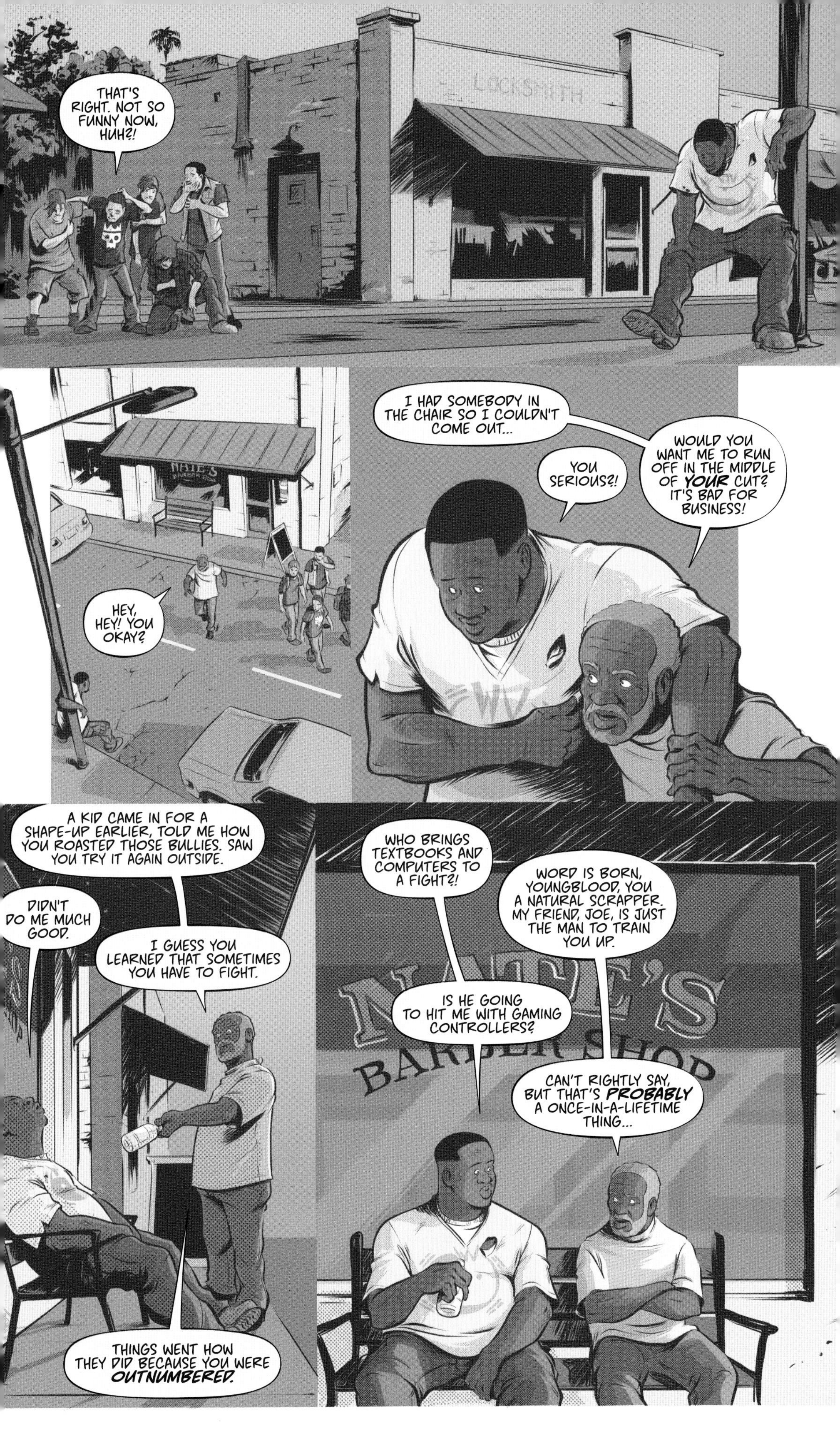
LOCKSMITH
THAT'S RIGHT. NOT SO FUNNY NOW, HUH?!
NATE'S BARBER SHOP
HEY, HEY! YOU OKAY?
I HAD SOMEBODY IN THE CHAIR SO I COULDN'T COME OUT...
YOU SERIOUS?!
WOULD YOU WANT ME TO RUN OFF IN THE MIDDLE OF **YOUR** CUT? IT'S BAD FOR BUSINESS!
A KID CAME IN FOR A SHAPE-UP EARLIER, TOLD ME HOW YOU ROASTED THOSE BULLIES. SAW YOU TRY IT AGAIN OUTSIDE.
DIDN'T DO ME MUCH GOOD.
I GUESS YOU LEARNED THAT SOMETIMES YOU HAVE TO FIGHT.
THINGS WENT HOW THEY DID BECAUSE YOU WERE **OUTNUMBERED.**
WHO BRINGS TEXTBOOKS AND COMPUTERS TO A FIGHT?!
WORD IS BORN, YOUNGBLOOD, YOU A NATURAL SCRAPPER. MY FRIEND, JOE, IS JUST THE MAN TO TRAIN YOU UP.
IS HE GOING TO HIT ME WITH GAMING CONTROLLERS?
CAN'T RIGHTLY SAY, BUT THAT'S **PROBABLY** A ONCE-IN-A-LIFETIME THING...

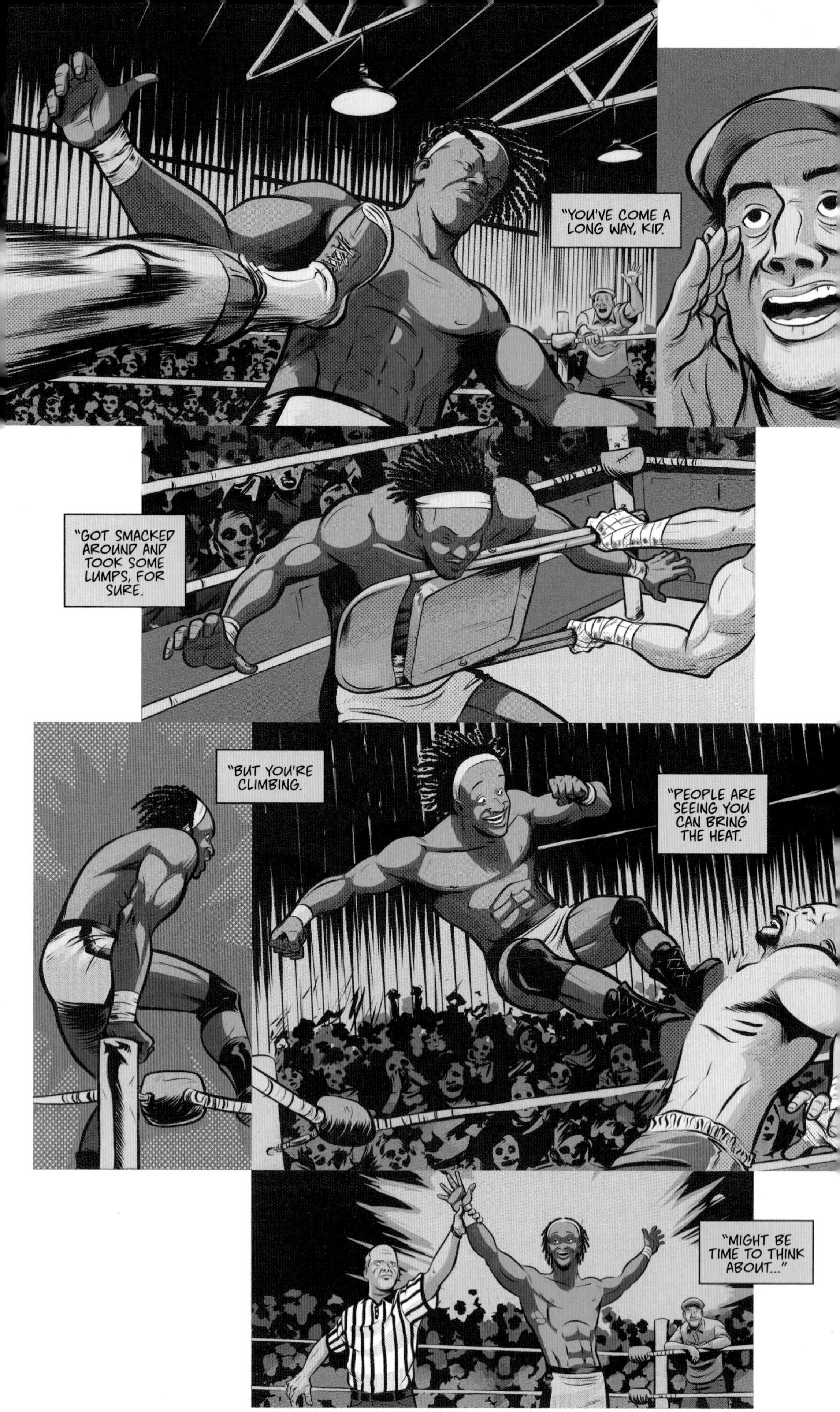
"YOU'VE COME A LONG WAY, KID.
"GOT SMACKED AROUND AND TOOK SOME LUMPS, FOR SURE.
"BUT YOU'RE CLIMBING.
"PEOPLE ARE SEEING YOU CAN BRING THE HEAT.
"MIGHT BE TIME TO THINK ABOUT..."

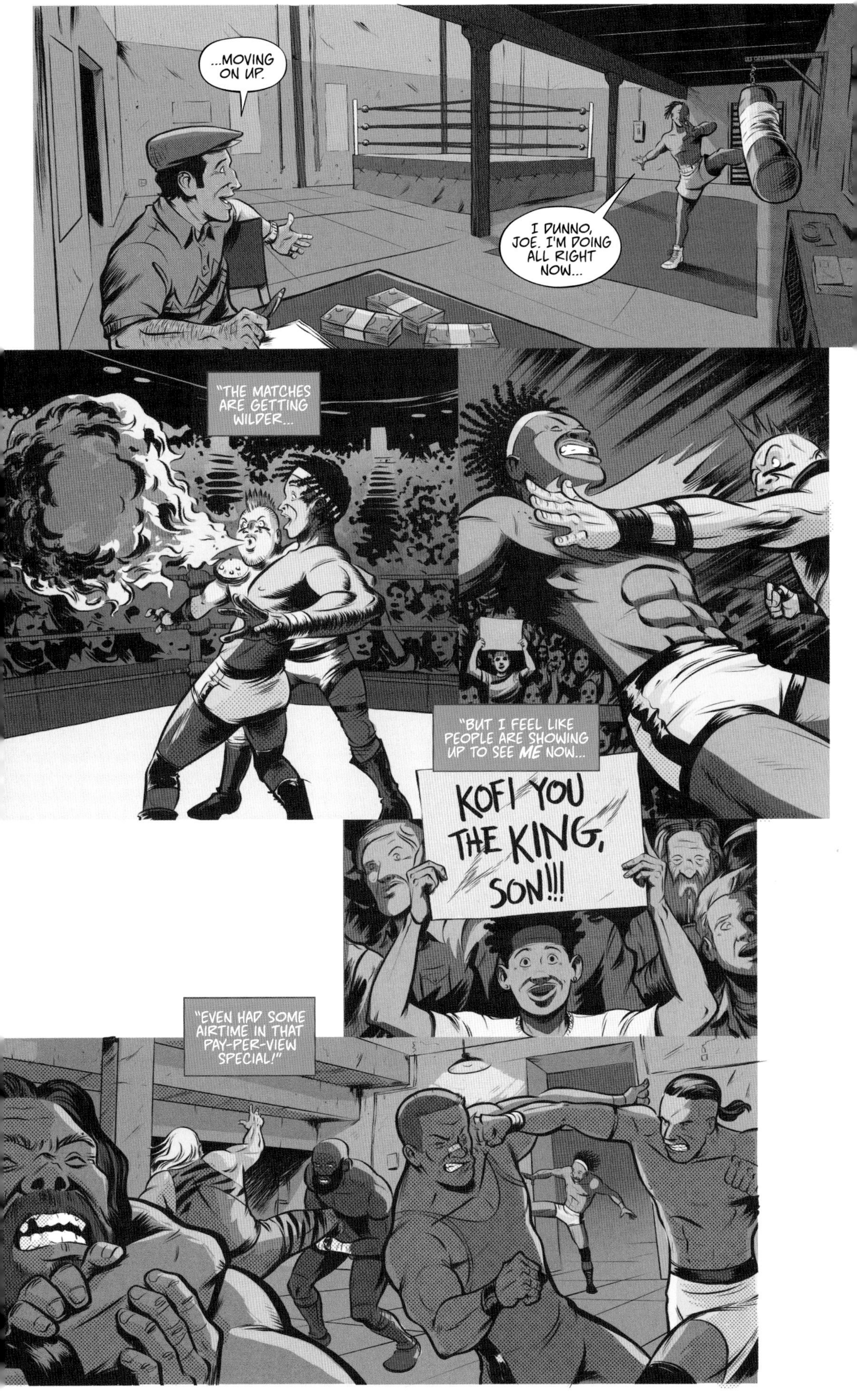
...MOVING ON UP.
I DUNNO, JOE. I'M DOING ALL RIGHT NOW...
"THE MATCHES ARE GETTING WILDER...
"BUT I FEEL LIKE PEOPLE ARE SHOWING UP TO SEE ME NOW...
KOFI YOU THE KING, SON!!!
"EVEN HAD SOME AIRTIME IN THAT PAY-PER-VIEW SPECIAL!"

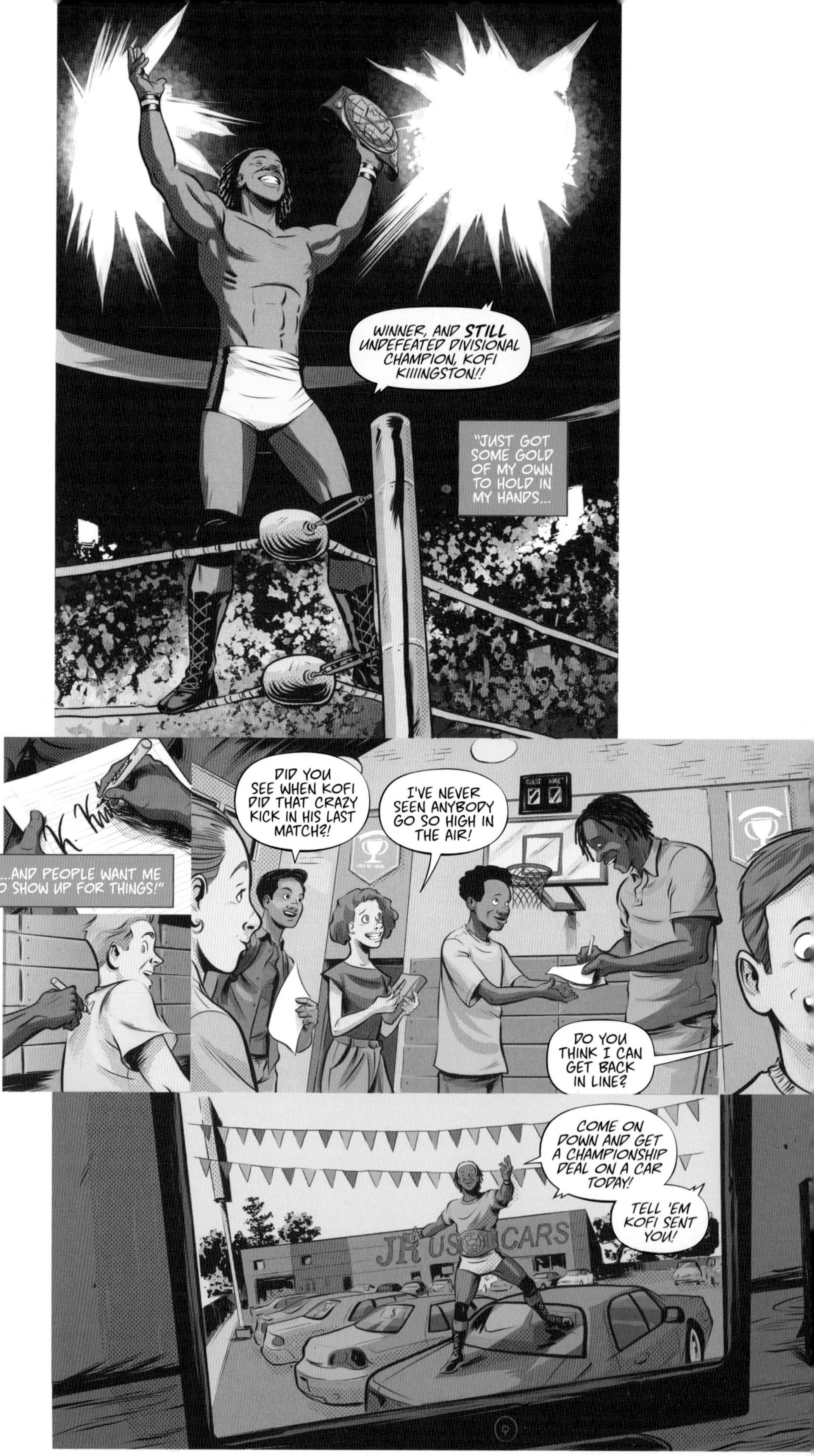
WINNER, AND **STILL** UNDEFEATED DIVISIONAL CHAMPION, KOFI KIIINGSTON!!
"JUST GOT SOME GOLD OF MY OWN TO HOLD IN MY HANDS...
"...AND PEOPLE WANT ME TO SHOW UP FOR THINGS!"
DID YOU SEE WHEN KOFI DID THAT CRAZY KICK IN HIS LAST MATCH?!
I'VE NEVER SEEN ANYBODY GO SO HIGH IN THE AIR!
DO YOU THINK I CAN GET BACK IN LINE?
COME ON DOWN AND GET A CHAMPIONSHIP DEAL ON A CAR TODAY!
TELL 'EM KOFI SENT YOU!

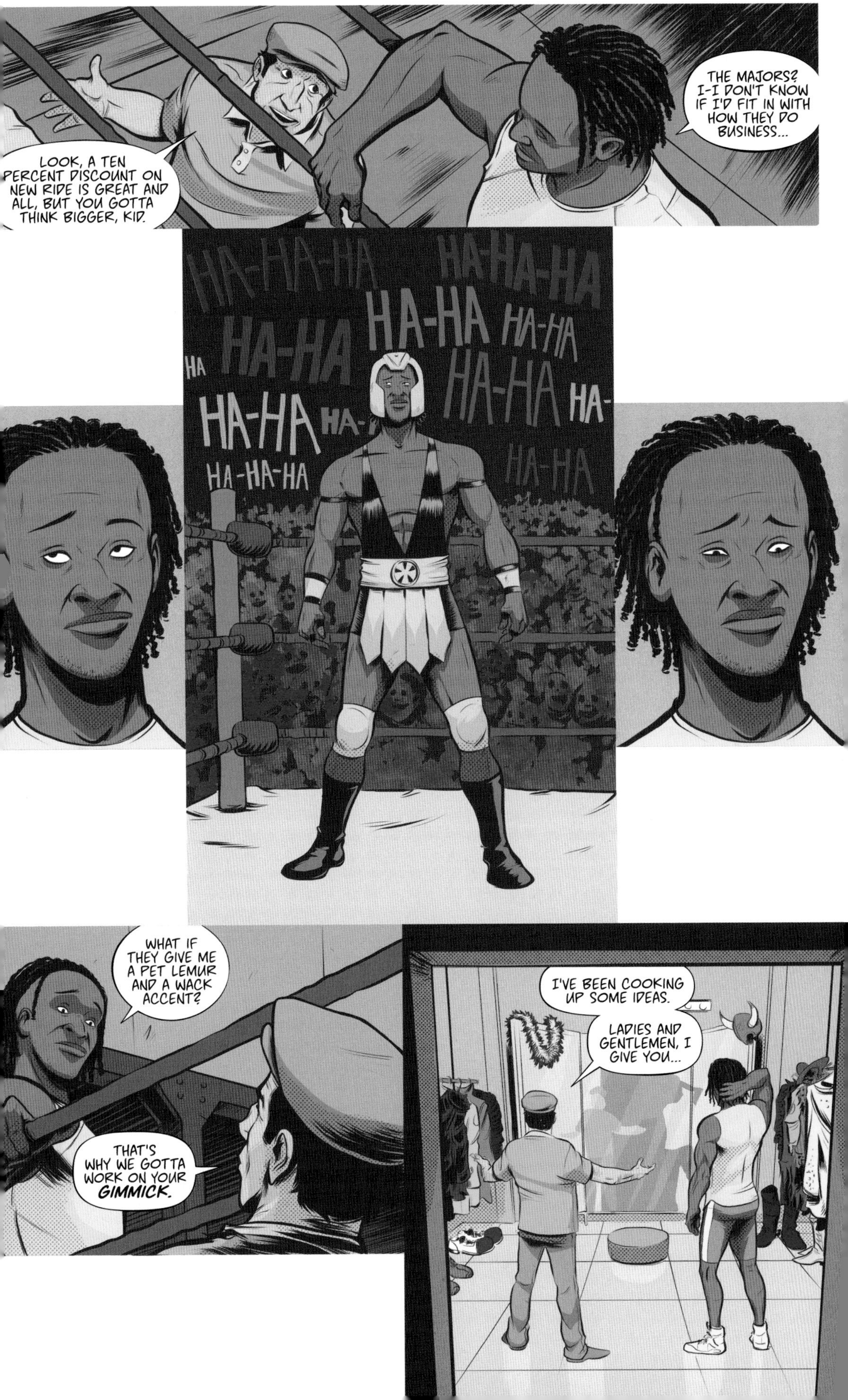
LOOK, A TEN PERCENT DISCOUNT ON NEW RIDE IS GREAT AND ALL, BUT YOU GOTTA THINK BIGGER, KID.
THE MAJORS? I-I DON'T KNOW IF I'D FIT IN WITH HOW THEY DO BUSINESS...
HA-HA-HA HA-HA-HA
HA-HA HA-HA HA-HA
HA
HA-HA HA- HA-HA HA-
HA-HA-HA HA-HA
WHAT IF THEY GIVE ME A PET LEMUR AND A WACK ACCENT?
THAT'S WHY WE GOTTA WORK ON YOUR **GIMMICK.**
I'VE BEEN COOKING UP SOME IDEAS.
LADIES AND GENTLEMEN, I GIVE YOU...

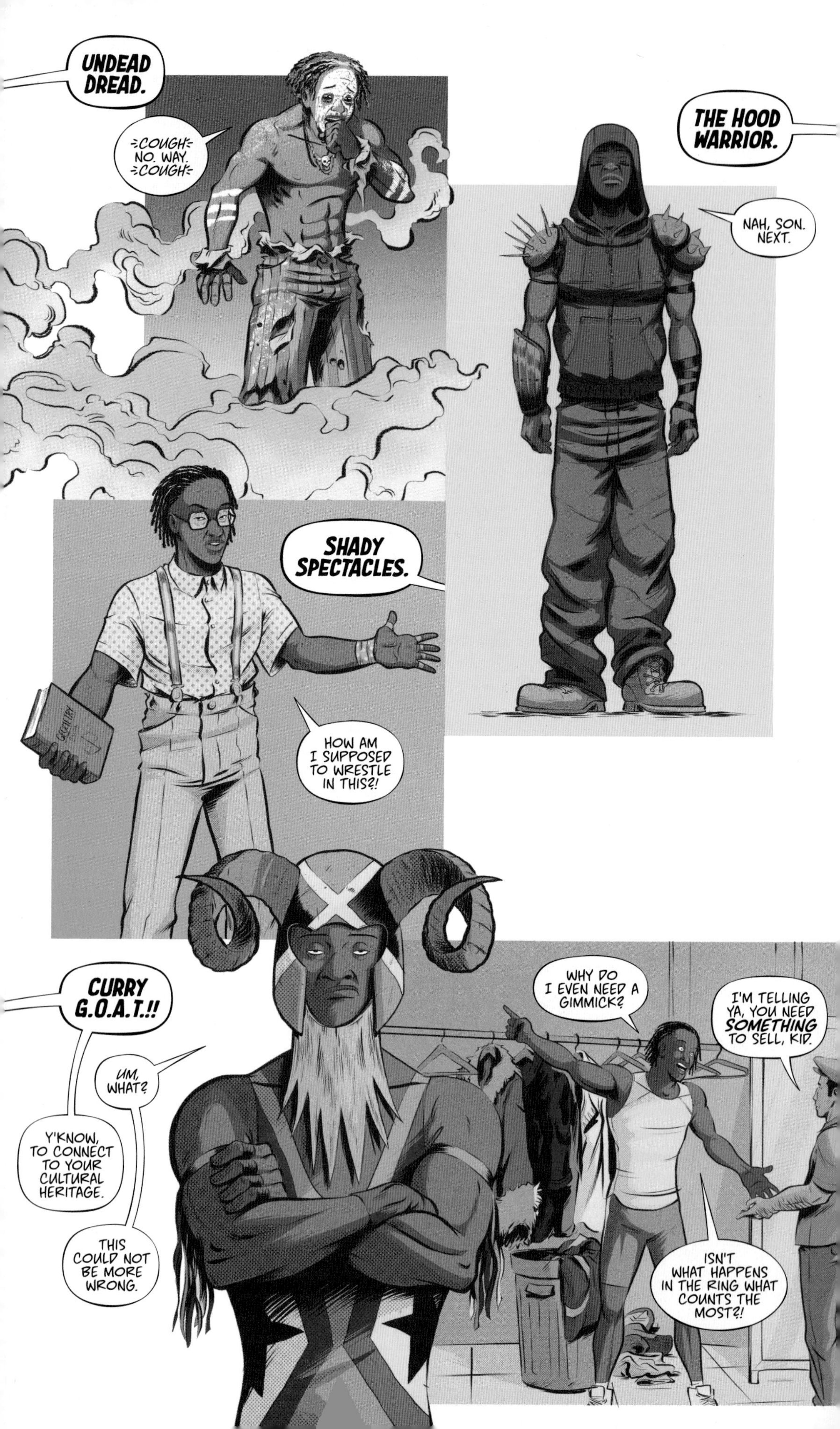
UNDEAD DREAD.
=COUGH= NO. WAY. =COUGH=
THE HOOD WARRIOR.
NAH, SON. NEXT.
SHADY SPECTACLES.
HOW AM I SUPPOSED TO WRESTLE IN THIS?!
CURRY G.O.A.T.!!
UM, WHAT?
Y'KNOW, TO CONNECT TO YOUR CULTURAL HERITAGE.
THIS COULD NOT BE MORE WRONG.
WHY DO I EVEN NEED A GIMMICK?
I'M TELLING YA, YOU NEED SOMETHING TO SELL, KID.
ISN'T WHAT HAPPENS IN THE RING WHAT COUNTS THE MOST?!

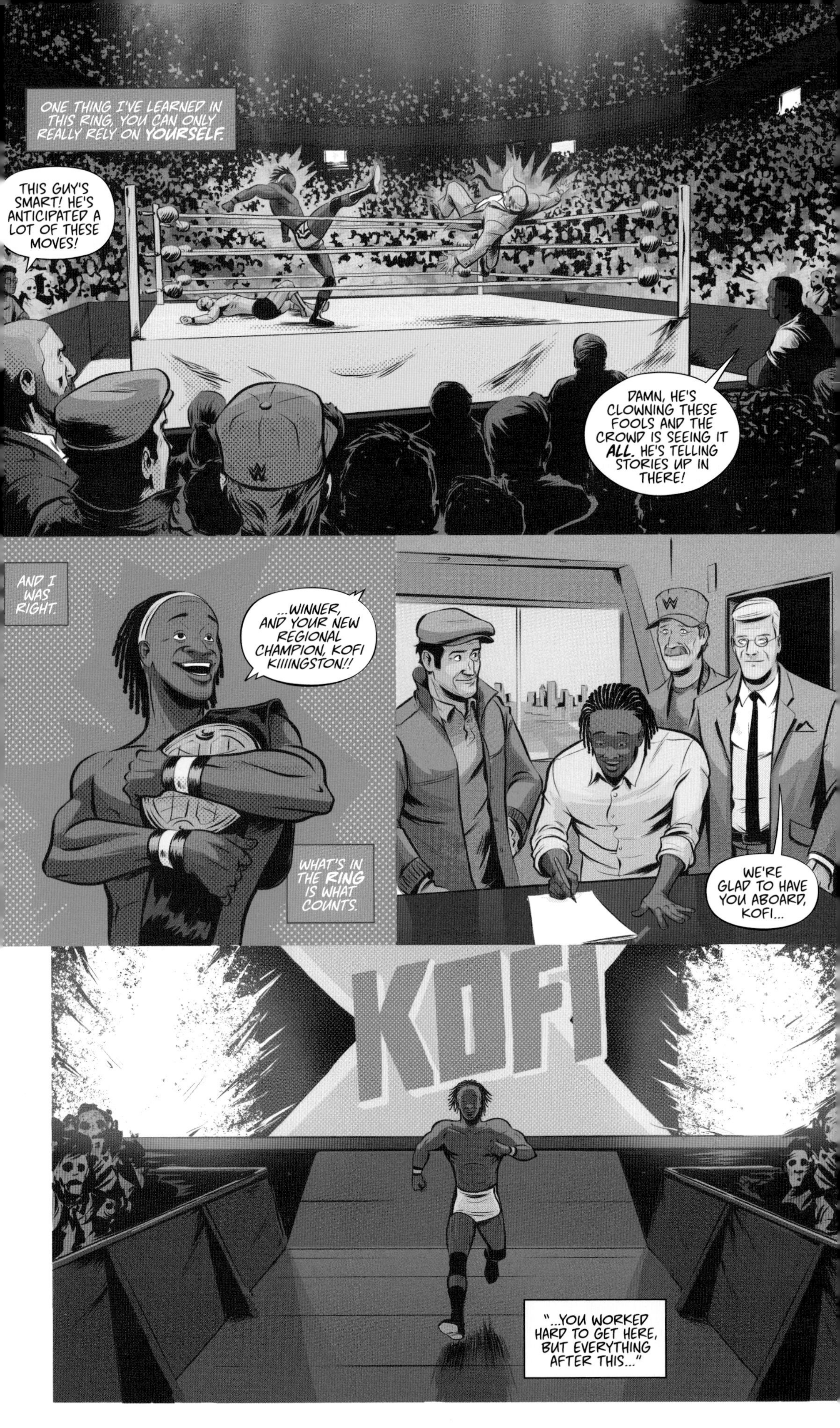
ONE THING I'VE LEARNED IN THIS RING, YOU CAN ONLY REALLY RELY ON YOURSELF.
THIS GUY'S SMART! HE'S ANTICIPATED A LOT OF THESE MOVES!
DAMN, HE'S CLOWNING THESE FOOLS AND THE CROWD IS SEEING IT ALL. HE'S TELLING STORIES UP IN THERE!
AND I WAS RIGHT.
...WINNER, AND YOUR NEW REGIONAL CHAMPION, KOFI KIIINGSTON!!
WHAT'S IN THE RING IS WHAT COUNTS.
WE'RE GLAD TO HAVE YOU ABOARD, KOFI...
KOFI
"...YOU WORKED HARD TO GET HERE, BUT EVERYTHING AFTER THIS..."

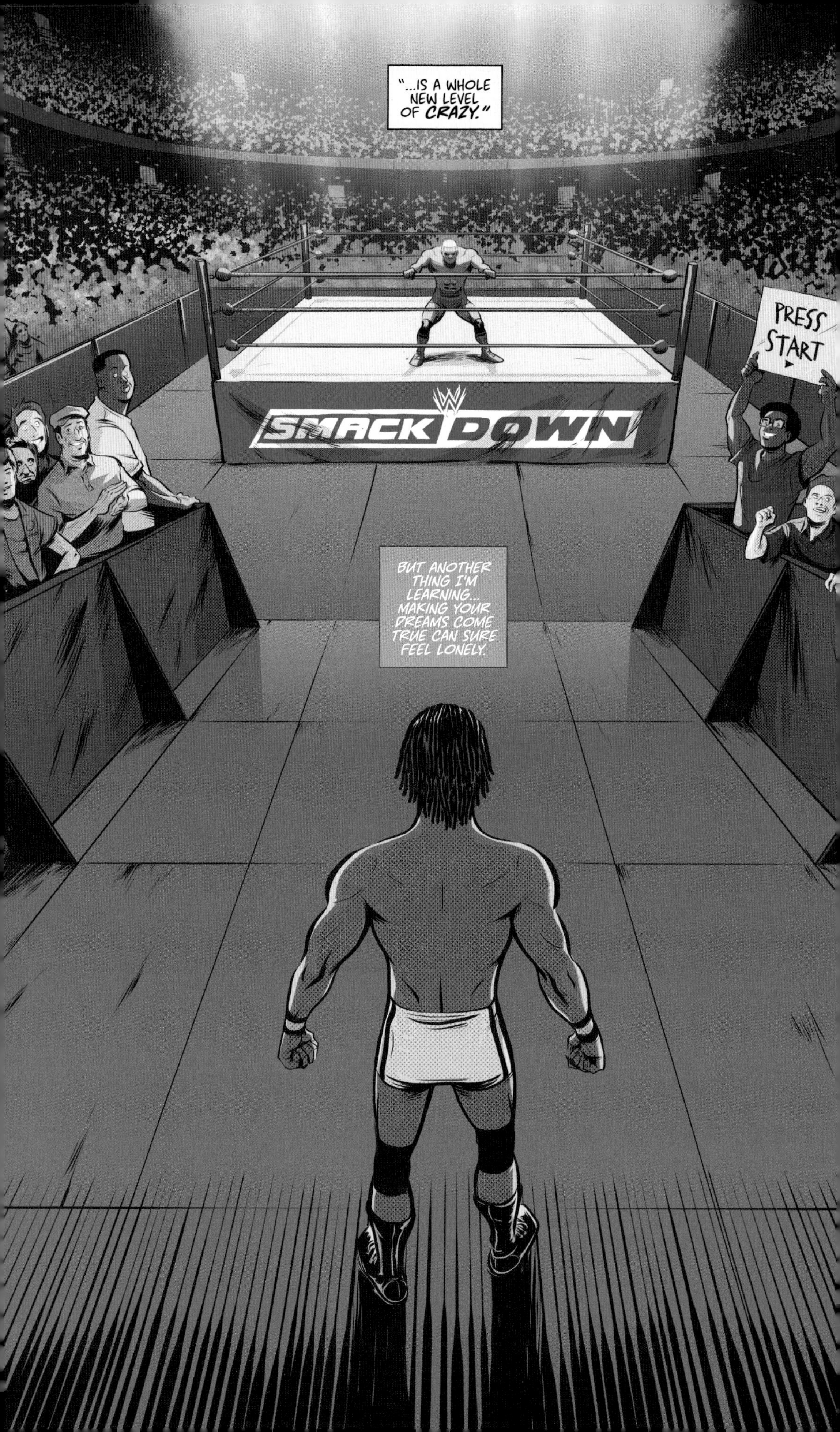
"...IS A WHOLE NEW LEVEL OF CRAZY."
PRESS START
SMACKDOWN
BUT ANOTHER THING I'M LEARNING... MAKING YOUR DREAMS COME TRUE CAN SURE FEEL LONELY.

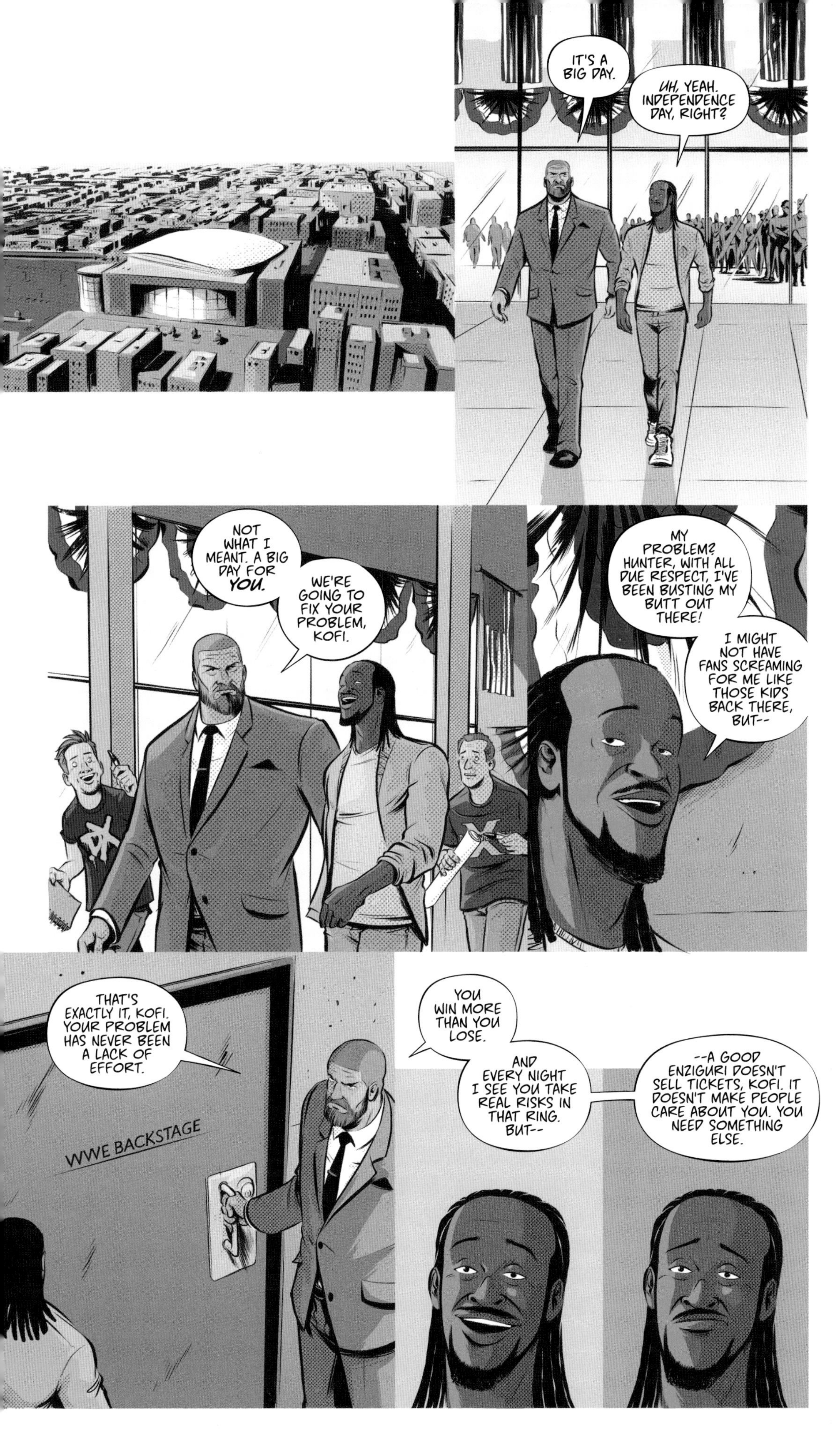
IT'S A BIG DAY.
UH, YEAH. INDEPENDENCE DAY, RIGHT?
NOT WHAT I MEANT. A BIG DAY FOR YOU.
WE'RE GOING TO FIX YOUR PROBLEM, KOFI.
MY PROBLEM? HUNTER, WITH ALL DUE RESPECT, I'VE BEEN BUSTING MY BUTT OUT THERE!
I MIGHT NOT HAVE FANS SCREAMING FOR ME LIKE THOSE KIDS BACK THERE, BUT--
THAT'S EXACTLY IT, KOFI. YOUR PROBLEM HAS NEVER BEEN A LACK OF EFFORT.
WWE BACKSTAGE
YOU WIN MORE THAN YOU LOSE.
AND EVERY NIGHT I SEE YOU TAKE REAL RISKS IN THAT RING. BUT--
--A GOOD ENZIGURI DOESN'T SELL TICKETS, KOFI. IT DOESN'T MAKE PEOPLE CARE ABOUT YOU. YOU NEED SOMETHING ELSE.

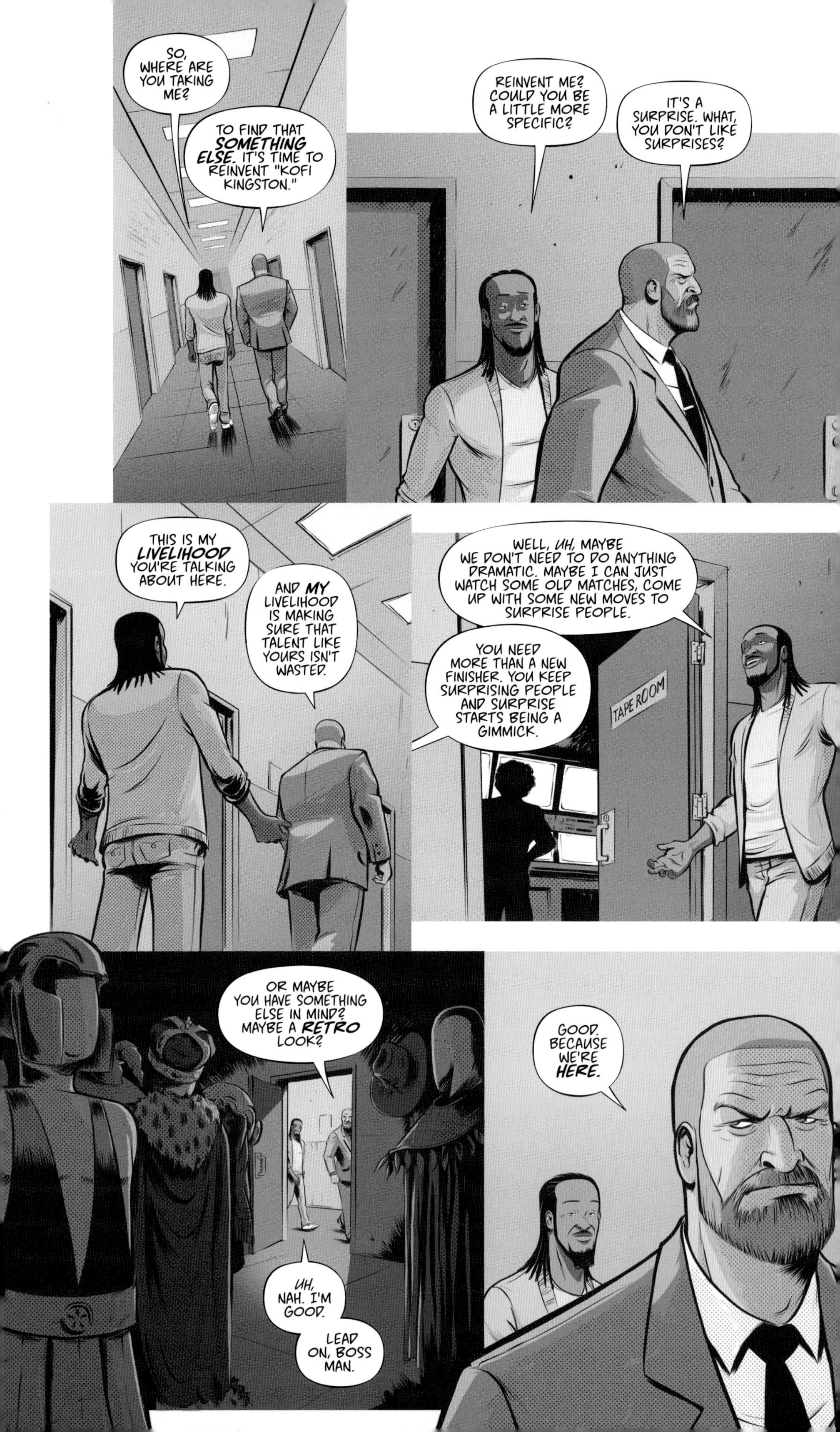
SO, WHERE ARE YOU TAKING ME?
TO FIND THAT **SOMETHING ELSE.** IT'S TIME TO REINVENT "KOFI KINGSTON."
REINVENT ME? COULD YOU BE A LITTLE MORE SPECIFIC?
IT'S A SURPRISE. WHAT, YOU DON'T LIKE SURPRISES?
THIS IS MY **LIVELIHOOD** YOU'RE TALKING ABOUT HERE.
AND **MY** LIVELIHOOD IS MAKING SURE THAT TALENT LIKE YOURS ISN'T WASTED.
WELL, *UH,* MAYBE WE DON'T NEED TO DO ANYTHING DRAMATIC. MAYBE I CAN JUST WATCH SOME OLD MATCHES, COME UP WITH SOME NEW MOVES TO SURPRISE PEOPLE.
YOU NEED MORE THAN A NEW FINISHER. YOU KEEP SURPRISING PEOPLE AND SURPRISE STARTS BEING A GIMMICK.
TAPE ROOM
OR MAYBE YOU HAVE SOMETHING ELSE IN MIND? MAYBE A **RETRO** LOOK?
UH, NAH. I'M GOOD.
LEAD ON, BOSS MAN.
GOOD. BECAUSE WE'RE **HERE.**

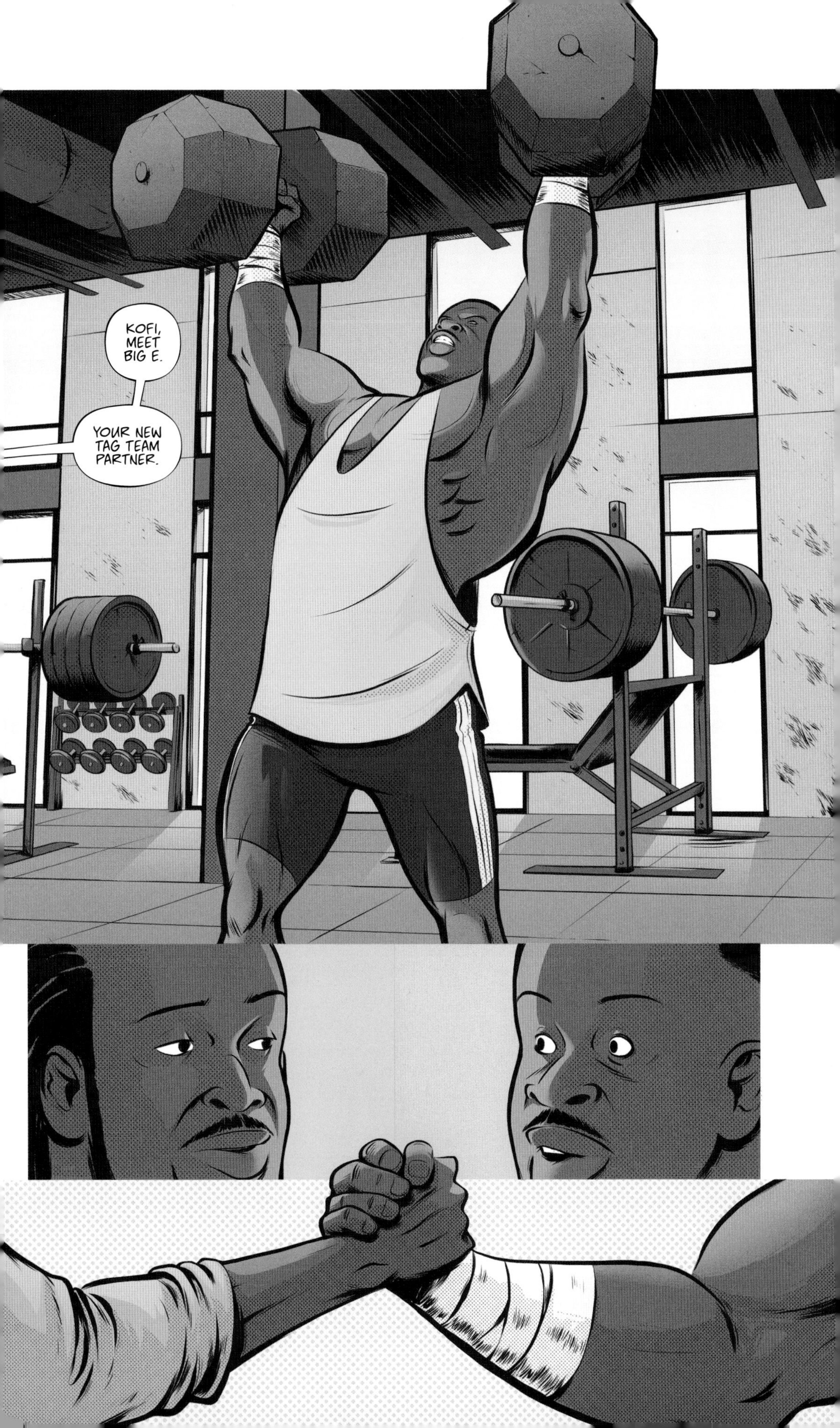
KOFI, MEET BIG E.
YOUR NEW TAG TEAM PARTNER.

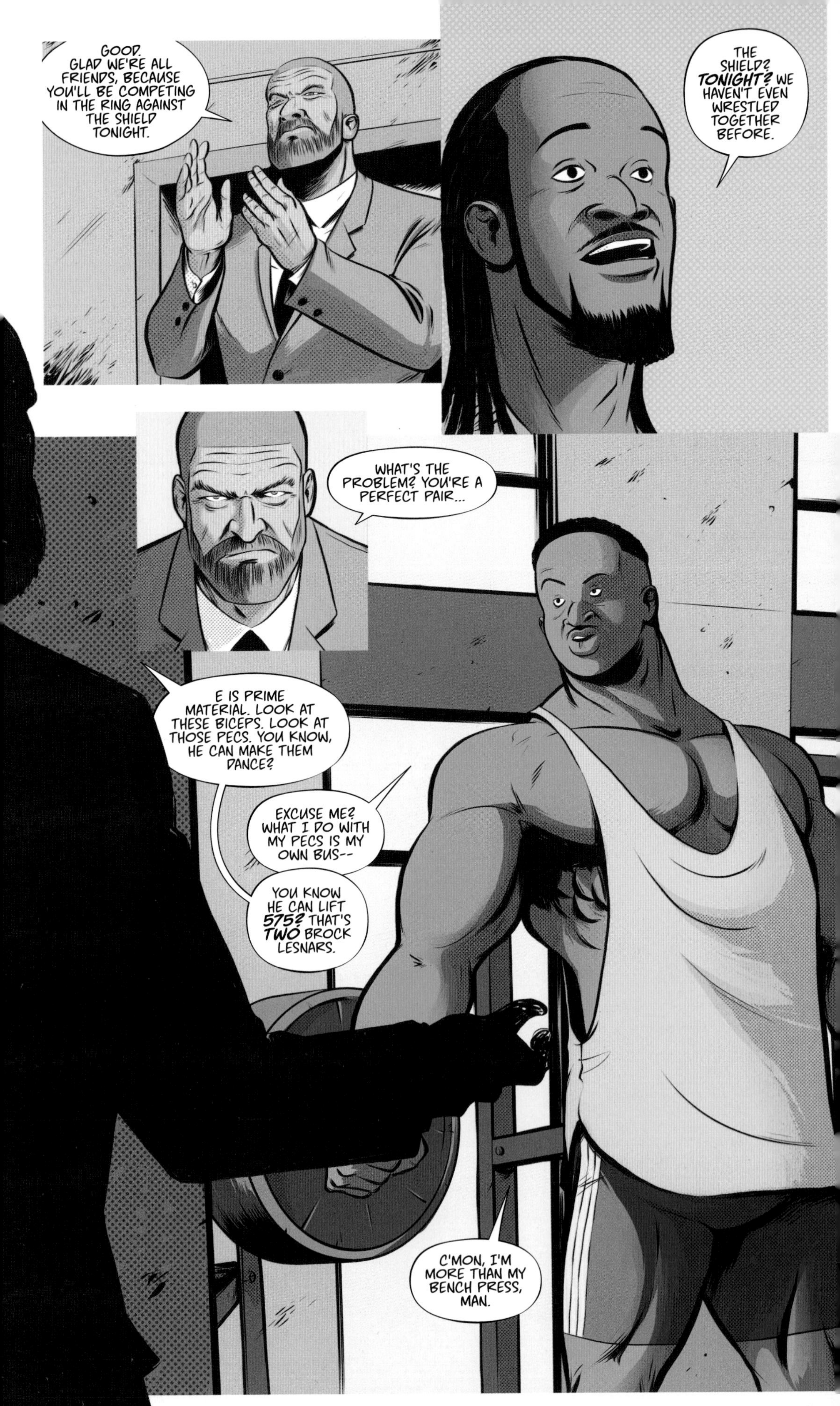
GOOD. GLAD WE'RE ALL FRIENDS, BECAUSE YOU'LL BE COMPETING IN THE RING AGAINST THE SHIELD TONIGHT.
THE SHIELD? TONIGHT? WE HAVEN'T EVEN WRESTLED TOGETHER BEFORE.
WHAT'S THE PROBLEM? YOU'RE A PERFECT PAIR...
E IS PRIME MATERIAL. LOOK AT THESE BICEPS. LOOK AT THOSE PECS. YOU KNOW, HE CAN MAKE THEM DANCE?
EXCUSE ME? WHAT I DO WITH MY PECS IS MY OWN BUS--
YOU KNOW HE CAN LIFT 575? THAT'S TWO BROCK LESNARS.
C'MON, I'M MORE THAN MY BENCH PRESS, MAN.

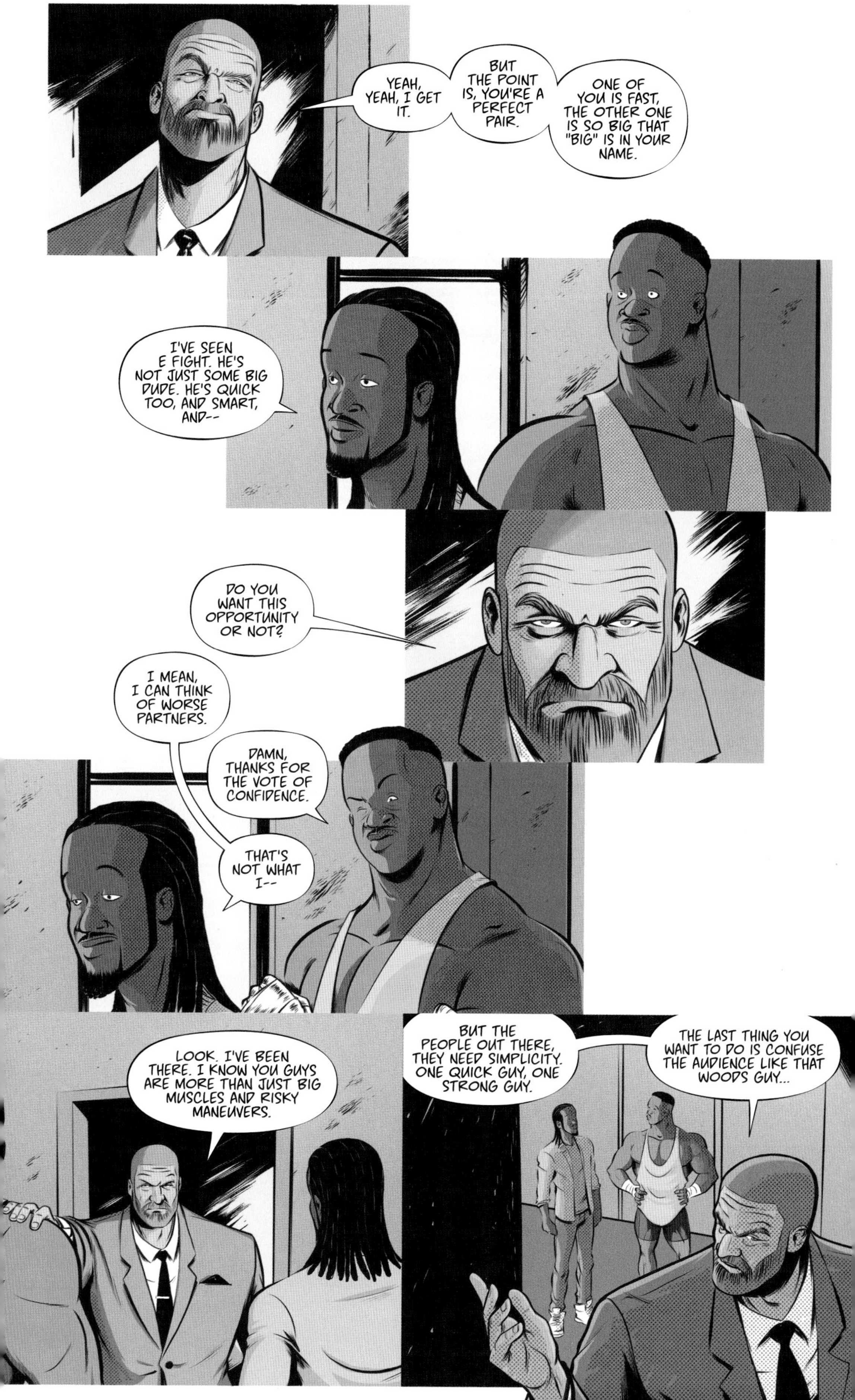
YEAH, YEAH, I GET IT.
BUT THE POINT IS, YOU'RE A PERFECT PAIR.
ONE OF YOU IS FAST, THE OTHER ONE IS SO BIG THAT "BIG" IS IN YOUR NAME.
I'VE SEEN E FIGHT. HE'S NOT JUST SOME BIG DUDE. HE'S QUICK TOO, AND SMART, AND--
DO YOU WANT THIS OPPORTUNITY OR NOT?
I MEAN, I CAN THINK OF WORSE PARTNERS.
DAMN, THANKS FOR THE VOTE OF CONFIDENCE.
THAT'S NOT WHAT I--
LOOK. I'VE BEEN THERE. I KNOW YOU GUYS ARE MORE THAN JUST BIG MUSCLES AND RISKY MANEUVERS.
BUT THE PEOPLE OUT THERE, THEY NEED SIMPLICITY. ONE QUICK GUY, ONE STRONG GUY.
THE LAST THING YOU WANT TO DO IS CONFUSE THE AUDIENCE LIKE THAT WOODS GUY...

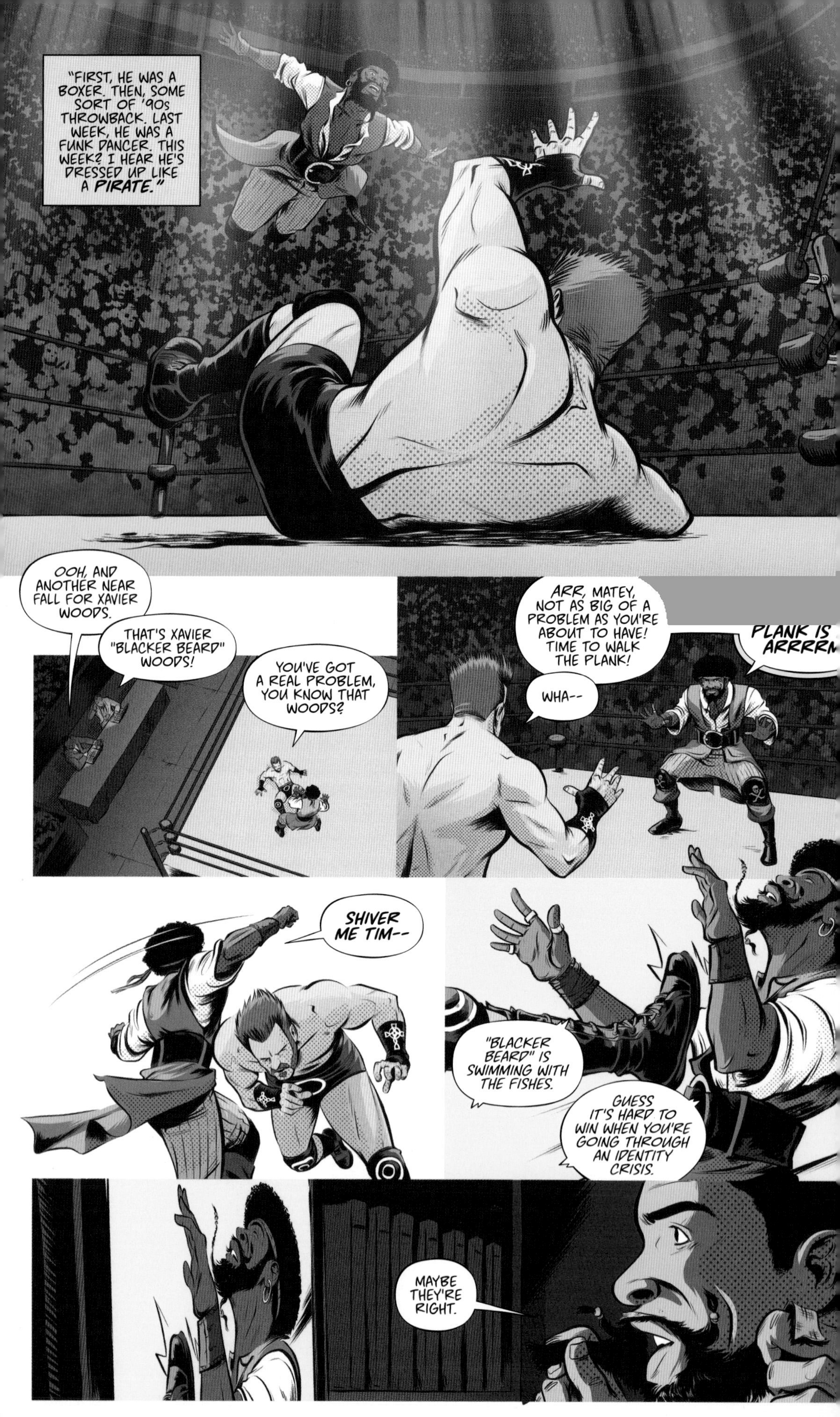
"FIRST, HE WAS A BOXER. THEN, SOME SORT OF '90s THROWBACK. LAST WEEK, HE WAS A FUNK DANCER. THIS WEEK? I HEAR HE'S DRESSED UP LIKE A *PIRATE.*"
OOH, AND ANOTHER NEAR FALL FOR XAVIER WOODS.
THAT'S XAVIER "BLACKER BEARD" WOODS!
YOU'VE GOT A REAL PROBLEM, YOU KNOW THAT WOODS?
ARR, MATEY, NOT AS BIG OF A PROBLEM AS YOU'RE ABOUT TO HAVE! TIME TO WALK THE PLANK!
WHA--
PLANK IS ARRRRM
SHIVER ME TIM--
"BLACKER BEARD" IS SWIMMING WITH THE FISHES.
GUESS IT'S HARD TO WIN WHEN YOU'RE GOING THROUGH AN IDENTITY CRISIS.
MAYBE THEY'RE RIGHT.

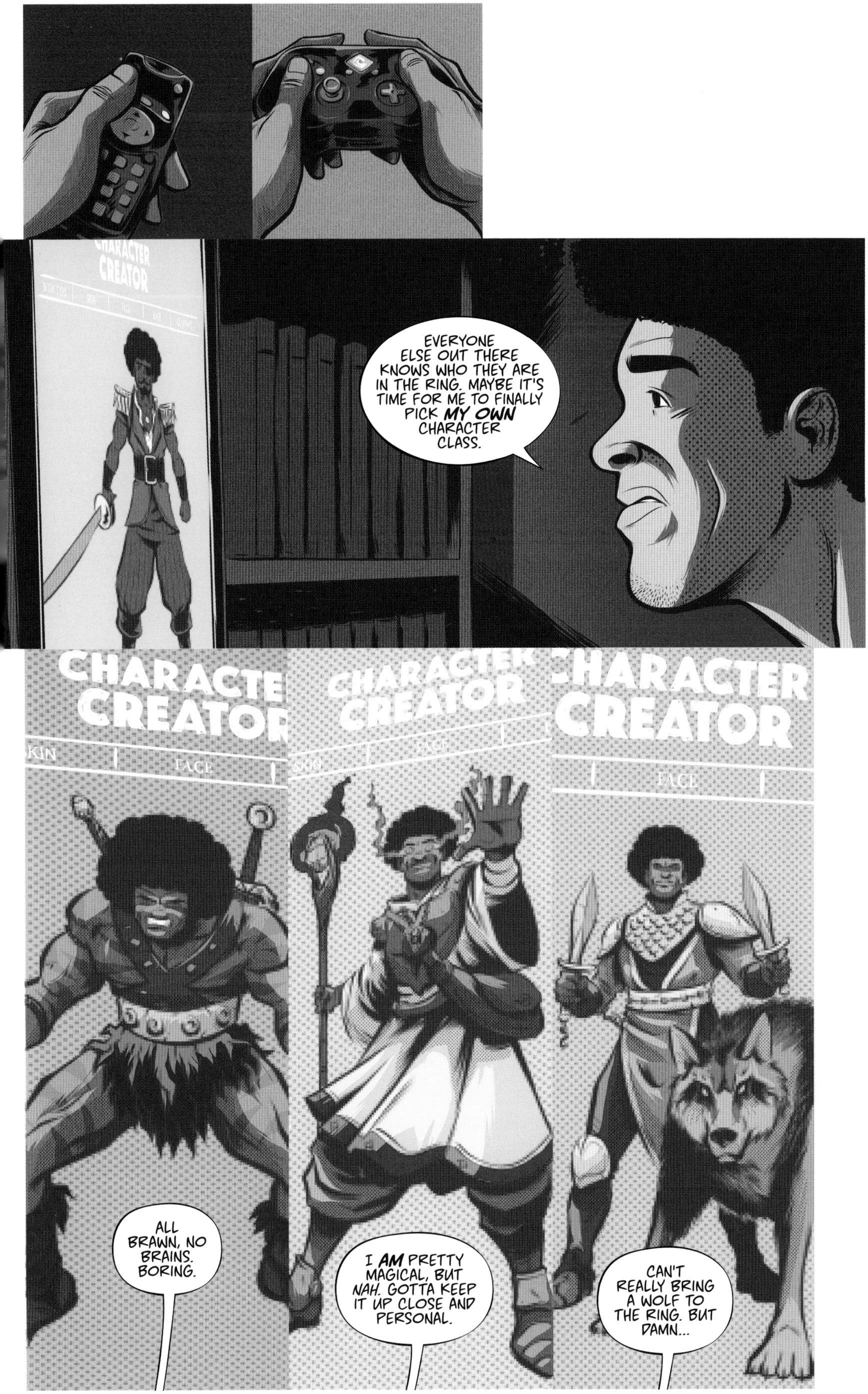
CHARACTER CREATOR
EVERYONE ELSE OUT THERE KNOWS WHO THEY ARE IN THE RING. MAYBE IT'S TIME FOR ME TO FINALLY PICK **MY OWN** CHARACTER CLASS.
CHARACTER CREATOR
FACE
ALL BRAWN, NO BRAINS. BORING.
CHARACTER CREATOR
FACE
I **AM** PRETTY MAGICAL, BUT NAH. GOTTA KEEP IT UP CLOSE AND PERSONAL.
CHARACTER CREATOR
FACE
CAN'T REALLY BRING A WOLF TO THE RING. BUT DAMN...

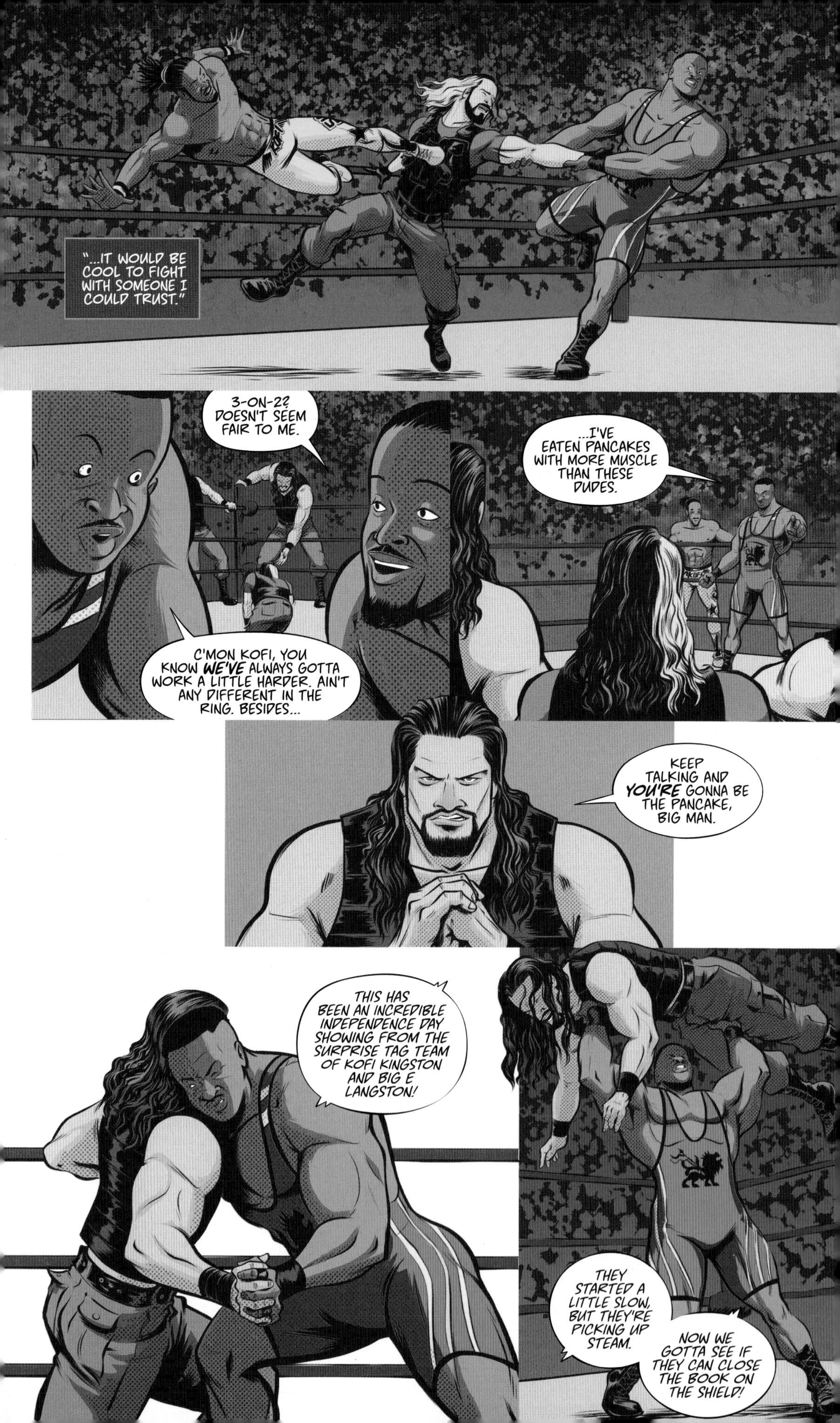
"...IT WOULD BE COOL TO FIGHT WITH SOMEONE I COULD TRUST."
3-ON-2? DOESN'T SEEM FAIR TO ME.
C'MON KOFI, YOU KNOW **WE'VE** ALWAYS GOTTA WORK A LITTLE HARDER. AIN'T ANY DIFFERENT IN THE RING. BESIDES...
...I'VE EATEN PANCAKES WITH MORE MUSCLE THAN THESE DUDES.
KEEP TALKING AND **YOU'RE** GONNA BE THE PANCAKE, BIG MAN.
THIS HAS BEEN AN INCREDIBLE INDEPENDENCE DAY SHOWING FROM THE SURPRISE TAG TEAM OF KOFI KINGSTON AND BIG E LANGSTON!
THEY STARTED A LITTLE SLOW, BUT THEY'RE PICKING UP STEAM.
NOW WE GOTTA SEE IF THEY CAN CLOSE THE BOOK ON THE SHIELD!

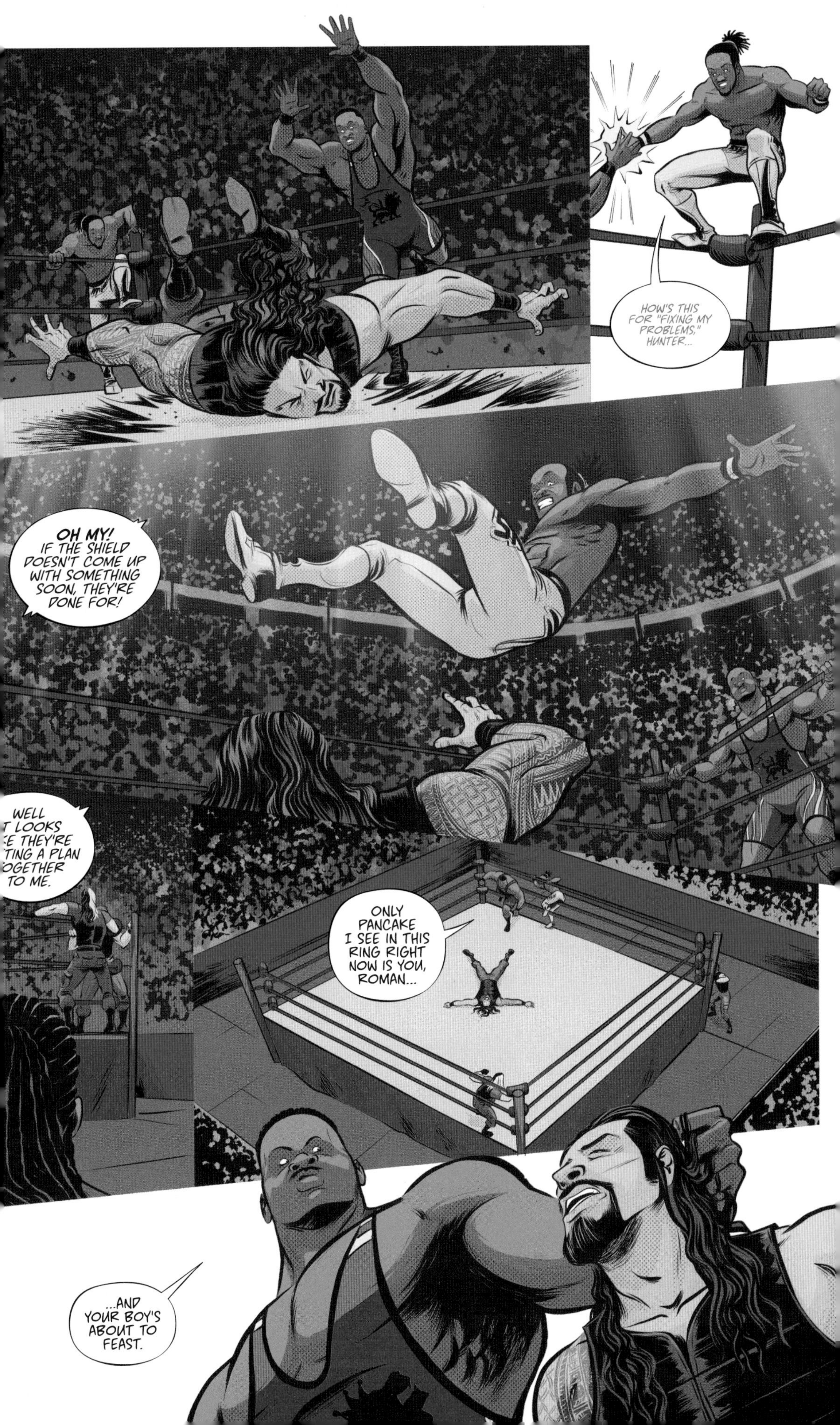
HOW'S THIS FOR "FIXING MY PROBLEMS," HUNTER...
OH MY! IF THE SHIELD DOESN'T COME UP WITH SOMETHING SOON, THEY'RE DONE FOR!
WELL T LOOKS E THEY'RE TING A PLAN OGETHER TO ME.
ONLY PANCAKE I SEE IN THIS RING RIGHT NOW IS YOU, ROMAN...
...AND YOUR BOY'S ABOUT TO FEAST.

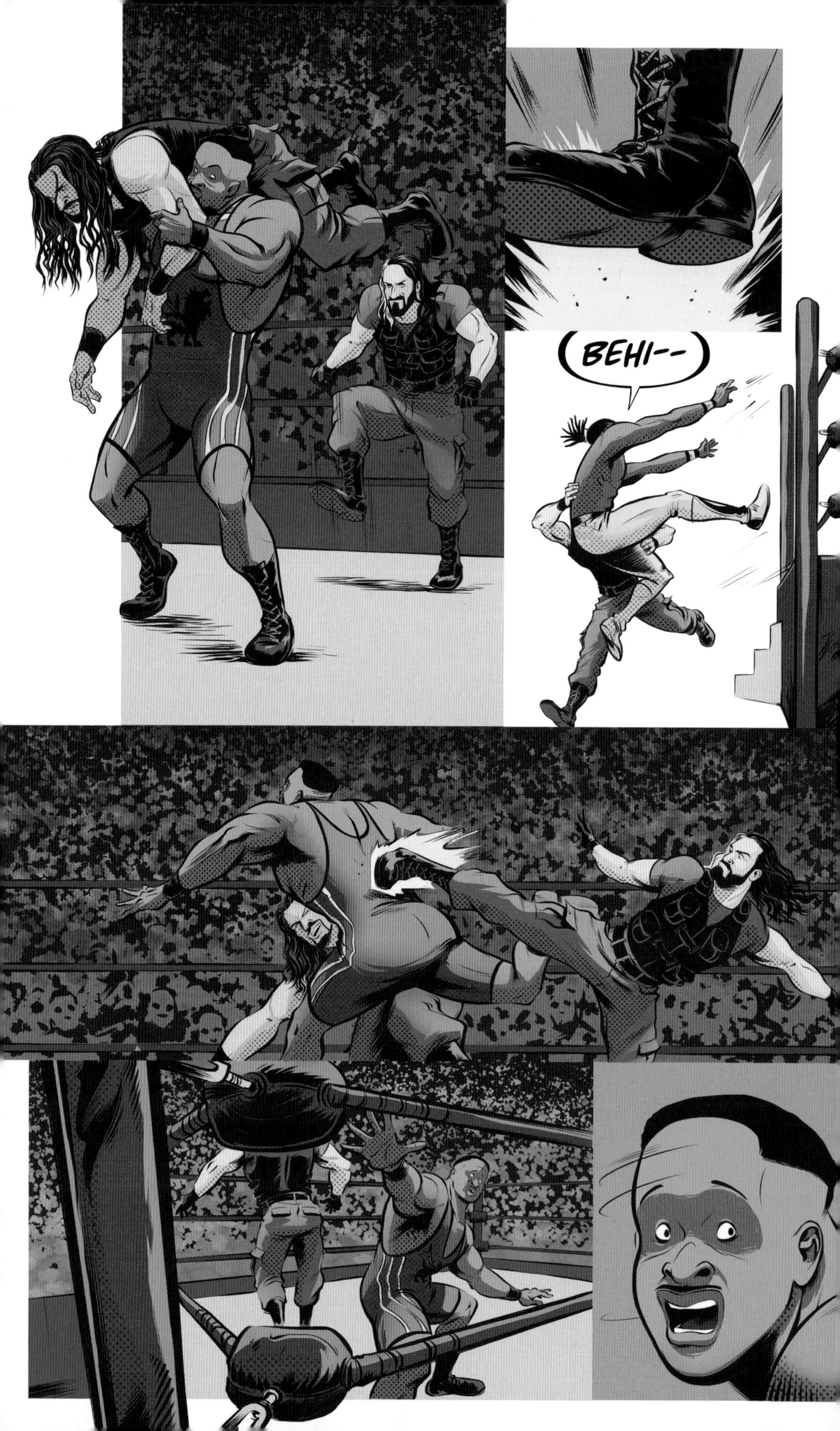
BEHI--

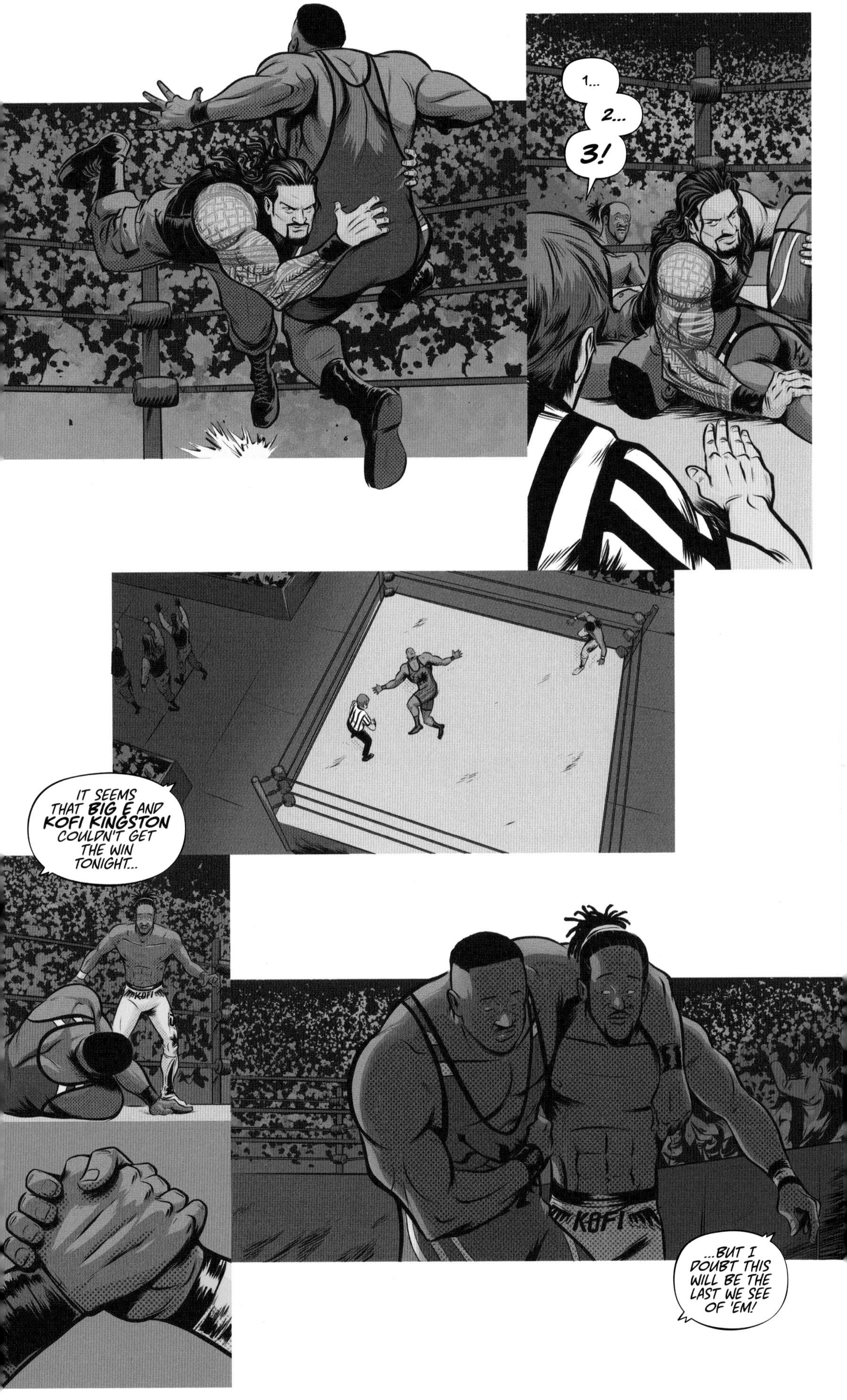
1...
2...
3!
IT SEEMS THAT BIG E AND KOFI KINGSTON COULDN'T GET THE WIN TONIGHT...
KOFI
KOFI
...BUT I DOUBT THIS WILL BE THE LAST WE SEE OF 'EM!

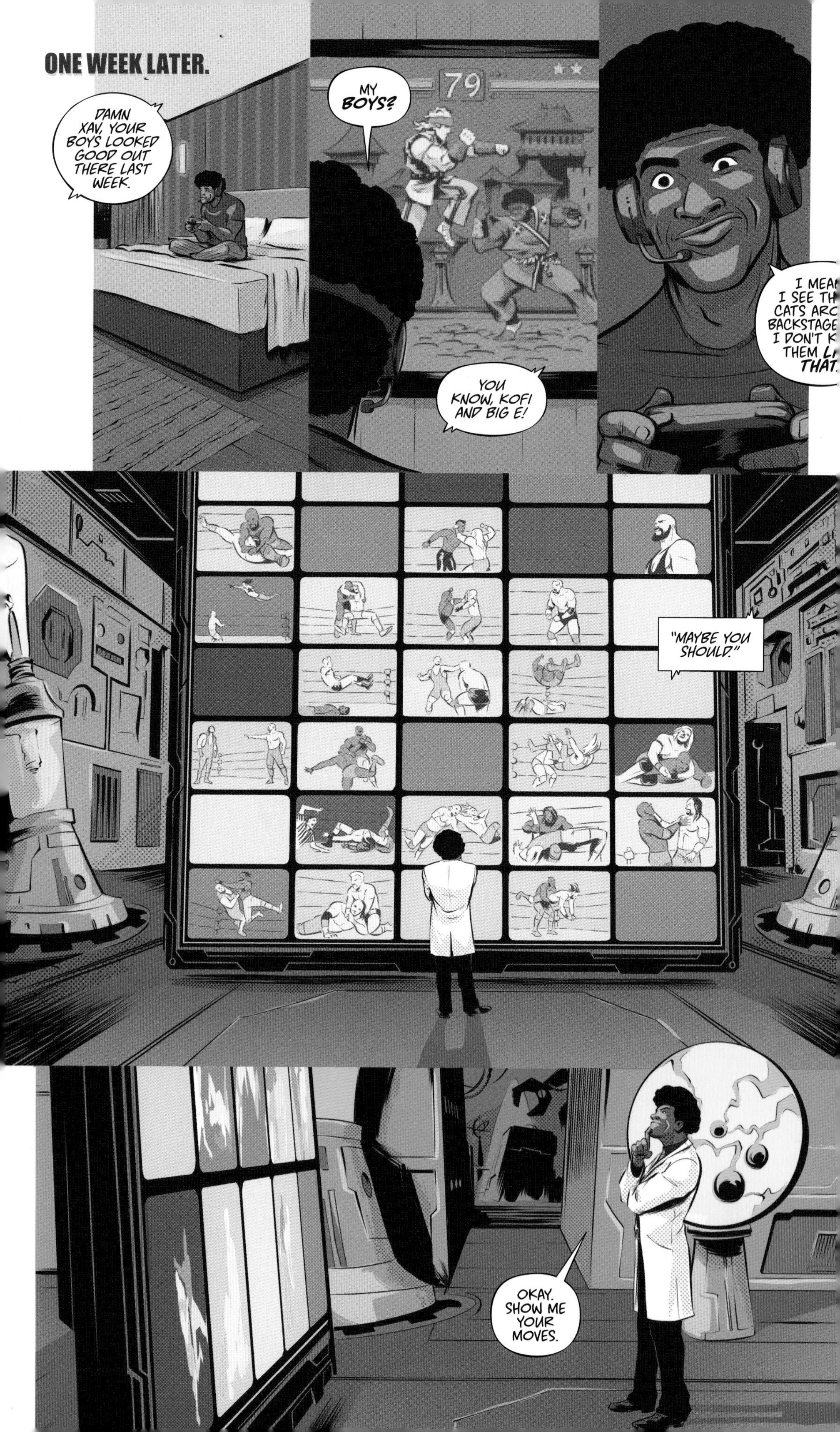
ONE WEEK LATER.
DAMN XAV, YOUR BOYS LOOKED GOOD OUT THERE LAST WEEK.
MY BOYS?
YOU KNOW, KOFI AND BIG E!
79
I MEA
I SEE TH
CATS ARO
BACKSTAGE
I DON'T K
THEM LI
THAT.
"MAYBE YOU SHOULD."
OKAY. SHOW ME YOUR MOVES.

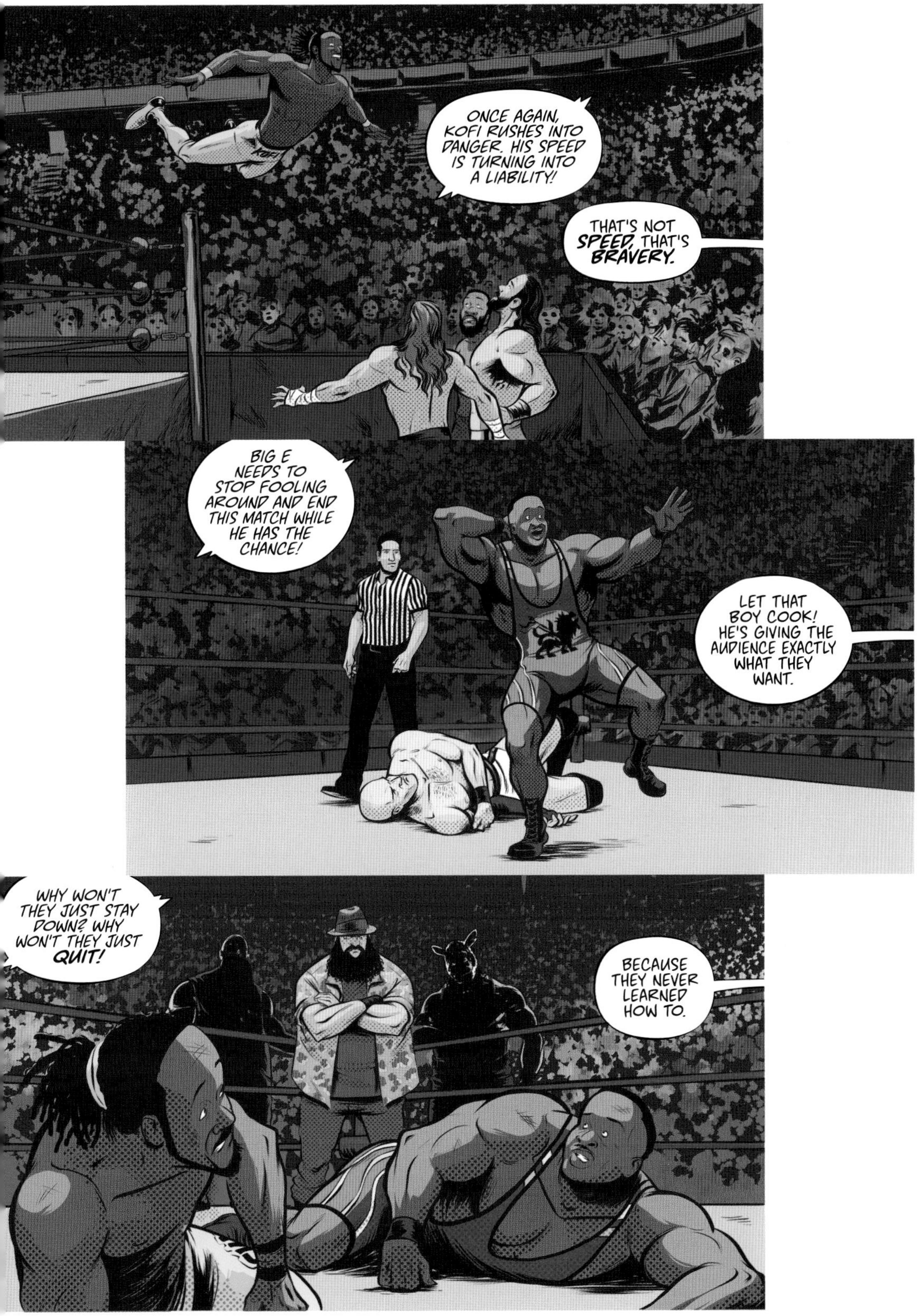
ONCE AGAIN, KOFI RUSHES INTO DANGER. HIS SPEED IS TURNING INTO A LIABILITY!
THAT'S NOT SPEED, THAT'S BRAVERY.
BIG E NEEDS TO STOP FOOLING AROUND AND END THIS MATCH WHILE HE HAS THE CHANCE!
LET THAT BOY COOK! HE'S GIVING THE AUDIENCE EXACTLY WHAT THEY WANT.
WHY WON'T THEY JUST STAY DOWN? WHY WON'T THEY JUST QUIT!
BECAUSE THEY NEVER LEARNED HOW TO.

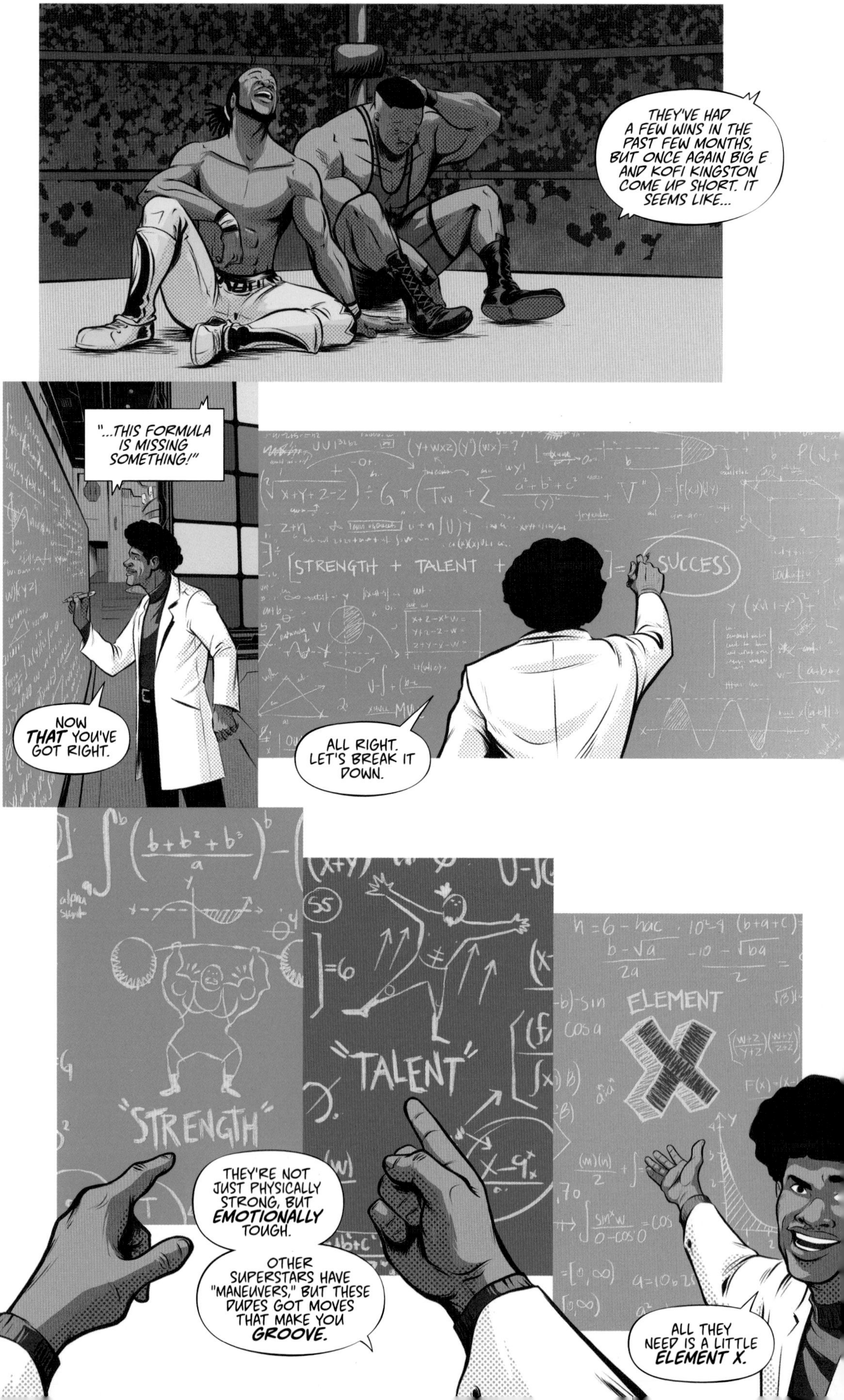
THEY'VE HAD A FEW WINS IN THE PAST FEW MONTHS, BUT ONCE AGAIN BIG E AND KOFI KINGSTON COME UP SHORT. IT SEEMS LIKE...
"...THIS FORMULA IS MISSING SOMETHING!"
NOW **THAT** YOU'VE GOT RIGHT.
STRENGTH + TALENT + = SUCCESS
ALL RIGHT. LET'S BREAK IT DOWN.
"STRENGTH"
"TALENT"
ELEMENT X
THEY'RE NOT JUST PHYSICALLY STRONG, BUT **EMOTIONALLY** TOUGH.
OTHER SUPERSTARS HAVE "MANEUVERS," BUT THESE DUDES GOT MOVES THAT MAKE YOU **GROOVE.**
ALL THEY NEED IS A LITTLE **ELEMENT X.**

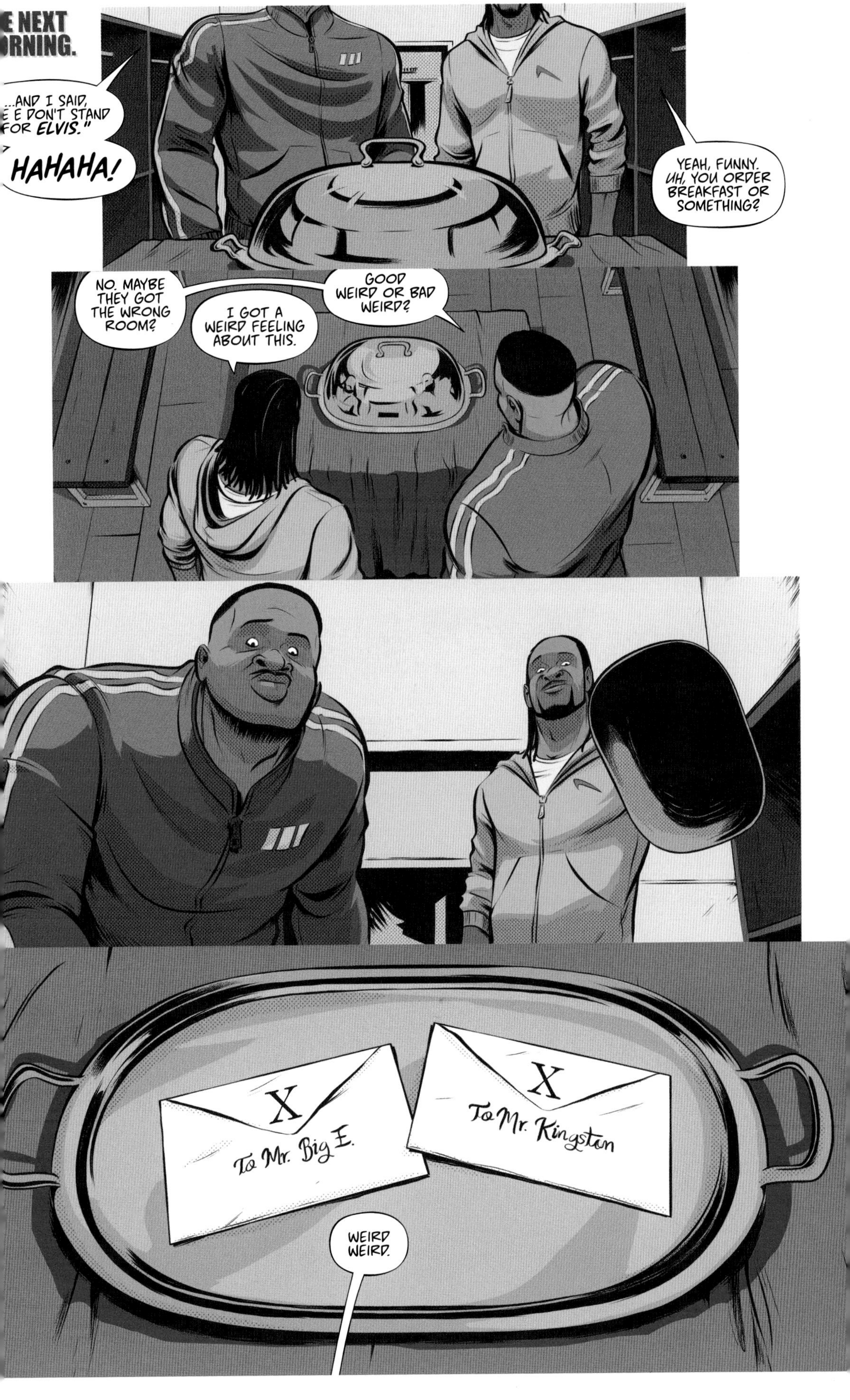
E NEXT
RNING.
...AND I SAID, E E DON'T STAND FOR *ELVIS*."
HAHAHA!
YEAH, FUNNY. UH, YOU ORDER BREAKFAST OR SOMETHING?
NO. MAYBE THEY GOT THE WRONG ROOM?
I GOT A WEIRD FEELING ABOUT THIS.
GOOD WEIRD OR BAD WEIRD?
X
To Mr. Big E.
X
To Mr. Kingston
WEIRD WEIRD.

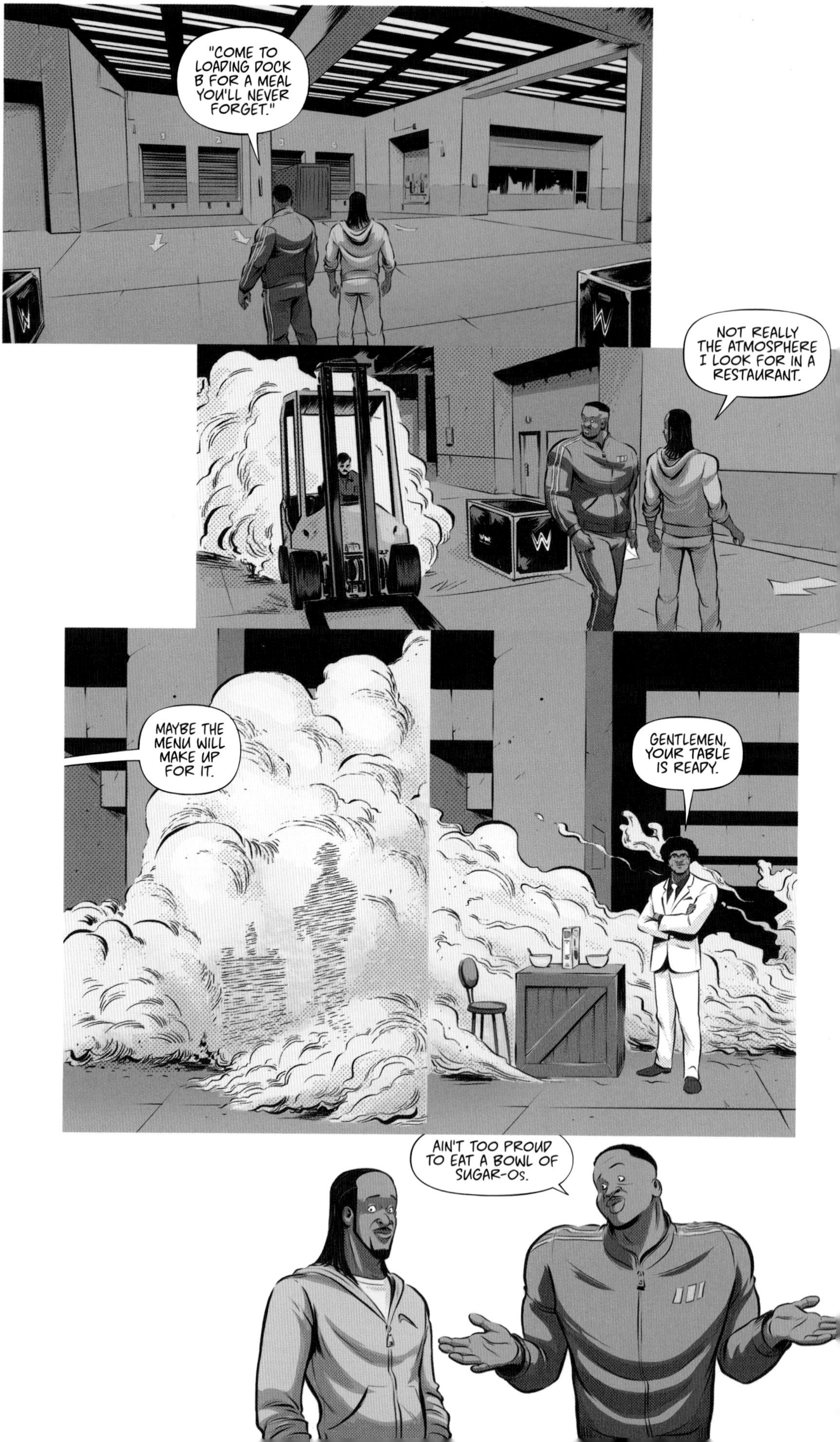
"COME TO LOADING DOCK B FOR A MEAL YOU'LL NEVER FORGET."
NOT REALLY THE ATMOSPHERE I LOOK FOR IN A RESTAURANT.
MAYBE THE MENU WILL MAKE UP FOR IT.
GENTLEMEN, YOUR TABLE IS READY.
AIN'T TOO PROUD TO EAT A BOWL OF SUGAR-Os.

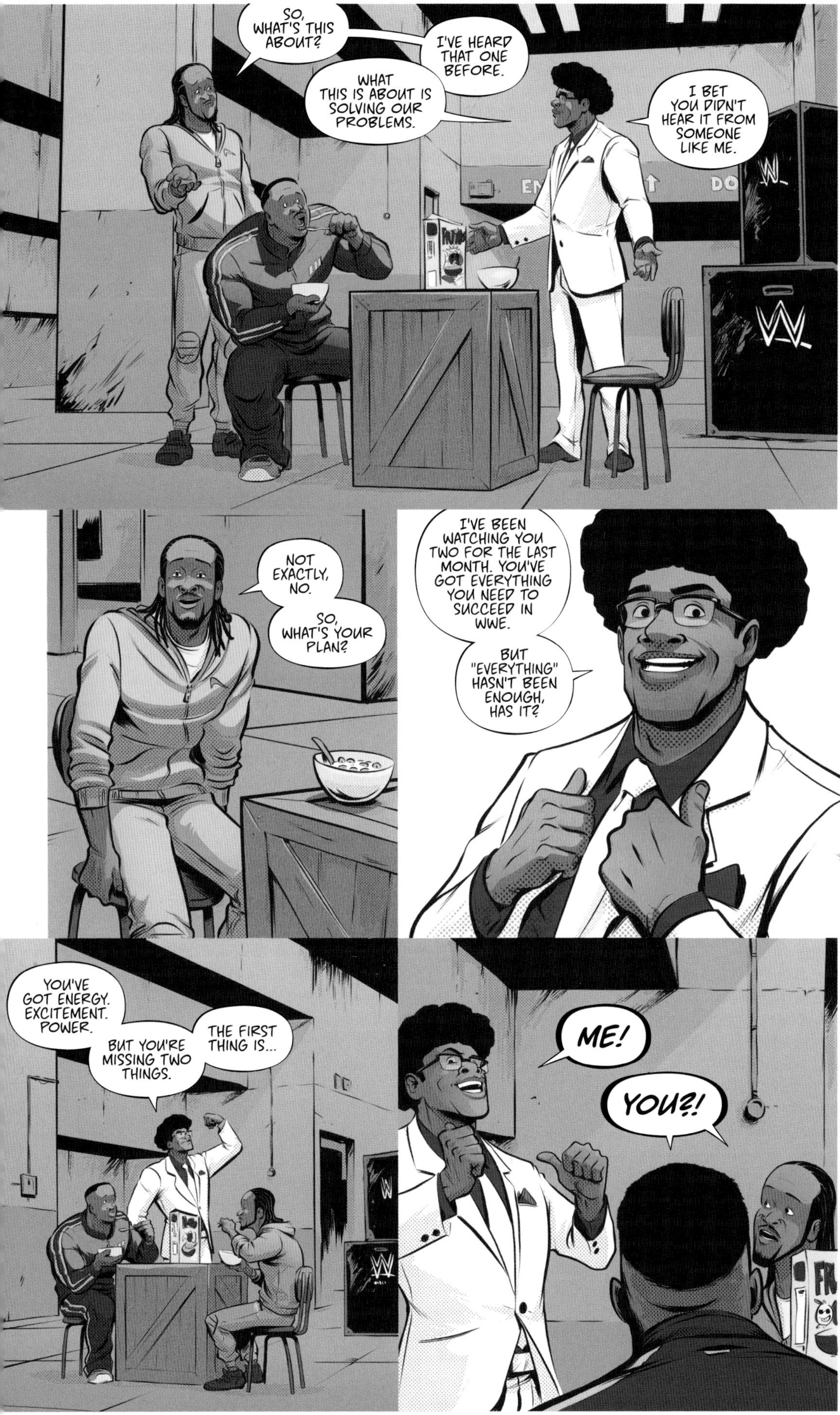
SO, WHAT'S THIS ABOUT?
I'VE HEARD THAT ONE BEFORE.
WHAT THIS IS ABOUT IS SOLVING OUR PROBLEMS.
I BET YOU DIDN'T HEAR IT FROM SOMEONE LIKE ME.
NOT EXACTLY, NO.
SO, WHAT'S YOUR PLAN?
I'VE BEEN WATCHING YOU TWO FOR THE LAST MONTH. YOU'VE GOT EVERYTHING YOU NEED TO SUCCEED IN WWE.
BUT "EVERYTHING" HASN'T BEEN ENOUGH, HAS IT?
YOU'VE GOT ENERGY. EXCITEMENT. POWER.
BUT YOU'RE MISSING TWO THINGS.
THE FIRST THING IS...
ME!
YOU?!

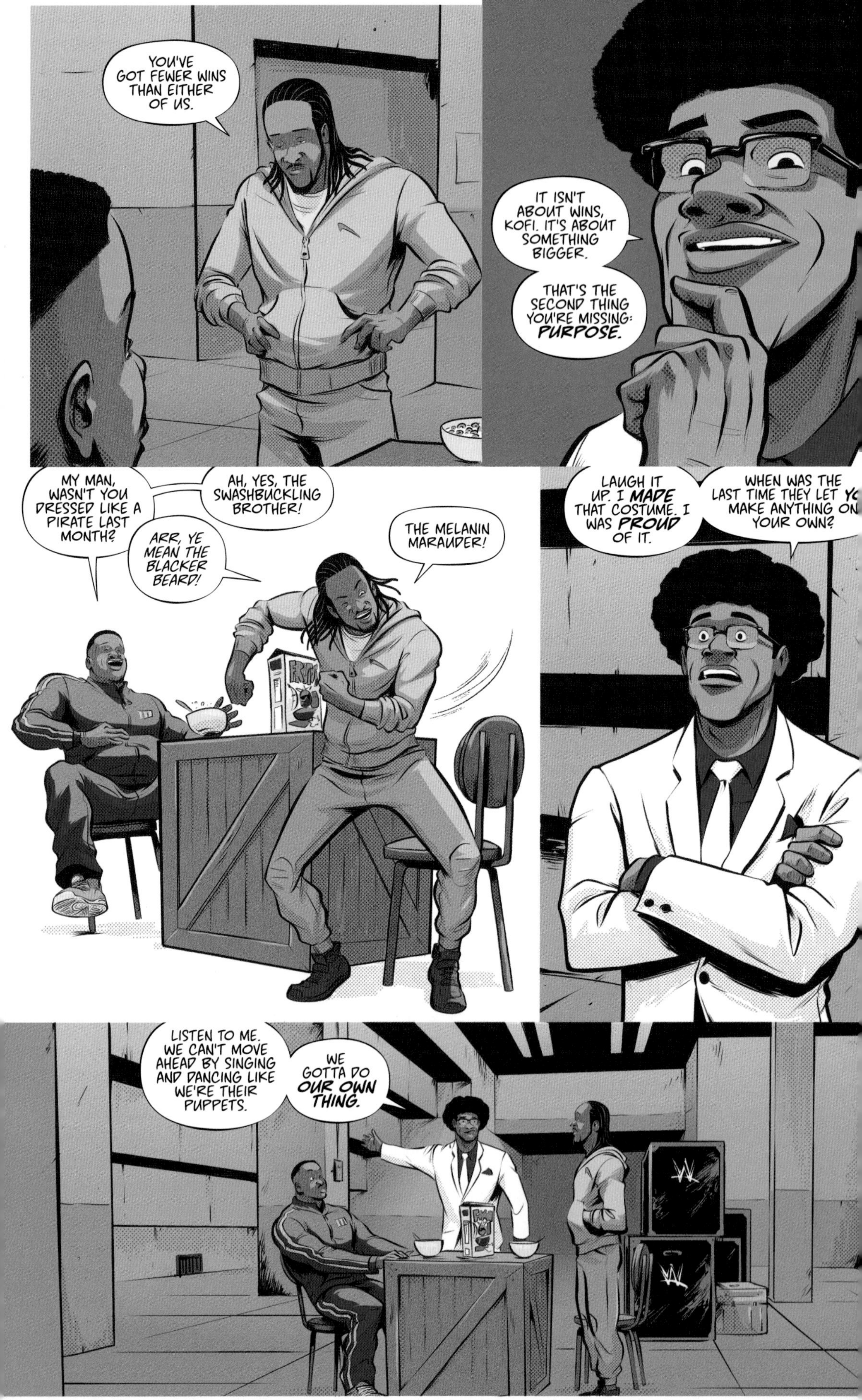
YOU'VE GOT FEWER WINS THAN EITHER OF US.
IT ISN'T ABOUT WINS, KOFI. IT'S ABOUT SOMETHING BIGGER.
THAT'S THE SECOND THING YOU'RE MISSING: PURPOSE.
MY MAN, WASN'T YOU DRESSED LIKE A PIRATE LAST MONTH?
AH, YES, THE SWASHBUCKLING BROTHER!
ARR, YE MEAN THE BLACKER BEARD!
THE MELANIN MARAUDER!
LAUGH IT UP. I MADE THAT COSTUME. I WAS PROUD OF IT.
LISTEN TO ME. WE CAN'T MOVE AHEAD BY SINGING AND DANCING LIKE WE'RE THEIR PUPPETS.
WE GOTTA DO OUR OWN THING.

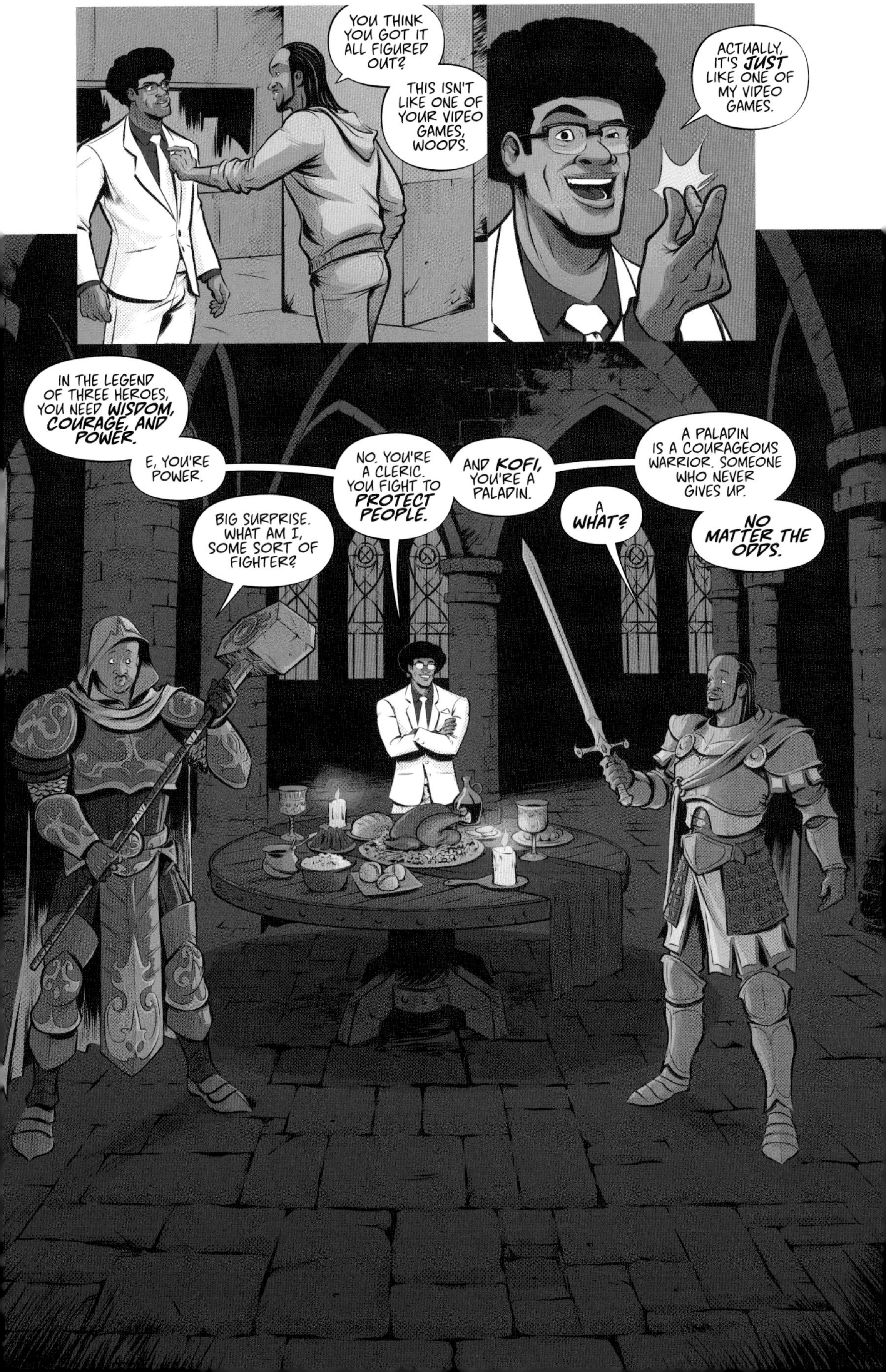
YOU THINK YOU GOT IT ALL FIGURED OUT?
THIS ISN'T LIKE ONE OF YOUR VIDEO GAMES, WOODS.
ACTUALLY, IT'S JUST LIKE ONE OF MY VIDEO GAMES.
IN THE LEGEND OF THREE HEROES, YOU NEED WISDOM, COURAGE, AND POWER.
E, YOU'RE POWER.
BIG SURPRISE. WHAT AM I, SOME SORT OF FIGHTER?
NO. YOU'RE A CLERIC. YOU FIGHT TO PROTECT PEOPLE.
AND KOFI, YOU'RE A PALADIN.
A WHAT?
A PALADIN IS A COURAGEOUS WARRIOR. SOMEONE WHO NEVER GIVES UP.
NO MATTER THE ODDS.

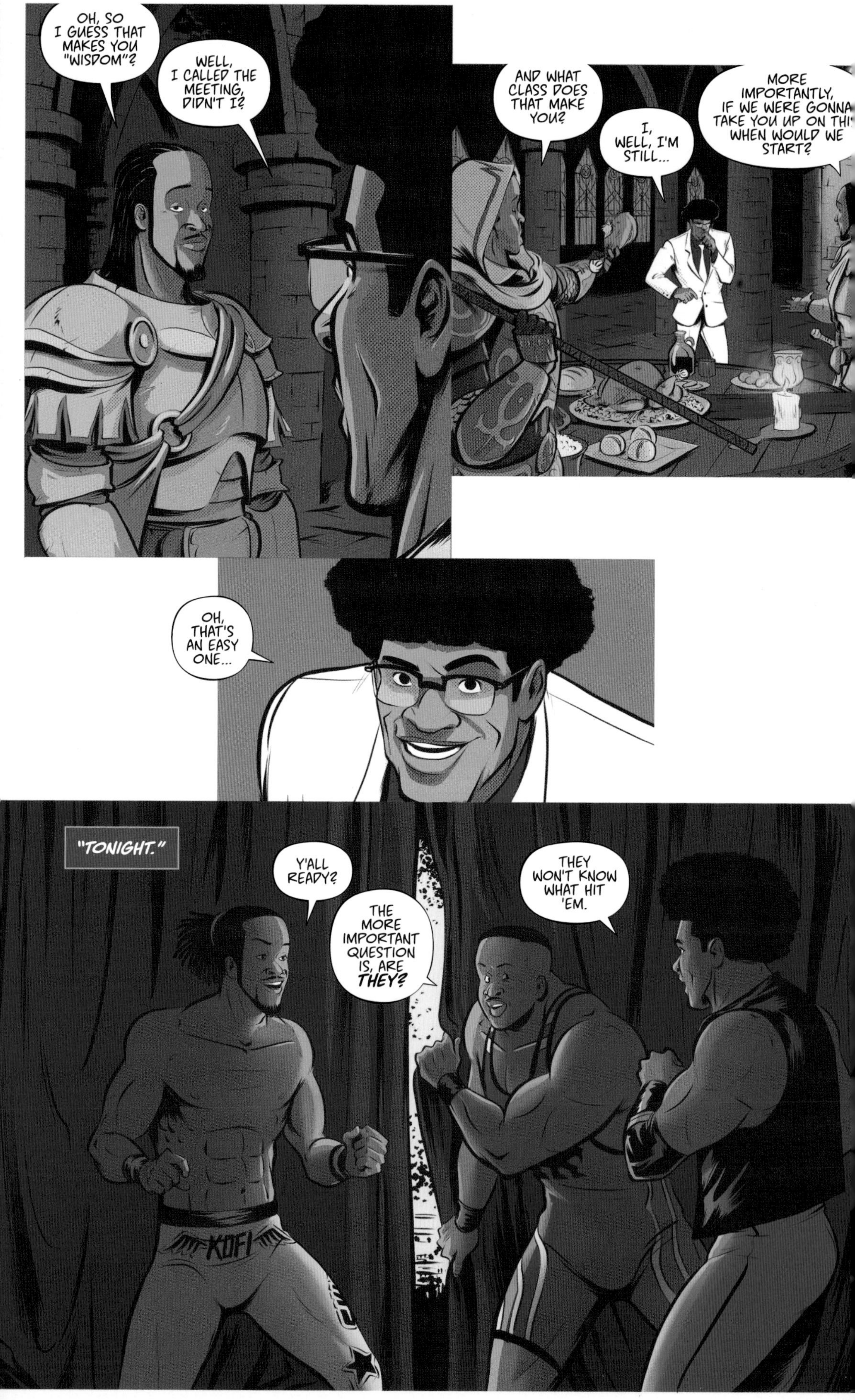
OH, SO I GUESS THAT MAKES YOU "WISDOM"?
WELL, I CALLED THE MEETING, DIDN'T I?
AND WHAT CLASS DOES THAT MAKE YOU?
I, WELL, I'M STILL...
MORE IMPORTANTLY, IF WE WERE GONNA TAKE YOU UP ON THI WHEN WOULD WE START?
OH, THAT'S AN EASY ONE...
"TONIGHT."
Y'ALL READY?
THE MORE IMPORTANT QUESTION IS, ARE *THEY*?
THEY WON'T KNOW WHAT HIT 'EM.
KOFI

WHEN WE CAME OUT ONTO THE RAMP, I FELT TERRIBLE. I TALKED A BIG GAME TO KOFI AND E, BUT I WAS SHOOK.

KOFI KINGSTON AND BIG E ARE SCHEDULED TO SQUARE OFF AGAINST THE USOS IN TAG TEAM ACTION, BUT IT LOOKS LIKE THEY'VE GOT A NEW FRIEND WITH THEM.

WHAT IF PEOPLE HATED US?

IS THAT XAVIER WOODS!?

WHAT IF I MADE KOFI AND E WORSE?

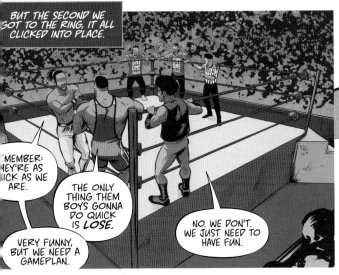

BUT THE SECOND WE GOT TO THE RING, IT ALL CLICKED INTO PLACE.

'MEMBER: THEY'RE AS QUICK AS WE ARE.

THE ONLY THING THEM BOYS GONNA DO QUICK IS LOSE.

VERY FUNNY, BUT WE NEED A GAMEPLAN.

NO. WE DON'T. WE JUST NEED TO HAVE FUN.

GUYS, THIS IS NOT A HANDICAPPED MATCH, I'M GOING TO NEED TO ASK YOU TO--

NOT A PROBLEM.

HAVE.

FUN.

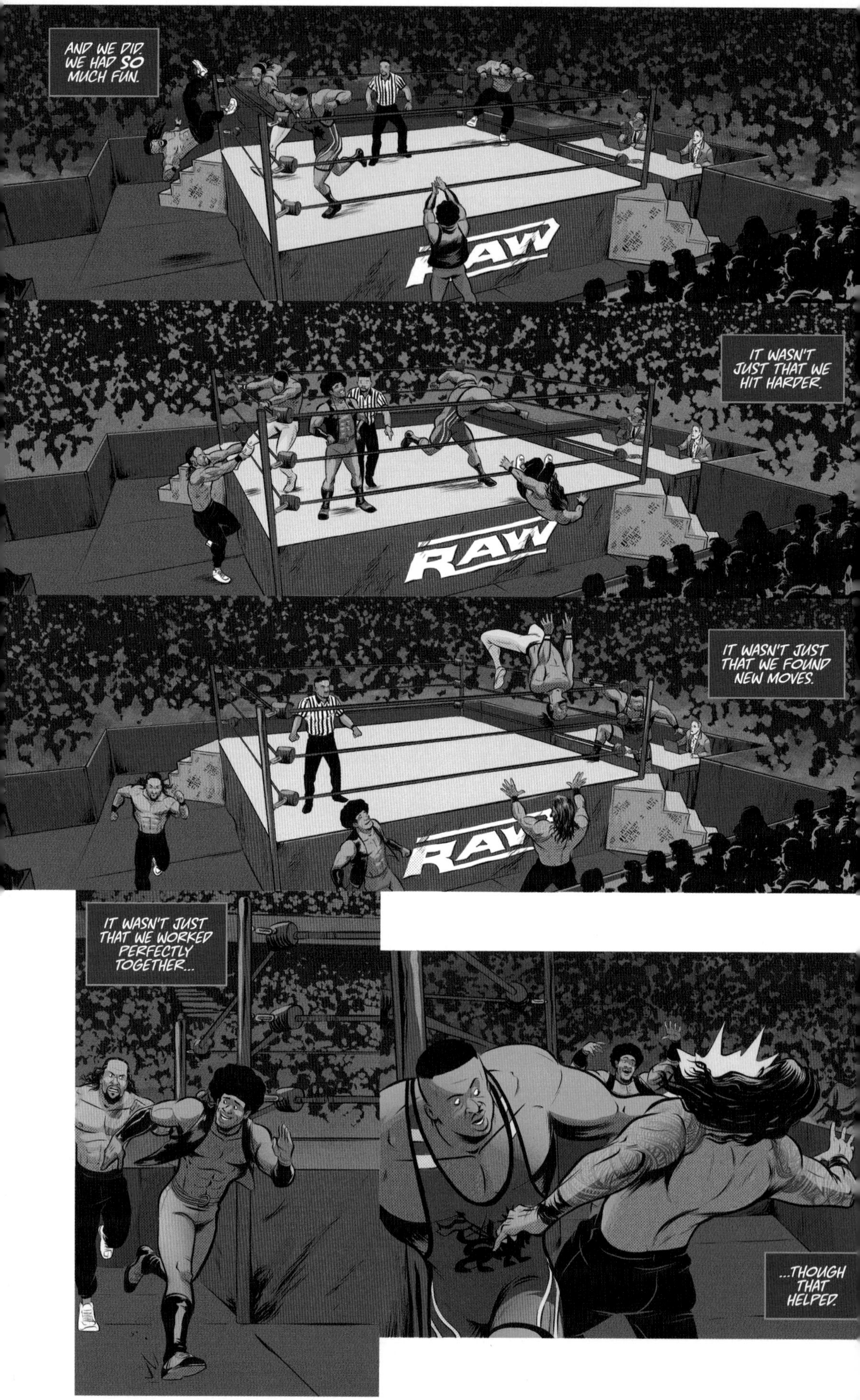
AND WE DID. WE HAD SO MUCH FUN.
RAW
IT WASN'T JUST THAT WE HIT HARDER.
RAW
IT WASN'T JUST THAT WE FOUND NEW MOVES.
RAW
IT WASN'T JUST THAT WE WORKED PERFECTLY TOGETHER...
...THOUGH THAT HELPED.

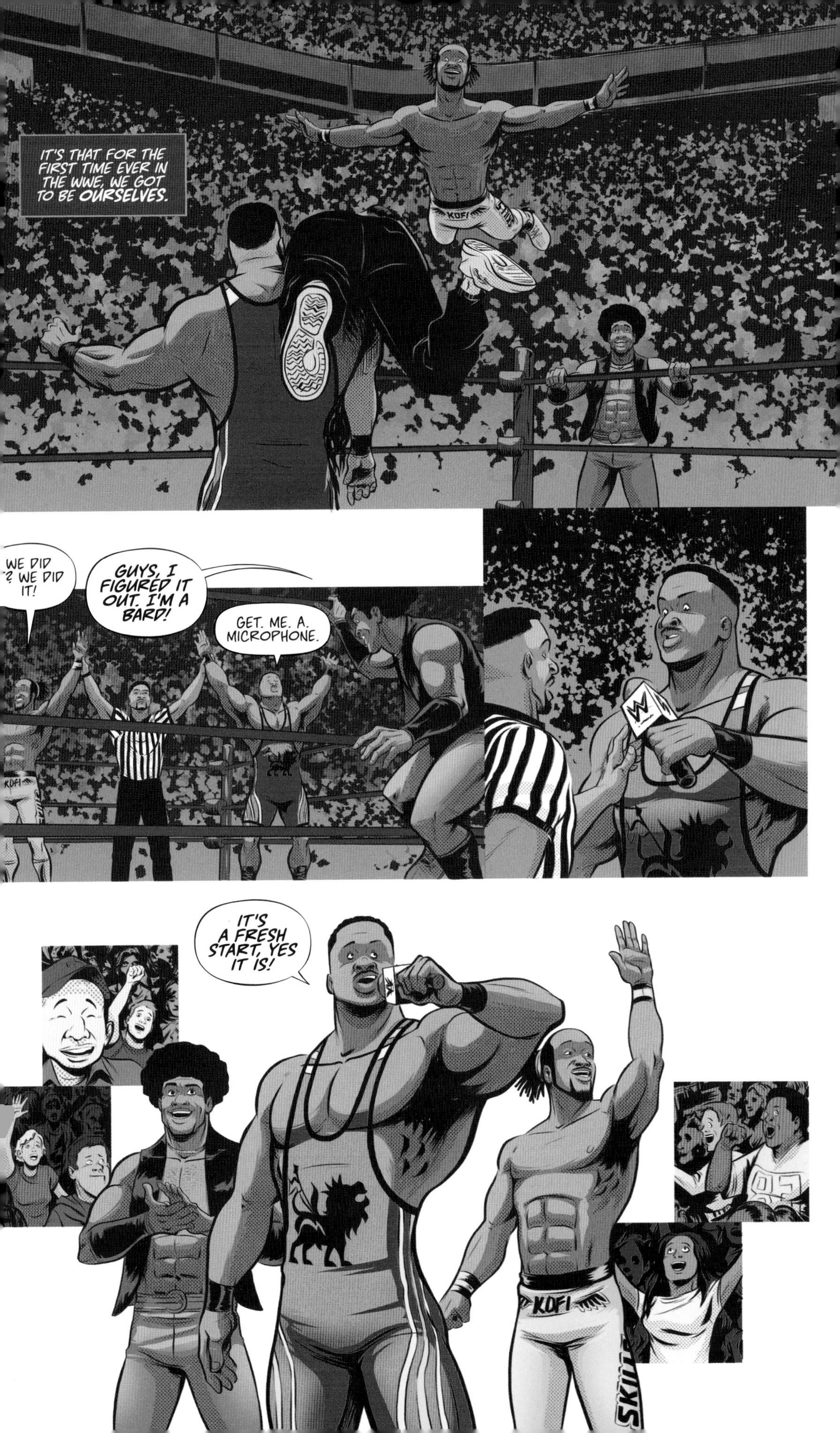
IT'S THAT FOR THE FIRST TIME EVER IN THE WWE, WE GOT TO BE OURSELVES.
WE DID ? WE DID IT!
GUYS, I FIGURED IT OUT. I'M A BARD!
GET. ME. A. MICROPHONE.
IT'S A FRESH START, YES IT IS!

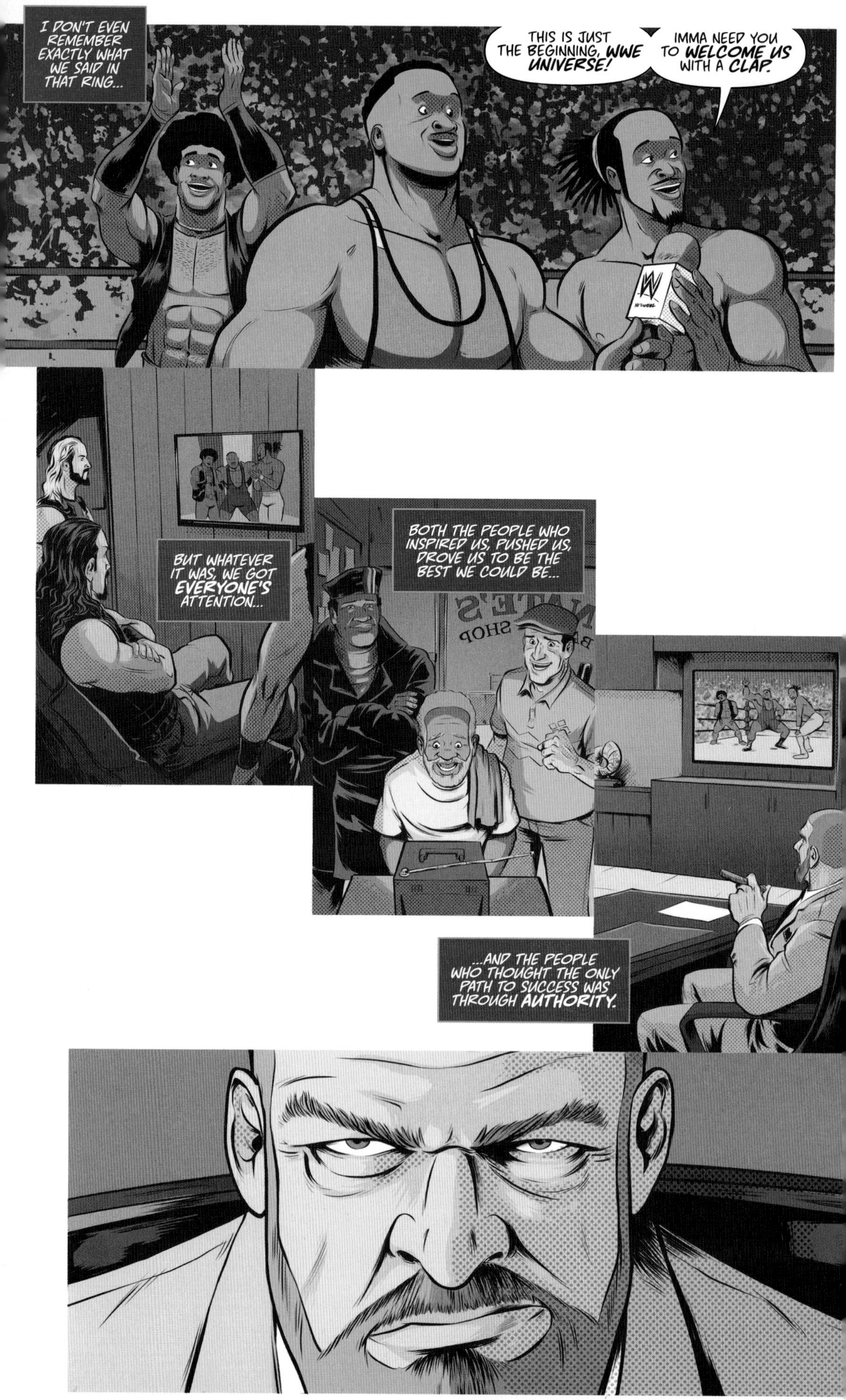
I DON'T EVEN REMEMBER EXACTLY WHAT WE SAID IN THAT RING...
THIS IS JUST THE BEGINNING, WWE UNIVERSE!
IMMA NEED YOU TO WELCOME US WITH A CLAP.
BUT WHATEVER IT WAS, WE GOT EVERYONE'S ATTENTION...
BOTH THE PEOPLE WHO INSPIRED US, PUSHED US, DROVE US TO BE THE BEST WE COULD BE...
...AND THE PEOPLE WHO THOUGHT THE ONLY PATH TO SUCCESS WAS THROUGH AUTHORITY.

CHAPTER
TWO

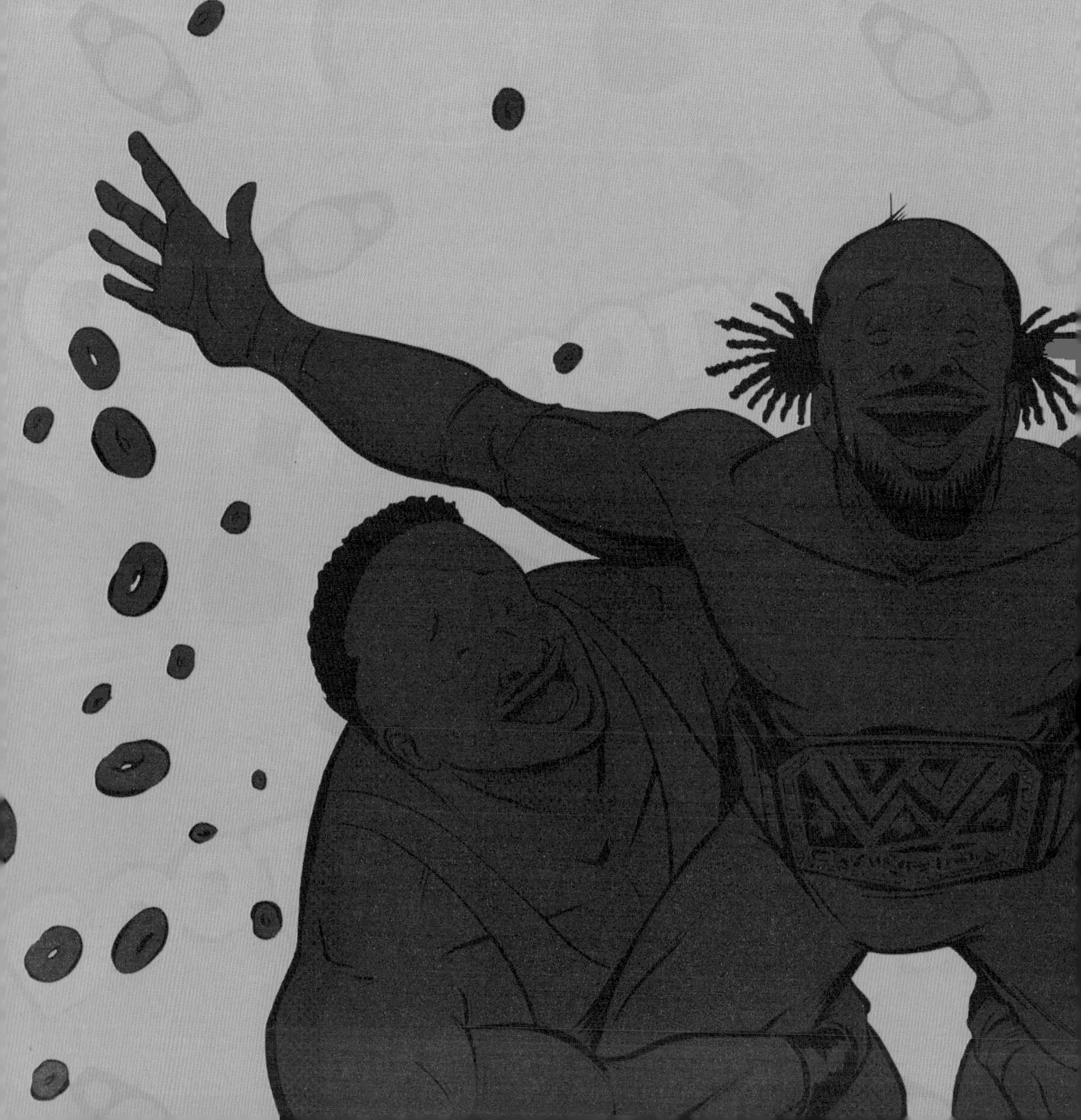

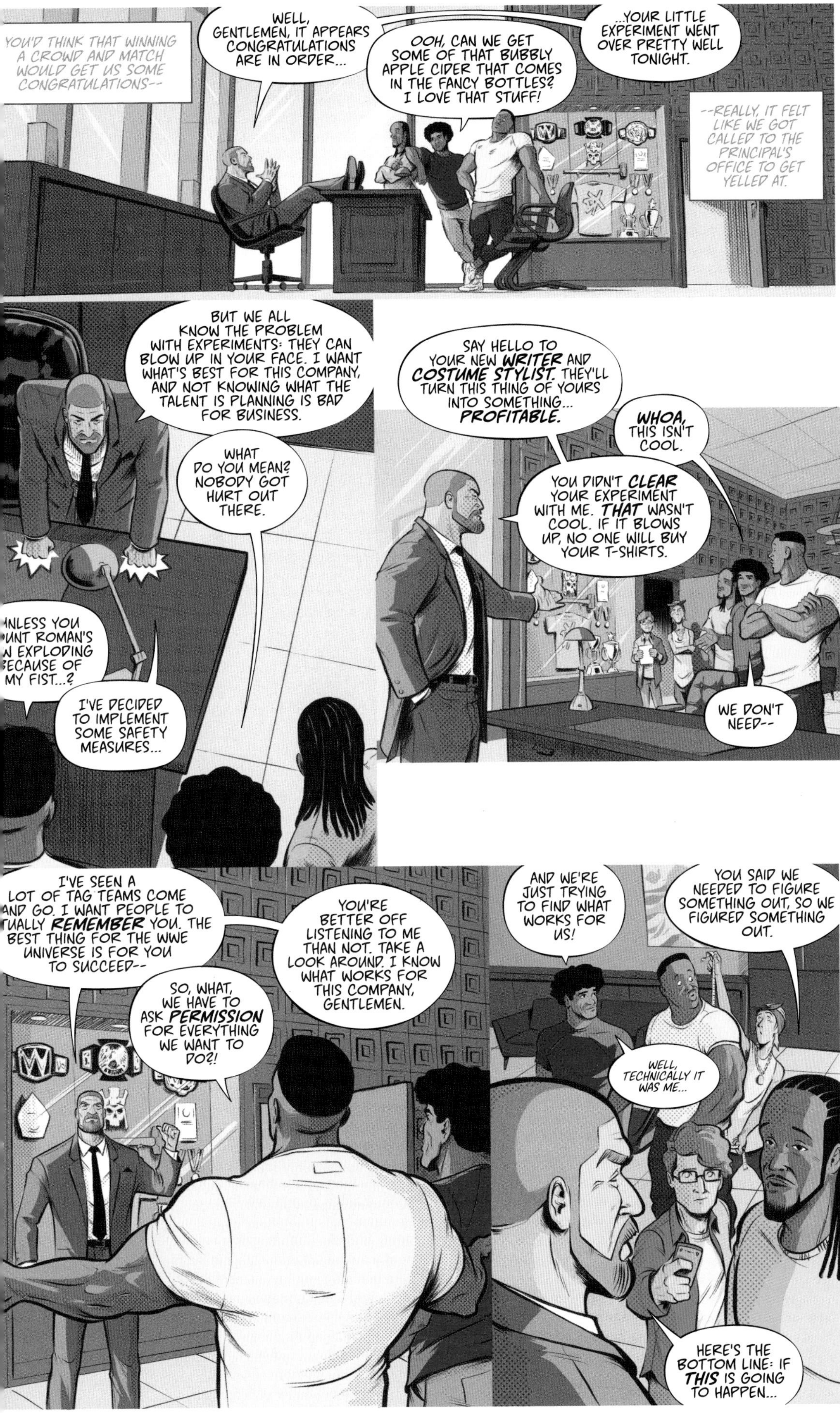
YOU'D THINK THAT WINNING A CROWD AND MATCH WOULD GET US SOME CONGRATULATIONS--
WELL, GENTLEMEN, IT APPEARS CONGRATULATIONS ARE IN ORDER...
OOH, CAN WE GET SOME OF THAT BUBBLY APPLE CIDER THAT COMES IN THE FANCY BOTTLES? I LOVE THAT STUFF!
...YOUR LITTLE EXPERIMENT WENT OVER PRETTY WELL TONIGHT.
--REALLY, IT FELT LIKE WE GOT CALLED TO THE PRINCIPAL'S OFFICE TO GET YELLED AT.
BUT WE ALL KNOW THE PROBLEM WITH EXPERIMENTS: THEY CAN BLOW UP IN YOUR FACE. I WANT WHAT'S BEST FOR THIS COMPANY, AND NOT KNOWING WHAT THE TALENT IS PLANNING IS BAD FOR BUSINESS.
WHAT DO YOU MEAN? NOBODY GOT HURT OUT THERE.
UNLESS YOU COUNT ROMAN'S ...N EXPLODING BECAUSE OF MY FIST...?
I'VE DECIDED TO IMPLEMENT SOME SAFETY MEASURES...
SAY HELLO TO YOUR NEW WRITER AND COSTUME STYLIST. THEY'LL TURN THIS THING OF YOURS INTO SOMETHING... PROFITABLE.
WHOA, THIS ISN'T COOL.
YOU DIDN'T CLEAR YOUR EXPERIMENT WITH ME. THAT WASN'T COOL. IF IT BLOWS UP, NO ONE WILL BUY YOUR T-SHIRTS.
WE DON'T NEED--
I'VE SEEN A LOT OF TAG TEAMS COME AND GO. I WANT PEOPLE TO ...TUALLY REMEMBER YOU. THE BEST THING FOR THE WWE UNIVERSE IS FOR YOU TO SUCCEED--
SO, WHAT, WE HAVE TO ASK PERMISSION FOR EVERYTHING WE WANT TO DO?!
YOU'RE BETTER OFF LISTENING TO ME THAN NOT. TAKE A LOOK AROUND. I KNOW WHAT WORKS FOR THIS COMPANY, GENTLEMEN.
AND WE'RE JUST TRYING TO FIND WHAT WORKS FOR US!
YOU SAID WE NEEDED TO FIGURE SOMETHING OUT, SO WE FIGURED SOMETHING OUT.
WELL, TECHNICALLY IT WAS ME...
HERE'S THE BOTTOM LINE: IF THIS IS GOING TO HAPPEN...

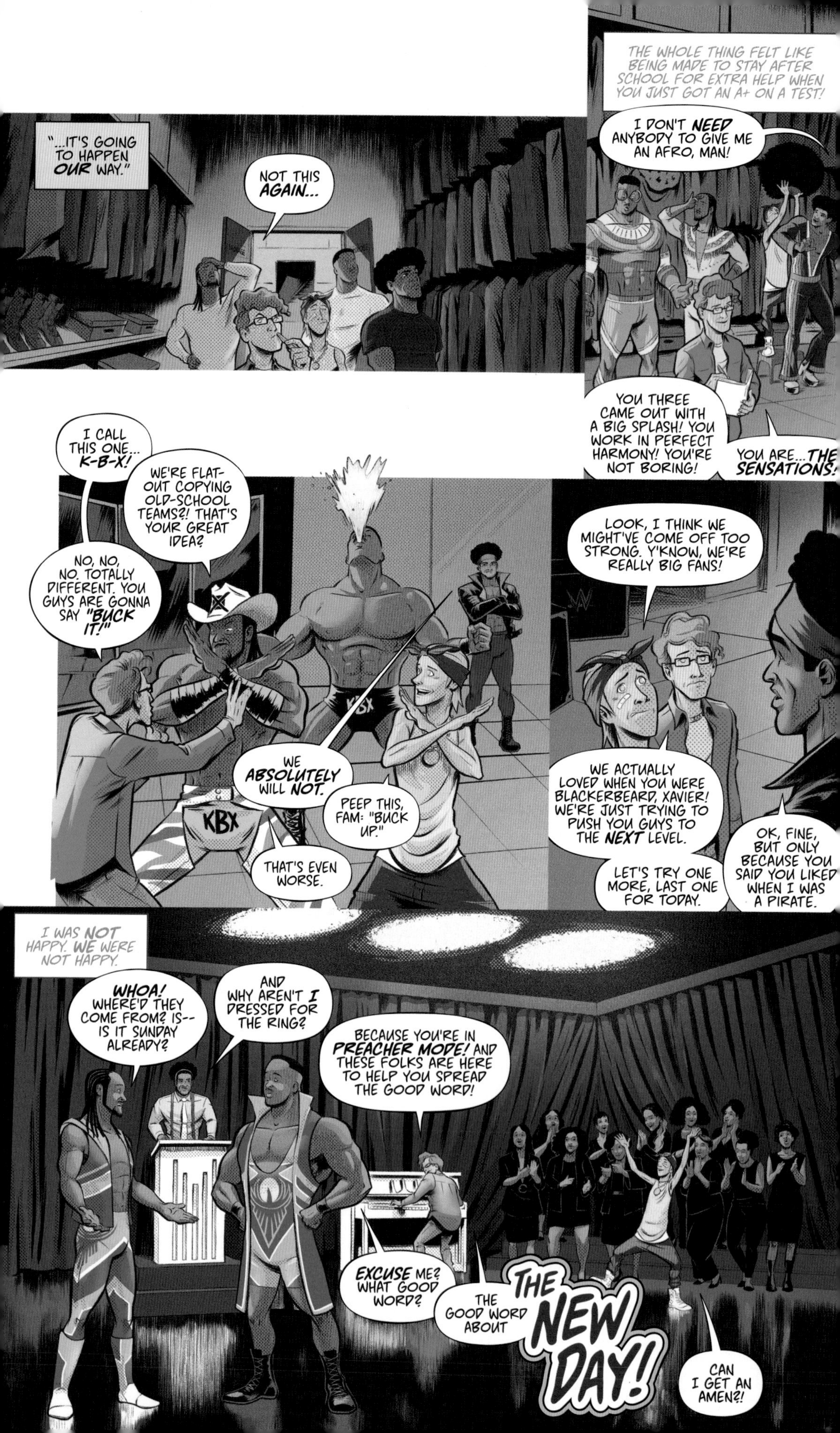

"...IT'S GOING TO HAPPEN **OUR** WAY."
NOT THIS **AGAIN...**
THE WHOLE THING FELT LIKE BEING MADE TO STAY AFTER SCHOOL FOR EXTRA HELP WHEN YOU JUST GOT AN A+ ON A TEST!
I DON'T **NEED** ANYBODY TO GIVE ME AN AFRO, MAN!
YOU THREE CAME OUT WITH A BIG SPLASH! YOU WORK IN PERFECT HARMONY! YOU'RE NOT BORING!
YOU ARE... **THE SENSATIONS!**
I CALL THIS ONE... **K-B-X!**
WE'RE FLAT-OUT COPYING OLD-SCHOOL TEAMS?! THAT'S YOUR GREAT IDEA?
NO, NO, NO. TOTALLY DIFFERENT. YOU GUYS ARE GONNA SAY **"BUCK IT!"**
KBX
KBX
WE **ABSOLUTELY** WILL **NOT.**
PEEP THIS, FAM: "BUCK UP."
THAT'S EVEN WORSE.
LOOK, I THINK WE MIGHT'VE COME OFF TOO STRONG. Y'KNOW, WE'RE REALLY BIG FANS!
WE ACTUALLY LOVED WHEN YOU WERE BLACKERBEARD, XAVIER! WE'RE JUST TRYING TO PUSH YOU GUYS TO THE **NEXT** LEVEL.
LET'S TRY ONE MORE, LAST ONE FOR TODAY.
OK, FINE, BUT ONLY BECAUSE YOU SAID YOU LIKED WHEN I WAS A PIRATE.
I WAS **NOT** HAPPY. **WE** WERE NOT HAPPY.
WHOA! WHERE'D THEY COME FROM? IS-- IS IT SUNDAY ALREADY?
AND WHY AREN'T **I** DRESSED FOR THE RING?
BECAUSE YOU'RE IN **PREACHER MODE!** AND THESE FOLKS ARE HERE TO HELP YOU SPREAD THE GOOD WORD!
EXCUSE ME? WHAT GOOD WORD?
THE GOOD WORD ABOUT **THE NEW DAY!**
CAN I GET AN AMEN?!

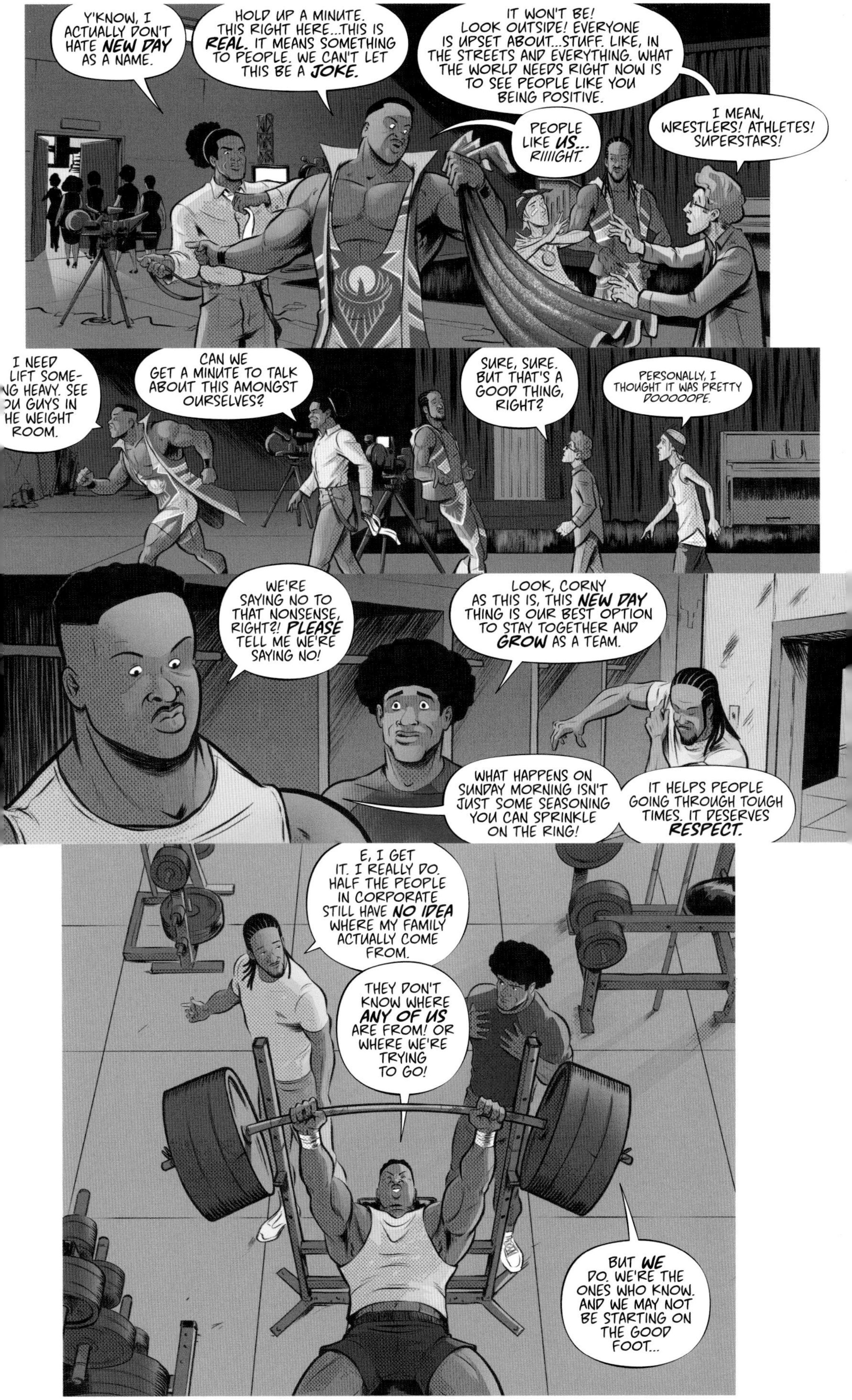

Y'KNOW, I ACTUALLY DON'T HATE NEW DAY AS A NAME.
HOLD UP A MINUTE. THIS RIGHT HERE...THIS IS REAL. IT MEANS SOMETHING TO PEOPLE. WE CAN'T LET THIS BE A JOKE.
IT WON'T BE! LOOK OUTSIDE! EVERYONE IS UPSET ABOUT...STUFF. LIKE, IN THE STREETS AND EVERYTHING. WHAT THE WORLD NEEDS RIGHT NOW IS TO SEE PEOPLE LIKE YOU BEING POSITIVE.
PEOPLE LIKE US... RIIIIGHT.
I MEAN, WRESTLERS! ATHLETES! SUPERSTARS!
I NEED LIFT SOME- NG HEAVY. SEE OU GUYS IN HE WEIGHT ROOM.
CAN WE GET A MINUTE TO TALK ABOUT THIS AMONGST OURSELVES?
SURE, SURE. BUT THAT'S A GOOD THING, RIGHT?
PERSONALLY, I THOUGHT IT WAS PRETTY DOOOOOPE.
WE'RE SAYING NO TO THAT NONSENSE, RIGHT?! PLEASE TELL ME WE'RE SAYING NO!
LOOK, CORNY AS THIS IS, THIS NEW DAY THING IS OUR BEST OPTION TO STAY TOGETHER AND GROW AS A TEAM.
WHAT HAPPENS ON SUNDAY MORNING ISN'T JUST SOME SEASONING YOU CAN SPRINKLE ON THE RING!
IT HELPS PEOPLE GOING THROUGH TOUGH TIMES. IT DESERVES RESPECT.
E, I GET IT. I REALLY DO. HALF THE PEOPLE IN CORPORATE STILL HAVE NO IDEA WHERE MY FAMILY ACTUALLY COME FROM.
THEY DON'T KNOW WHERE ANY OF US ARE FROM! OR WHERE WE'RE TRYING TO GO!
BUT WE DO. WE'RE THE ONES WHO KNOW. AND WE MAY NOT BE STARTING ON THE GOOD FOOT...

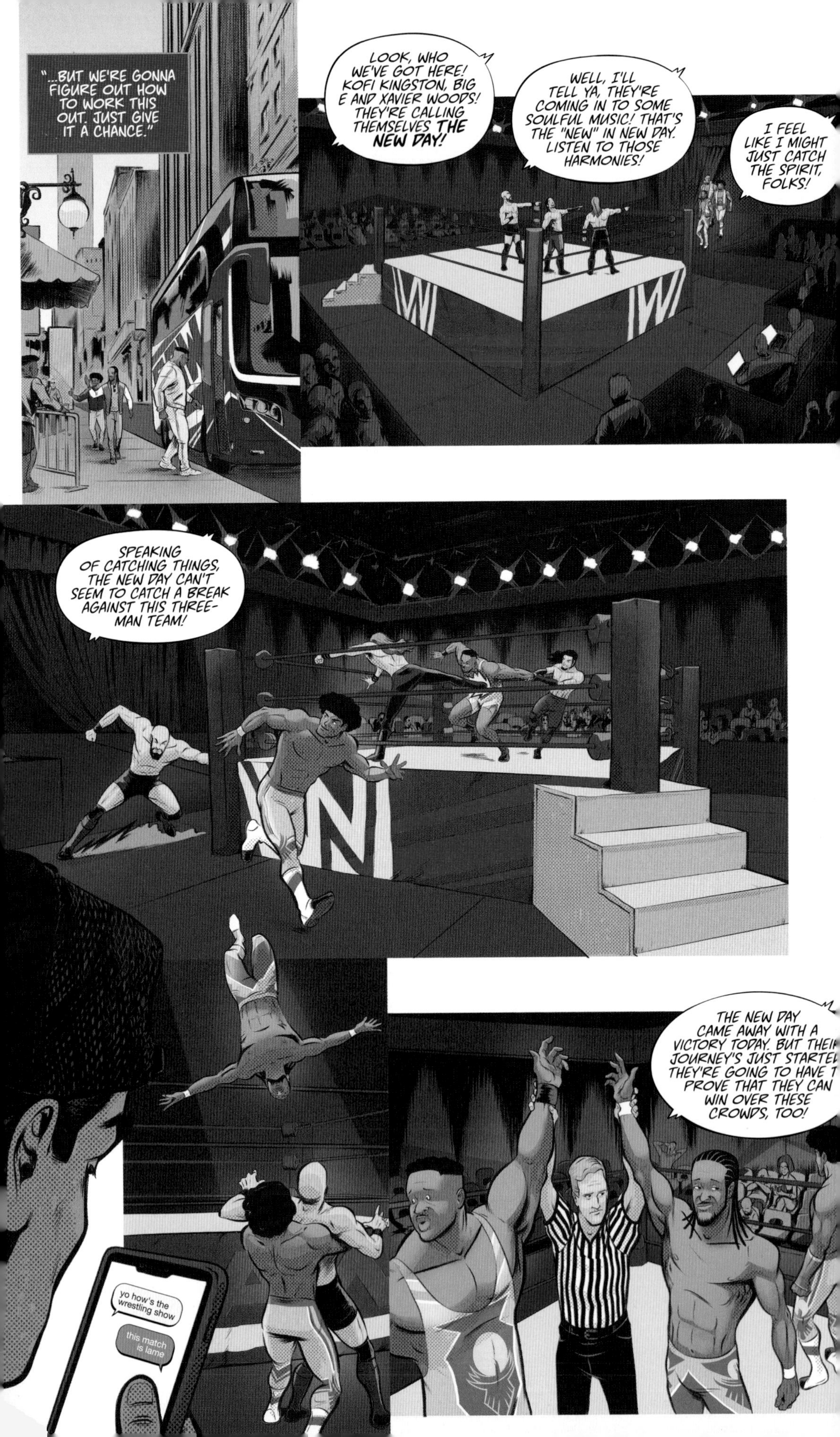

"...BUT WE'RE GONNA FIGURE OUT HOW TO WORK THIS OUT. JUST GIVE IT A CHANCE."
LOOK, WHO WE'VE GOT HERE! KOFI KINGSTON, BIG E AND XAVIER WOODS! THEY'RE CALLING THEMSELVES **THE NEW DAY!**
WELL, I'LL TELL YA, THEY'RE COMING IN TO SOME SOULFUL MUSIC! THAT'S THE "NEW" IN NEW DAY. LISTEN TO THOSE HARMONIES!
I FEEL LIKE I MIGHT JUST CATCH THE SPIRIT, FOLKS!
SPEAKING OF CATCHING THINGS, THE NEW DAY CAN'T SEEM TO CATCH A BREAK AGAINST THIS THREE-MAN TEAM!
yo how's the wrestling show
this match is lame
THE NEW DAY CAME AWAY WITH A VICTORY TODAY. BUT THEI JOURNEY'S JUST STARTE THEY'RE GOING TO HAVE T PROVE THAT THEY CAN WIN OVER THESE CROWDS, TOO!

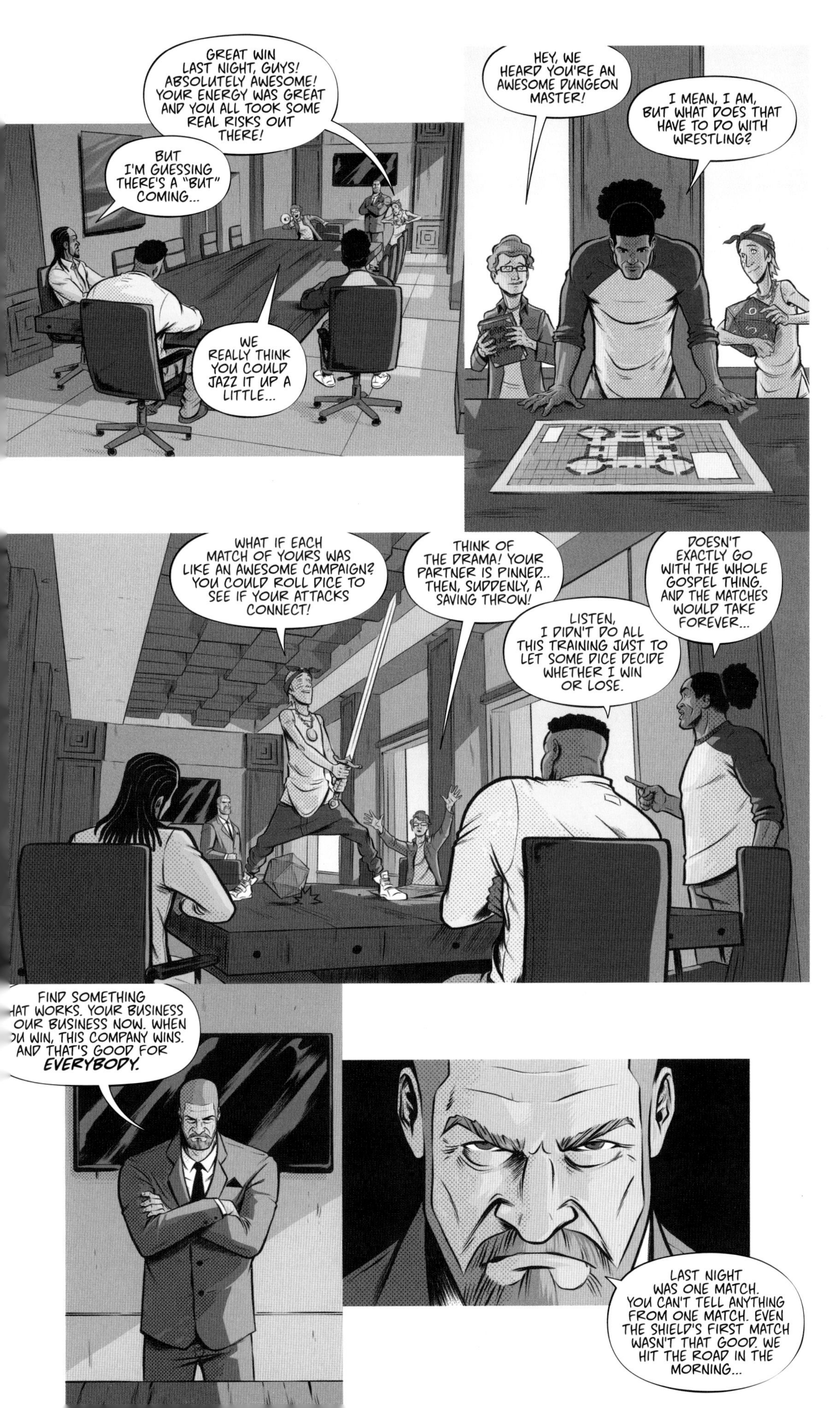
GREAT WIN LAST NIGHT, GUYS! ABSOLUTELY AWESOME! YOUR ENERGY WAS GREAT AND YOU ALL TOOK SOME REAL RISKS OUT THERE!
BUT I'M GUESSING THERE'S A "BUT" COMING...
WE REALLY THINK YOU COULD JAZZ IT UP A LITTLE...
HEY, WE HEARD YOU'RE AN AWESOME DUNGEON MASTER!
I MEAN, I AM, BUT WHAT DOES THAT HAVE TO DO WITH WRESTLING?
WHAT IF EACH MATCH OF YOURS WAS LIKE AN AWESOME CAMPAIGN? YOU COULD ROLL DICE TO SEE IF YOUR ATTACKS CONNECT!
THINK OF THE DRAMA! YOUR PARTNER IS PINNED... THEN, SUDDENLY, A SAVING THROW!
DOESN'T EXACTLY GO WITH THE WHOLE GOSPEL THING. AND THE MATCHES WOULD TAKE FOREVER...
LISTEN, I DIDN'T DO ALL THIS TRAINING JUST TO LET SOME DICE DECIDE WHETHER I WIN OR LOSE.
FIND SOMETHING HAT WORKS. YOUR BUSINESS OUR BUSINESS NOW. WHEN U WIN, THIS COMPANY WINS. AND THAT'S GOOD FOR *EVERYBODY.*
LAST NIGHT WAS ONE MATCH. YOU CAN'T TELL ANYTHING FROM ONE MATCH. EVEN THE SHIELD'S FIRST MATCH WASN'T THAT GOOD. WE HIT THE ROAD IN THE MORNING...

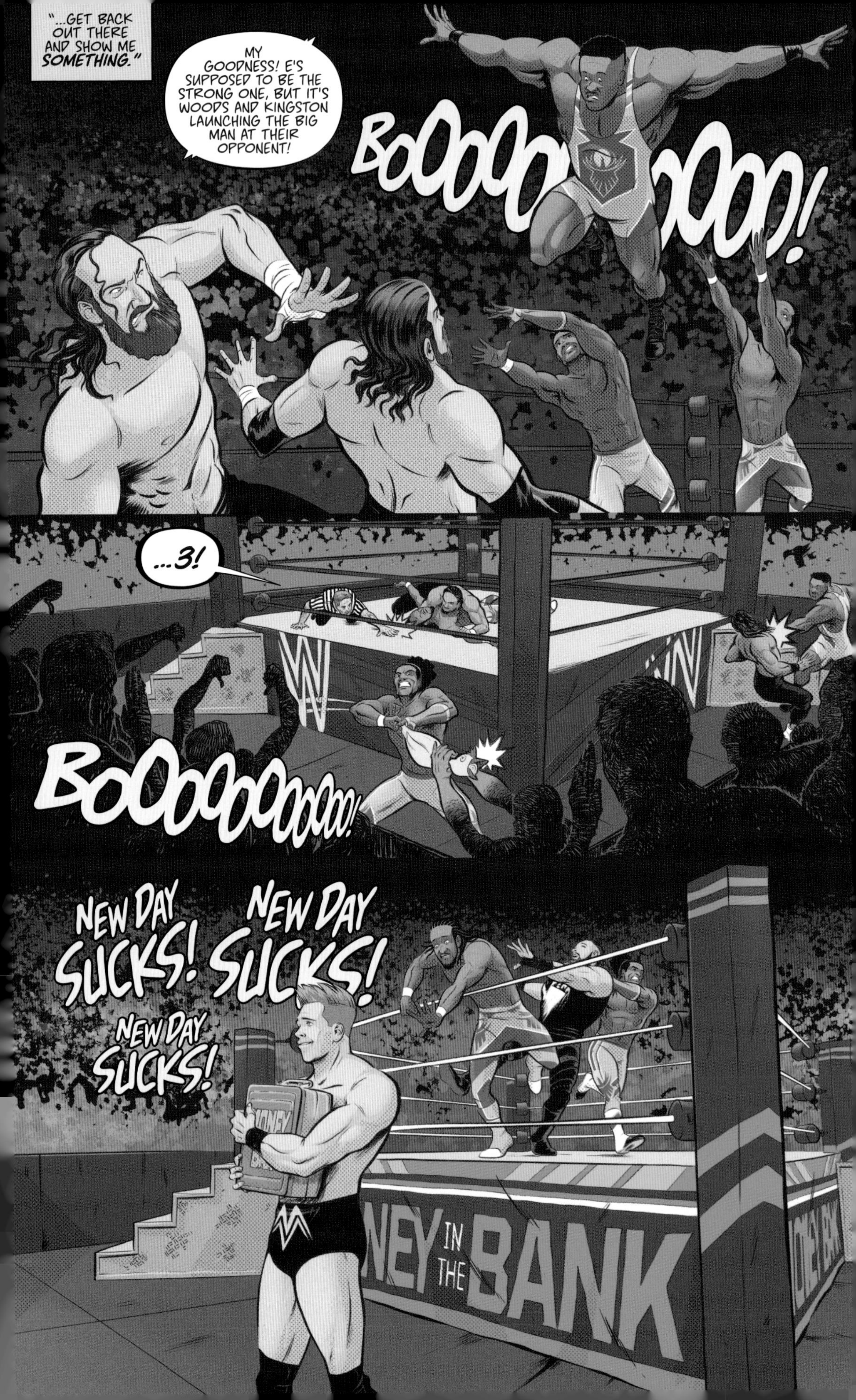
"...GET BACK OUT THERE AND SHOW ME SOMETHING."
MY GOODNESS! E'S SUPPOSED TO BE THE STRONG ONE, BUT IT'S WOODS AND KINGSTON LAUNCHING THE BIG MAN AT THEIR OPPONENT!
BOOOOOOOOOO!
...3!
BOOOOOOOOOO!
NEW DAY SUCKS!
NEW DAY SUCKS!
NEW DAY SUCKS!
IN THE BANK

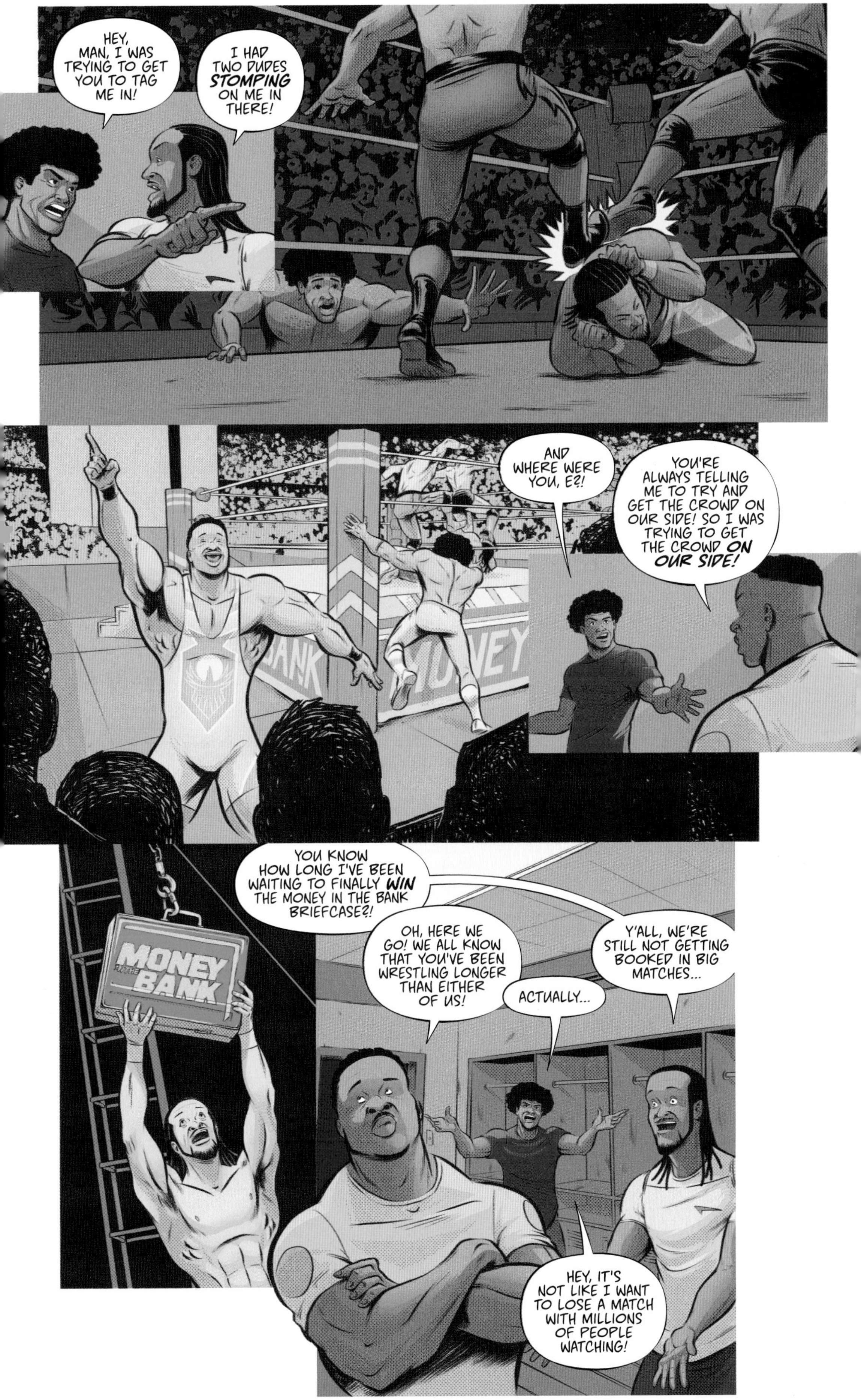
HEY, MAN, I WAS TRYING TO GET YOU TO TAG ME IN!
I HAD TWO DUDES STOMPING ON ME IN THERE!
AND WHERE WERE YOU, E?!
YOU'RE ALWAYS TELLING ME TO TRY AND GET THE CROWD ON OUR SIDE! SO I WAS TRYING TO GET THE CROWD ON OUR SIDE!
BANK
MONEY
YOU KNOW HOW LONG I'VE BEEN WAITING TO FINALLY WIN THE MONEY IN THE BANK BRIEFCASE?!
MONEY IN THE BANK
OH, HERE WE GO! WE ALL KNOW THAT YOU'VE BEEN WRESTLING LONGER THAN EITHER OF US!
Y'ALL, WE'RE STILL NOT GETTING BOOKED IN BIG MATCHES...
ACTUALLY...
HEY, IT'S NOT LIKE I WANT TO LOSE A MATCH WITH MILLIONS OF PEOPLE WATCHING!

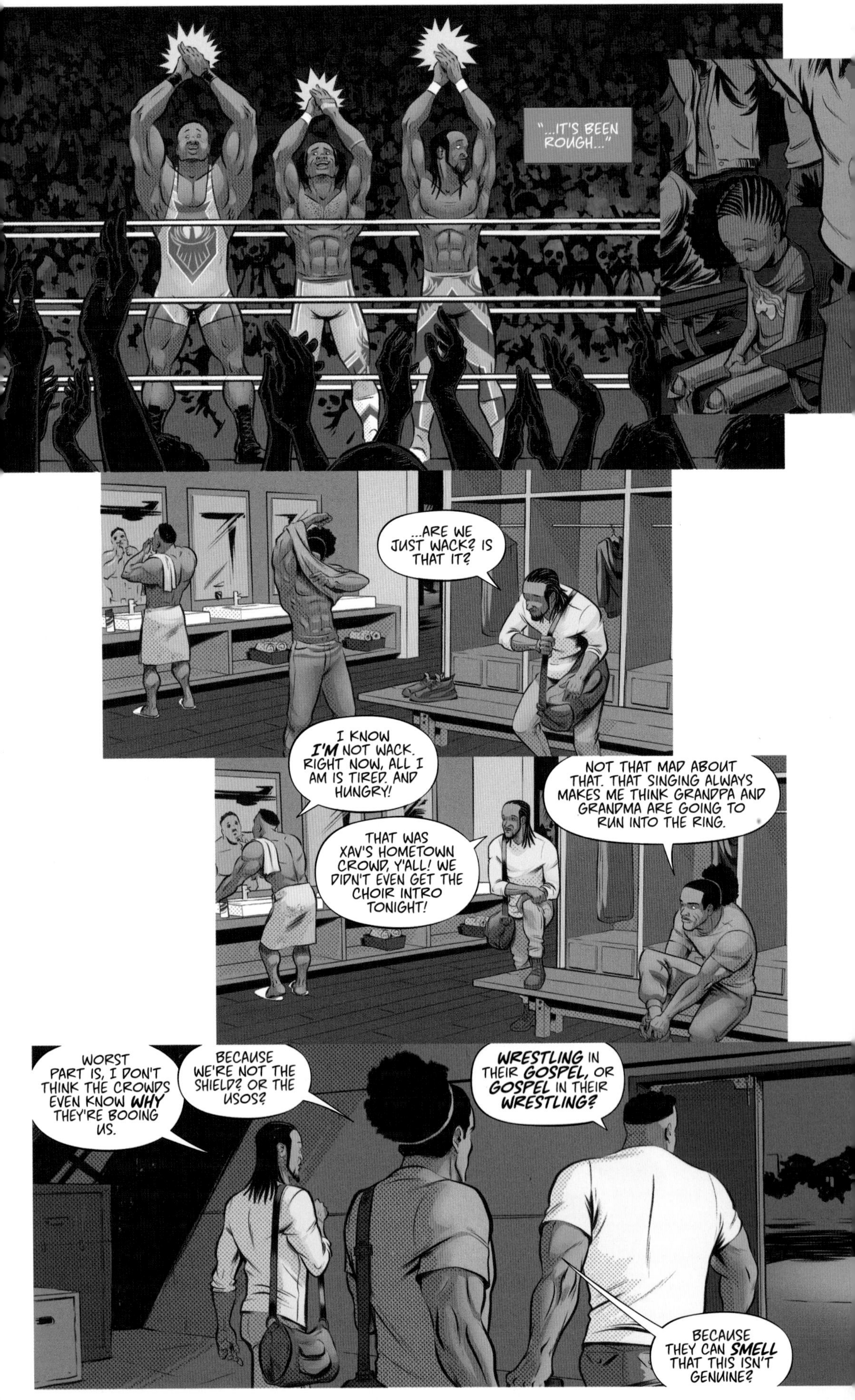
"...IT'S BEEN ROUGH..."
...ARE WE JUST WACK? IS THAT IT?
I KNOW ***I'M*** NOT WACK. RIGHT NOW, ALL I AM IS TIRED. AND HUNGRY!
THAT WAS XAV'S HOMETOWN CROWD, Y'ALL! WE DIDN'T EVEN GET THE CHOIR INTRO TONIGHT!
NOT THAT MAD ABOUT THAT. THAT SINGING ALWAYS MAKES ME THINK GRANDPA AND GRANDMA ARE GOING TO RUN INTO THE RING.
WORST PART IS, I DON'T THINK THE CROWDS EVEN KNOW ***WHY*** THEY'RE BOOING US.
BECAUSE WE'RE NOT THE SHIELD? OR THE USOS?
WRESTLING IN THEIR ***GOSPEL***, OR ***GOSPEL*** IN THEIR ***WRESTLING?***
BECAUSE THEY CAN ***SMELL*** THAT THIS ISN'T GENUINE?

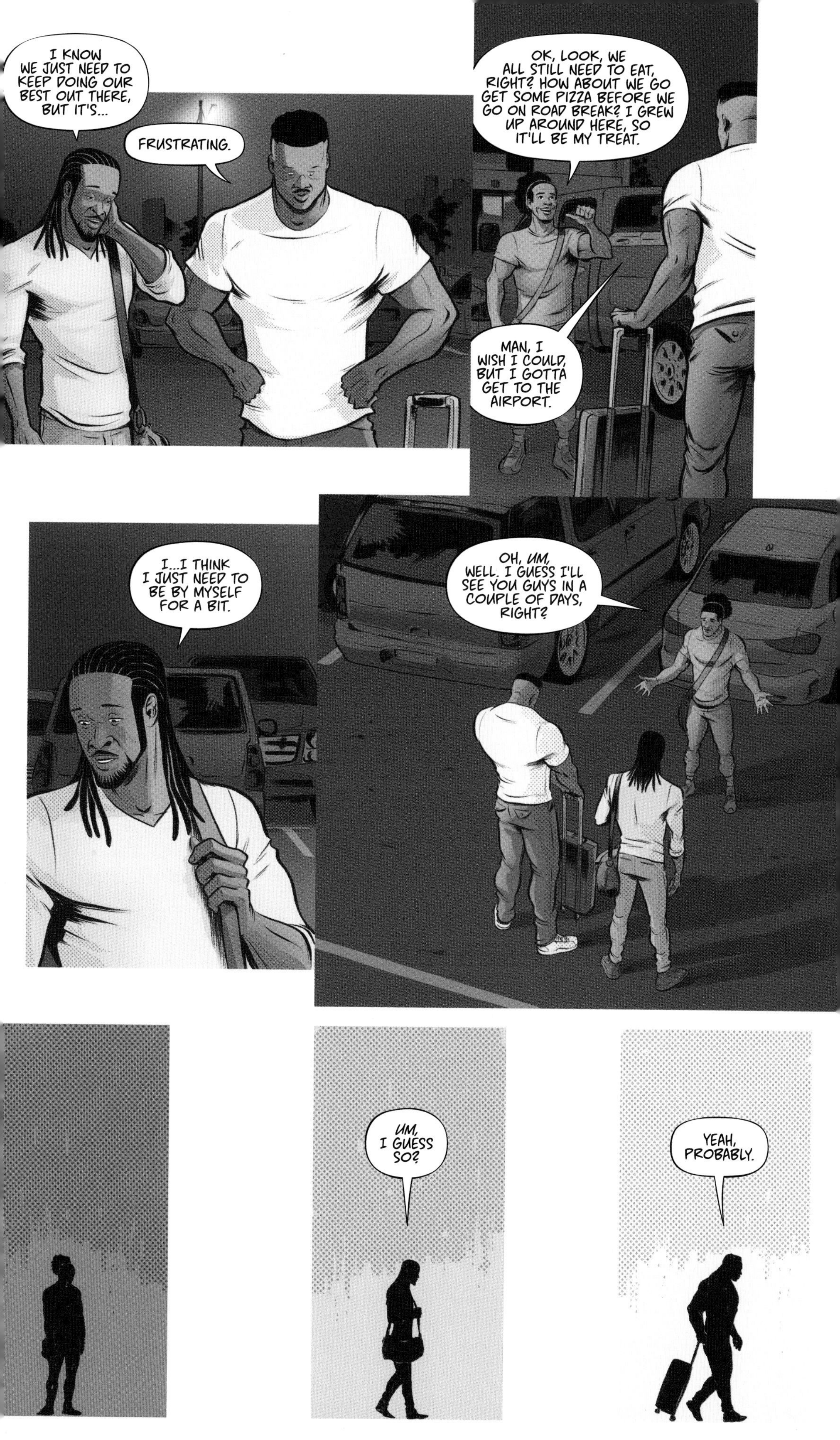
I KNOW WE JUST NEED TO KEEP DOING OUR BEST OUT THERE, BUT IT'S...
FRUSTRATING.
OK, LOOK, WE ALL STILL NEED TO EAT, RIGHT? HOW ABOUT WE GO GET SOME PIZZA BEFORE WE GO ON ROAD BREAK? I GREW UP AROUND HERE, SO IT'LL BE MY TREAT.
MAN, I WISH I COULD, BUT I GOTTA GET TO THE AIRPORT.
I...I THINK I JUST NEED TO BE BY MYSELF FOR A BIT.
OH, *UM*, WELL. I GUESS I'LL SEE YOU GUYS IN A COUPLE OF DAYS, RIGHT?
UM, I GUESS SO?
YEAH, PROBABLY.

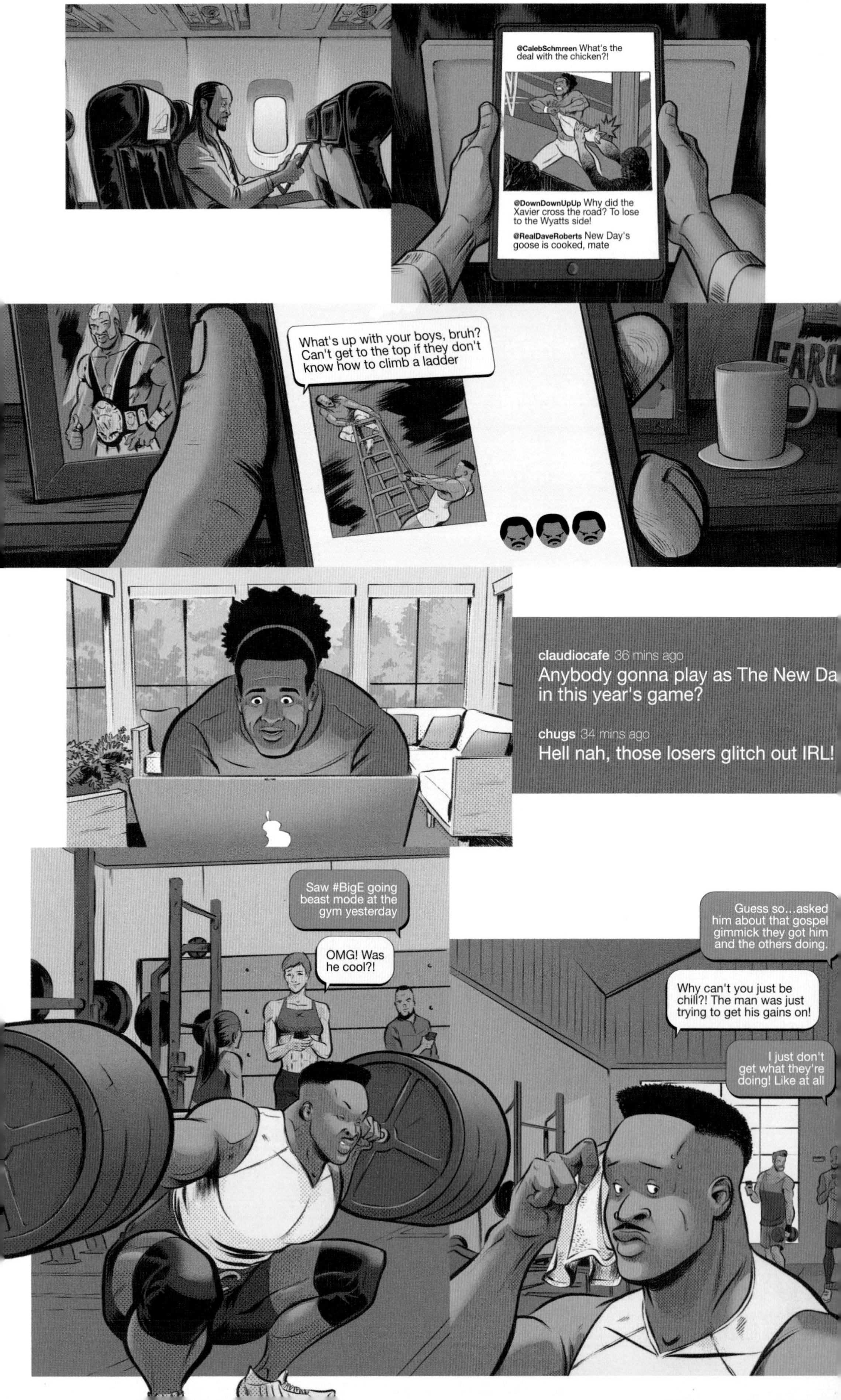

@CalebSchmreen What's the deal with the chicken?!
@DownDownUpUp Why did the Xavier cross the road? To lose to the Wyatts side!
@RealDaveRoberts New Day's goose is cooked, mate
What's up with your boys, bruh? Can't get to the top if they don't know how to climb a ladder
claudiocafe 36 mins ago
Anybody gonna play as The New Da
in this year's game?
chugs 34 mins ago
Hell nah, those losers glitch out IRL!
Saw #BigE going beast mode at the gym yesterday
OMG! Was he cool?!
Guess so...asked him about that gospel gimmick they got him and the others doing.
Why can't you just be chill?! The man was just trying to get his gains on!
I just don't get what they're doing! Like at all

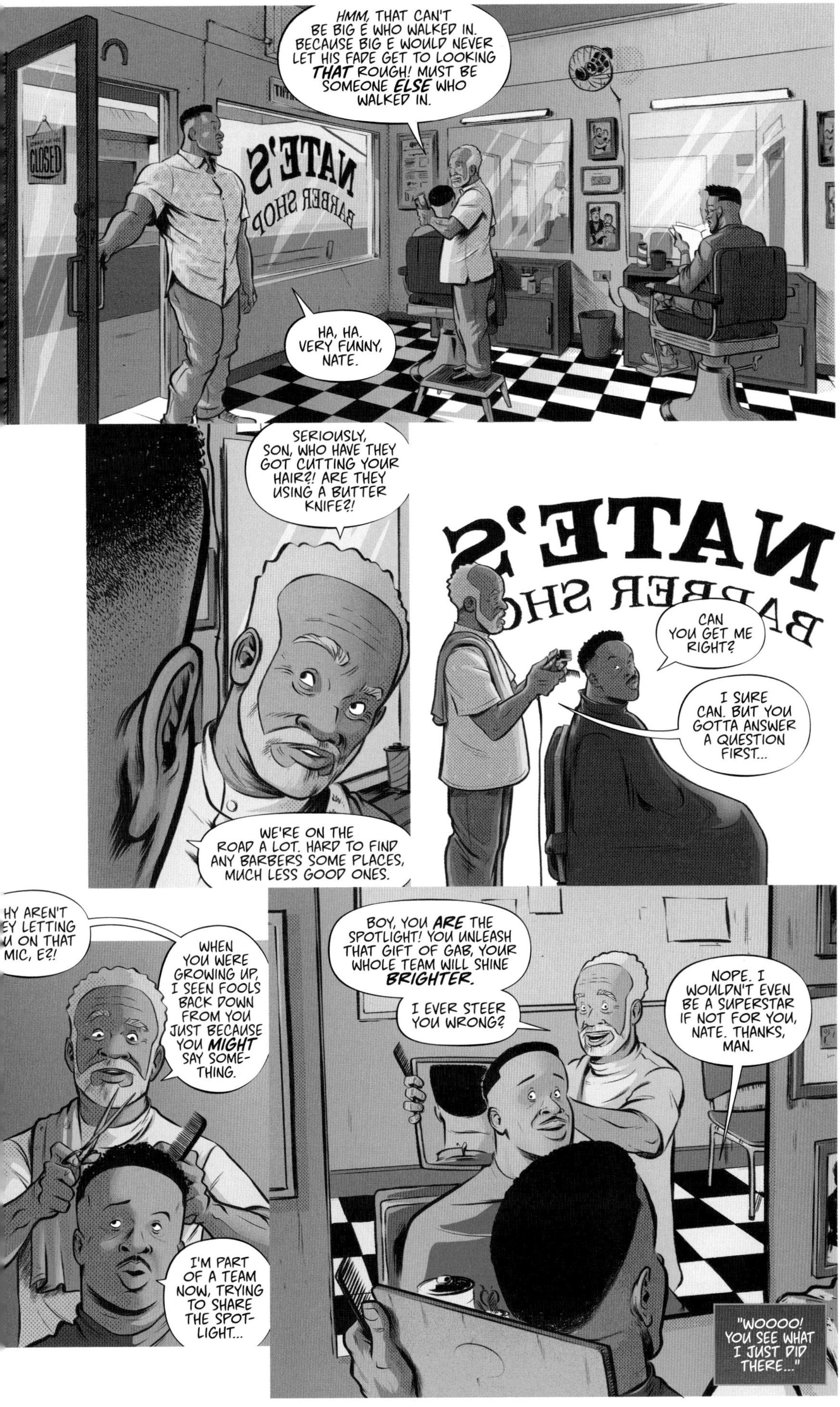
HMM, THAT CAN'T BE BIG E WHO WALKED IN. BECAUSE BIG E WOULD NEVER LET HIS FADE GET TO LOOKING **THAT** ROUGH! MUST BE SOMEONE **ELSE** WHO WALKED IN.
CLOSED
NATE'S BARBER SHOP
HA, HA. VERY FUNNY, NATE.
SERIOUSLY, SON, WHO HAVE THEY GOT CUTTING YOUR HAIR?! ARE THEY USING A BUTTER KNIFE?!
WE'RE ON THE ROAD A LOT. HARD TO FIND ANY BARBERS SOME PLACES, MUCH LESS GOOD ONES.
NATE'S BARBER SHO
CAN YOU GET ME RIGHT?
I SURE CAN. BUT YOU GOTTA ANSWER A QUESTION FIRST...
HY AREN'T EY LETTING U ON THAT MIC, E?!
WHEN YOU WERE GROWING UP, I SEEN FOOLS BACK DOWN FROM YOU JUST BECAUSE YOU **MIGHT** SAY SOME-THING.
I'M PART OF A TEAM NOW, TRYING TO SHARE THE SPOT-LIGHT...
BOY, YOU **ARE** THE SPOTLIGHT! YOU UNLEASH THAT GIFT OF GAB, YOUR WHOLE TEAM WILL SHINE **BRIGHTER.**
I EVER STEER YOU WRONG?
NOPE. I WOULDN'T EVEN BE A SUPERSTAR IF NOT FOR YOU, NATE. THANKS, MAN.
"WOOOO! YOU SEE WHAT I JUST DID THERE..."

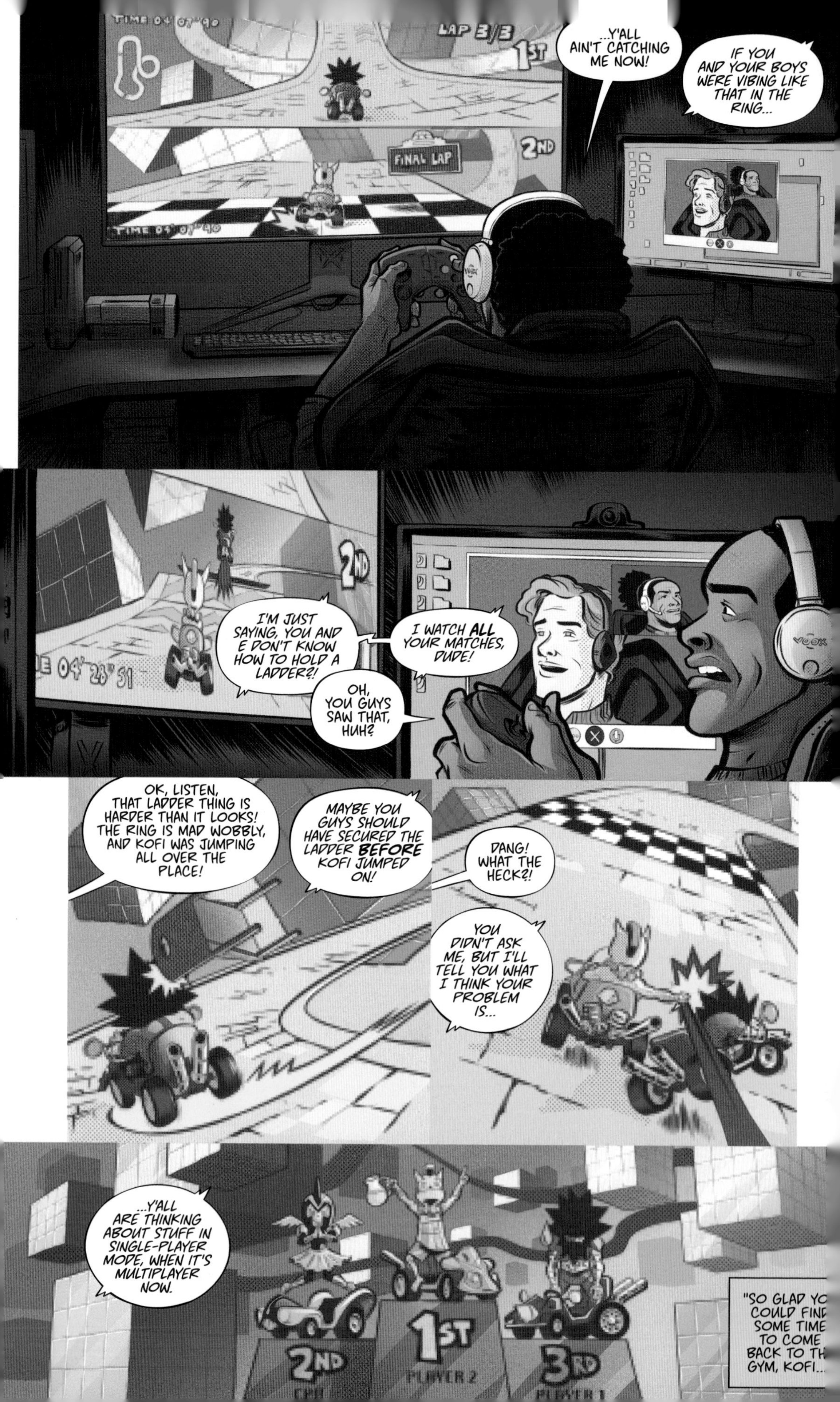
LAP 3/3
1ST
FINAL LAP
2ND
...Y'ALL AIN'T CATCHING ME NOW!
IF YOU AND YOUR BOYS WERE VIBING LIKE THAT IN THE RING...
2ND
I'M JUST SAYING, YOU AND E DON'T KNOW HOW TO HOLD A LADDER?!
I WATCH **ALL** YOUR MATCHES, DUDE!
OH, YOU GUYS SAW THAT, HUH?
OK, LISTEN, THAT LADDER THING IS HARDER THAN IT LOOKS! THE RING IS MAD WOBBLY, AND KOFI WAS JUMPING ALL OVER THE PLACE!
MAYBE YOU GUYS SHOULD HAVE SECURED THE LADDER **BEFORE** KOFI JUMPED ON!
DANG! WHAT THE HECK?!
YOU DIDN'T ASK ME, BUT I'LL TELL YOU WHAT I THINK YOUR PROBLEM IS...
...Y'ALL ARE THINKING ABOUT STUFF IN SINGLE-PLAYER MODE, WHEN IT'S MULTIPLAYER NOW.
2ND
1ST
PLAYER 2
3RD
"SO GLAD YO COULD FIND SOME TIME TO COME BACK TO TH GYM, KOFI...

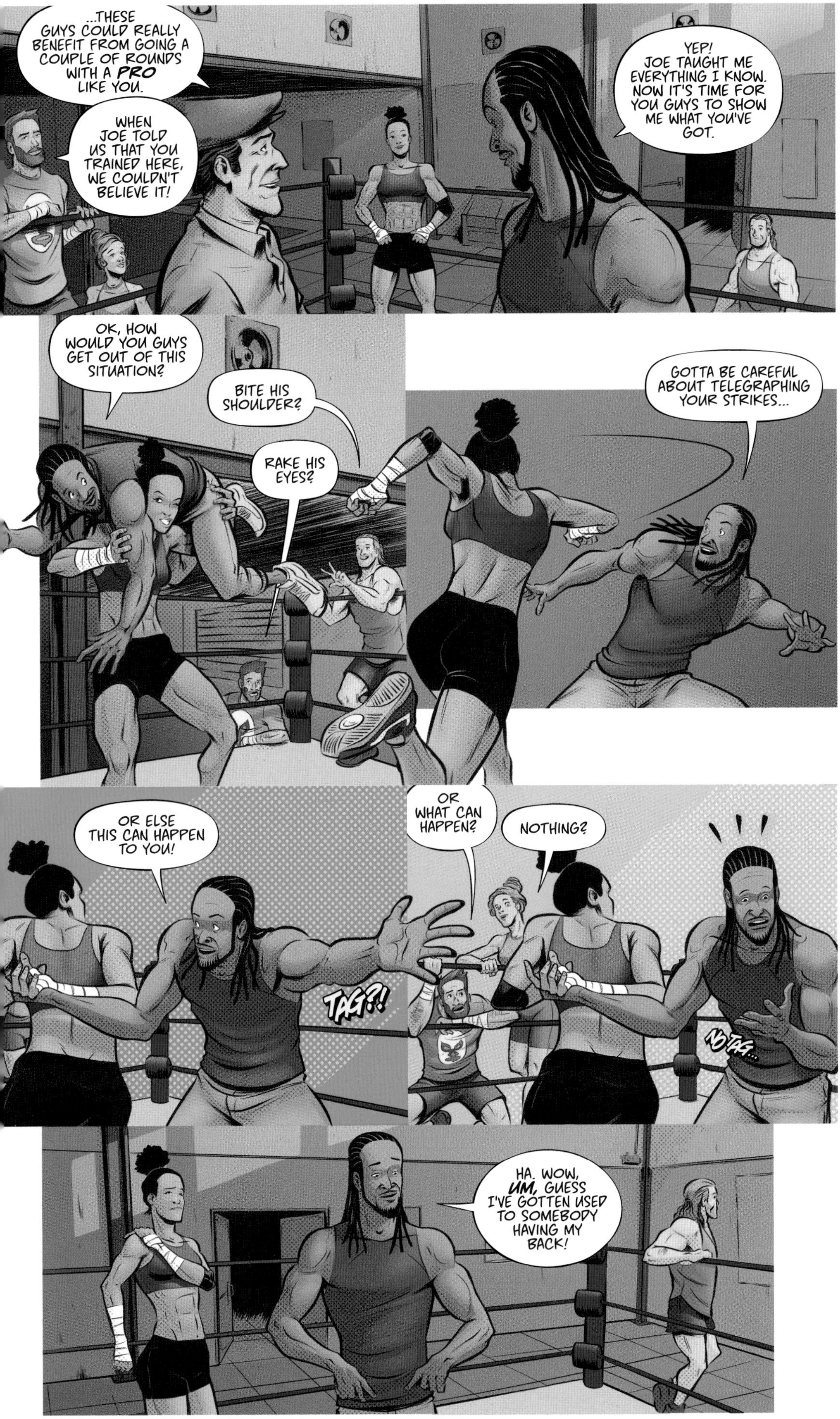
...THESE GUYS COULD REALLY BENEFIT FROM GOING A COUPLE OF ROUNDS WITH A PRO LIKE YOU.
WHEN JOE TOLD US THAT YOU TRAINED HERE, WE COULDN'T BELIEVE IT!
YEP! JOE TAUGHT ME EVERYTHING I KNOW. NOW IT'S TIME FOR YOU GUYS TO SHOW ME WHAT YOU'VE GOT.
OK, HOW WOULD YOU GUYS GET OUT OF THIS SITUATION?
BITE HIS SHOULDER?
RAKE HIS EYES?
GOTTA BE CAREFUL ABOUT TELEGRAPHING YOUR STRIKES...
OR ELSE THIS CAN HAPPEN TO YOU!
TAG?!
OR WHAT CAN HAPPEN?
NOTHING?
NO TAG...
HA. WOW, UM, GUESS I'VE GOTTEN USED TO SOMEBODY HAVING MY BACK!

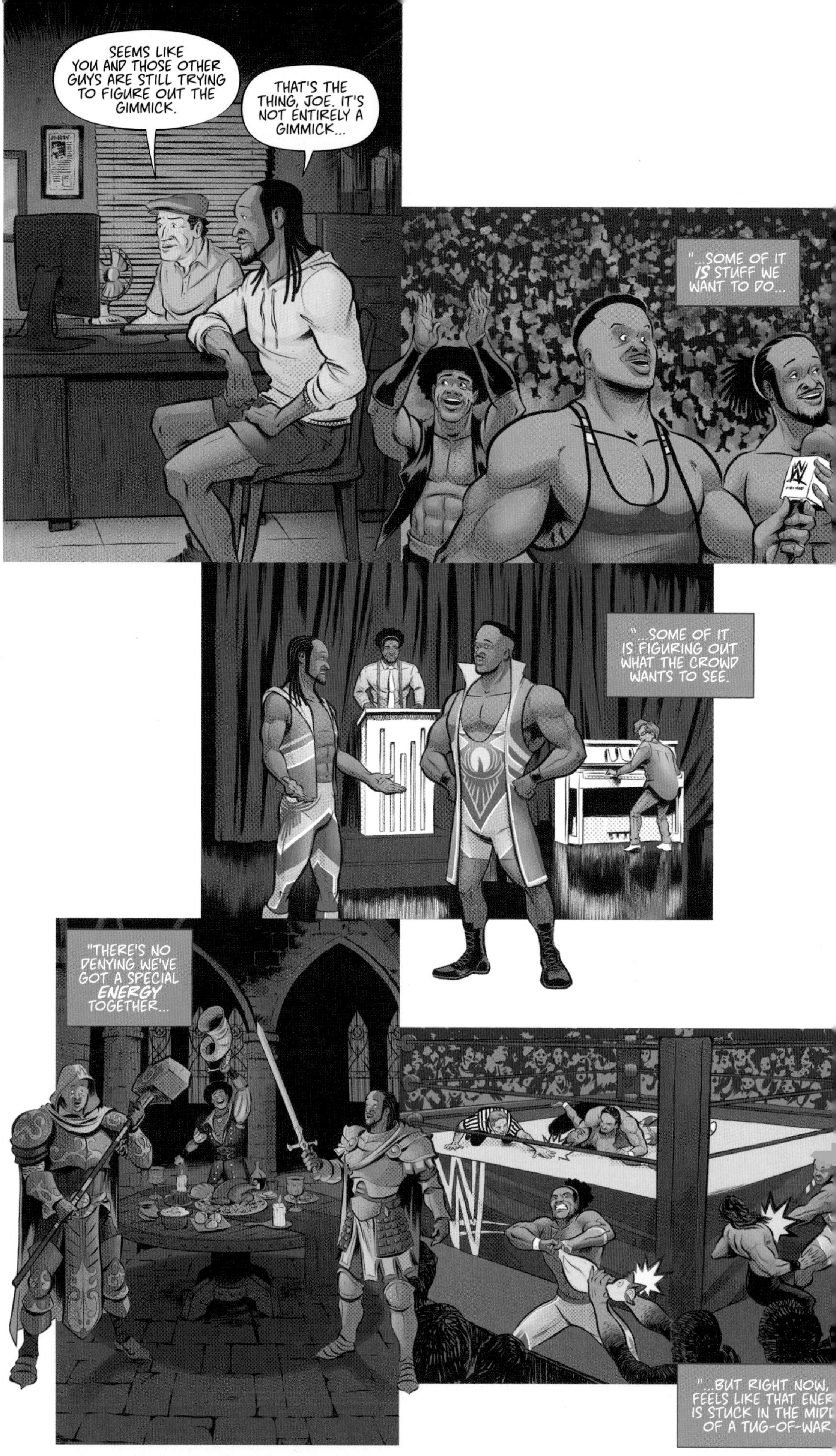
SEEMS LIKE YOU AND THOSE OTHER GUYS ARE STILL TRYING TO FIGURE OUT THE GIMMICK.
THAT'S THE THING, JOE. IT'S NOT ENTIRELY A GIMMICK...
"...SOME OF IT IS STUFF WE WANT TO DO...
"...SOME OF IT IS FIGURING OUT WHAT THE CROWD WANTS TO SEE.
"THERE'S NO DENYING WE'VE GOT A SPECIAL ENERGY TOGETHER...
"...BUT RIGHT NOW, FEELS LIKE THAT ENER
IS STUCK IN THE MID
OF A TUG-OF-WAR

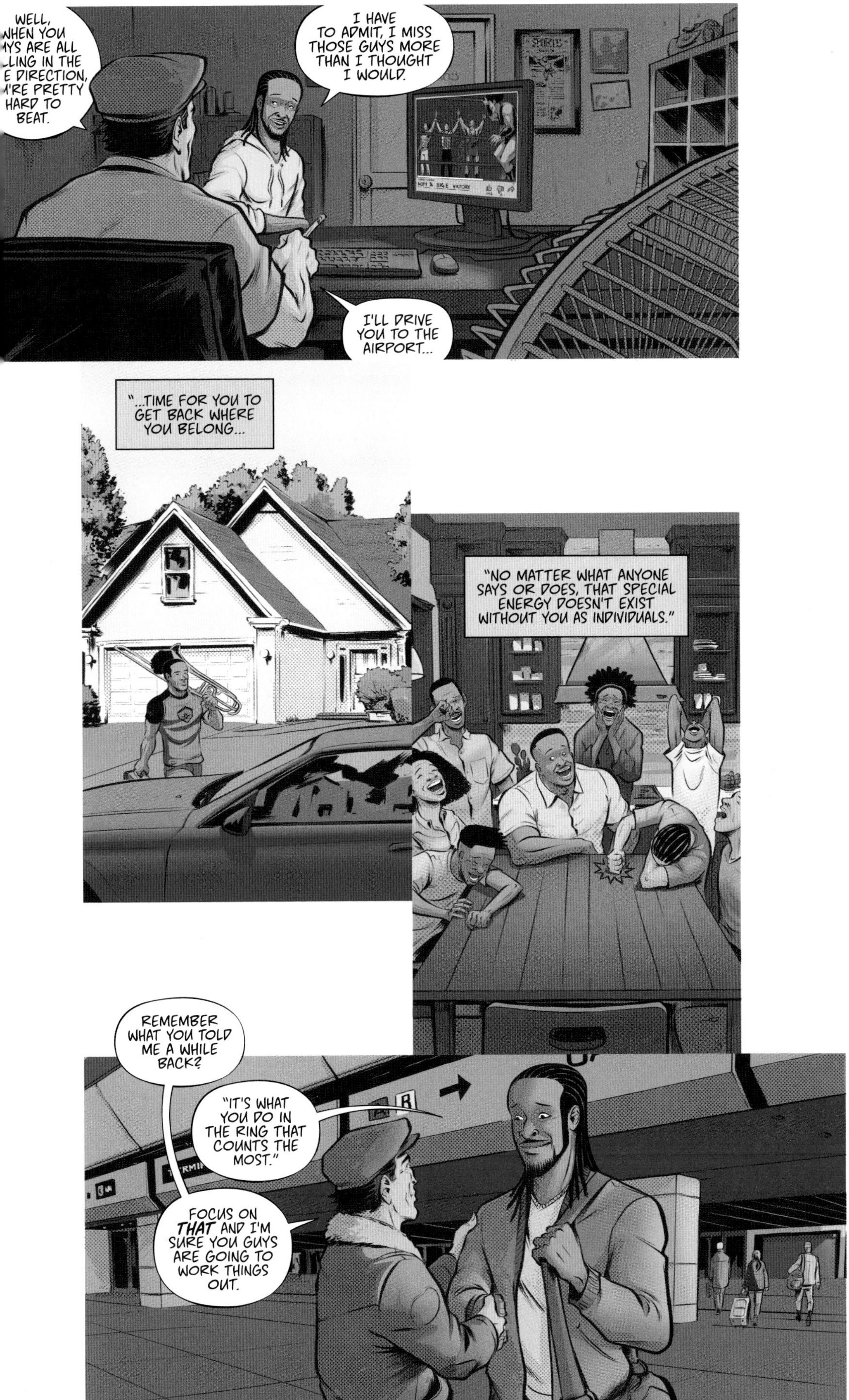
WELL, WHEN YOU YS ARE ALL LING IN THE E DIRECTION, 'RE PRETTY HARD TO BEAT.
I HAVE TO ADMIT, I MISS THOSE GUYS MORE THAN I THOUGHT I WOULD.
I'LL DRIVE YOU TO THE AIRPORT...
"...TIME FOR YOU TO GET BACK WHERE YOU BELONG...
"NO MATTER WHAT ANYONE SAYS OR DOES, THAT SPECIAL ENERGY DOESN'T EXIST WITHOUT YOU AS INDIVIDUALS."
REMEMBER WHAT YOU TOLD ME A WHILE BACK?
"IT'S WHAT YOU DO IN THE RING THAT COUNTS THE MOST."
FOCUS ON THAT AND I'M SURE YOU GUYS ARE GOING TO WORK THINGS OUT.

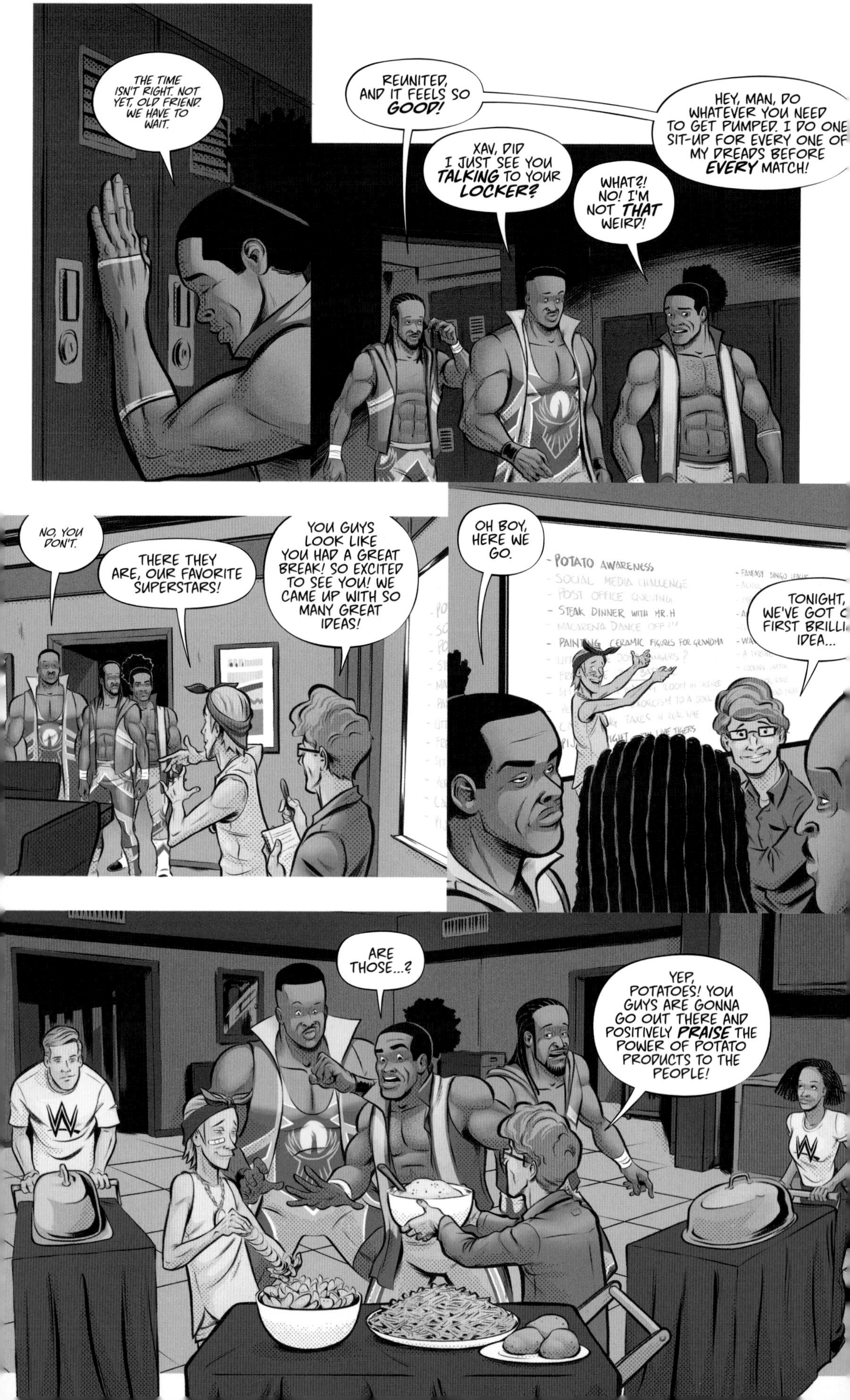

THE TIME ISN'T RIGHT. NOT YET, OLD FRIEND. WE HAVE TO WAIT.
REUNITED, AND IT FEELS SO GOOD!
HEY, MAN, DO WHATEVER YOU NEED TO GET PUMPED. I DO ONE SIT-UP FOR EVERY ONE OF MY DREADS BEFORE EVERY MATCH!
XAV, DID I JUST SEE YOU TALKING TO YOUR LOCKER?
WHAT?! NO! I'M NOT THAT WEIRD!
NO, YOU DON'T.
THERE THEY ARE, OUR FAVORITE SUPERSTARS!
YOU GUYS LOOK LIKE YOU HAD A GREAT BREAK! SO EXCITED TO SEE YOU! WE CAME UP WITH SO MANY GREAT IDEAS!
OH BOY, HERE WE GO.
- POTATO AWARENESS
- SOCIAL MEDIA CHALLENGE
- POST OFFICE QUEUING
- STEAK DINNER WITH MR. H
- MACARENA DANCE OFF!!!
- PAINTING CERAMIC FIGURES FOR GRANDMA
TONIGHT, WE'VE GOT O FIRST BRILLI IDEA...
ARE THOSE...?
YEP, POTATOES! YOU GUYS ARE GONNA GO OUT THERE AND POSITIVELY PRAISE THE POWER OF POTATO PRODUCTS TO THE PEOPLE!

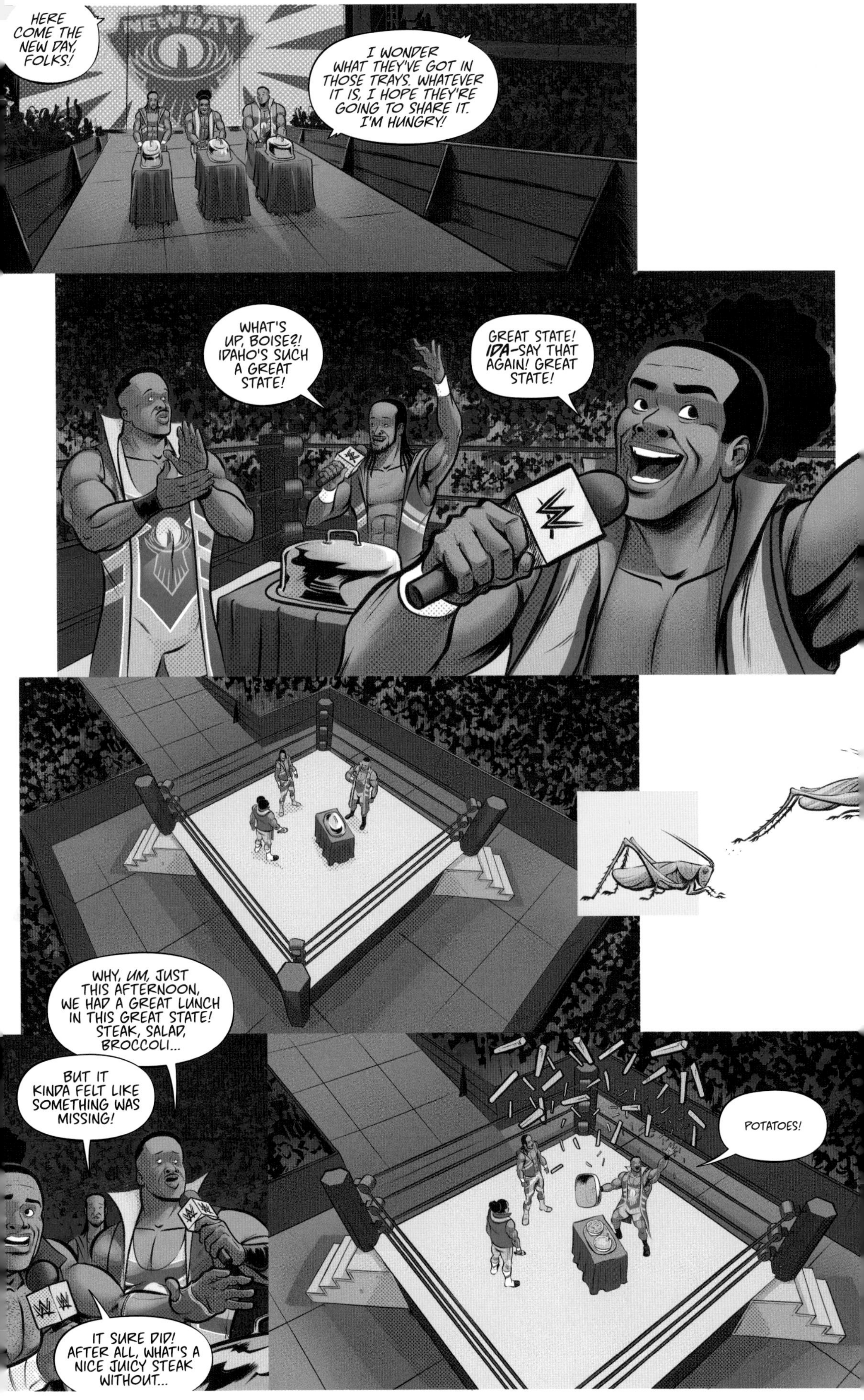
HERE COME THE NEW DAY, FOLKS!
I WONDER WHAT THEY'VE GOT IN THOSE TRAYS. WHATEVER IT IS, I HOPE THEY'RE GOING TO SHARE IT. I'M HUNGRY!
WHAT'S UP, BOISE?! IDAHO'S SUCH A GREAT STATE!
GREAT STATE! IDA–SAY THAT AGAIN! GREAT STATE!
WHY, UM, JUST THIS AFTERNOON, WE HAD A GREAT LUNCH IN THIS GREAT STATE! STEAK, SALAD, BROCCOLI...
BUT IT KINDA FELT LIKE SOMETHING WAS MISSING!
IT SURE DID! AFTER ALL, WHAT'S A NICE JUICY STEAK WITHOUT...
POTATOES!

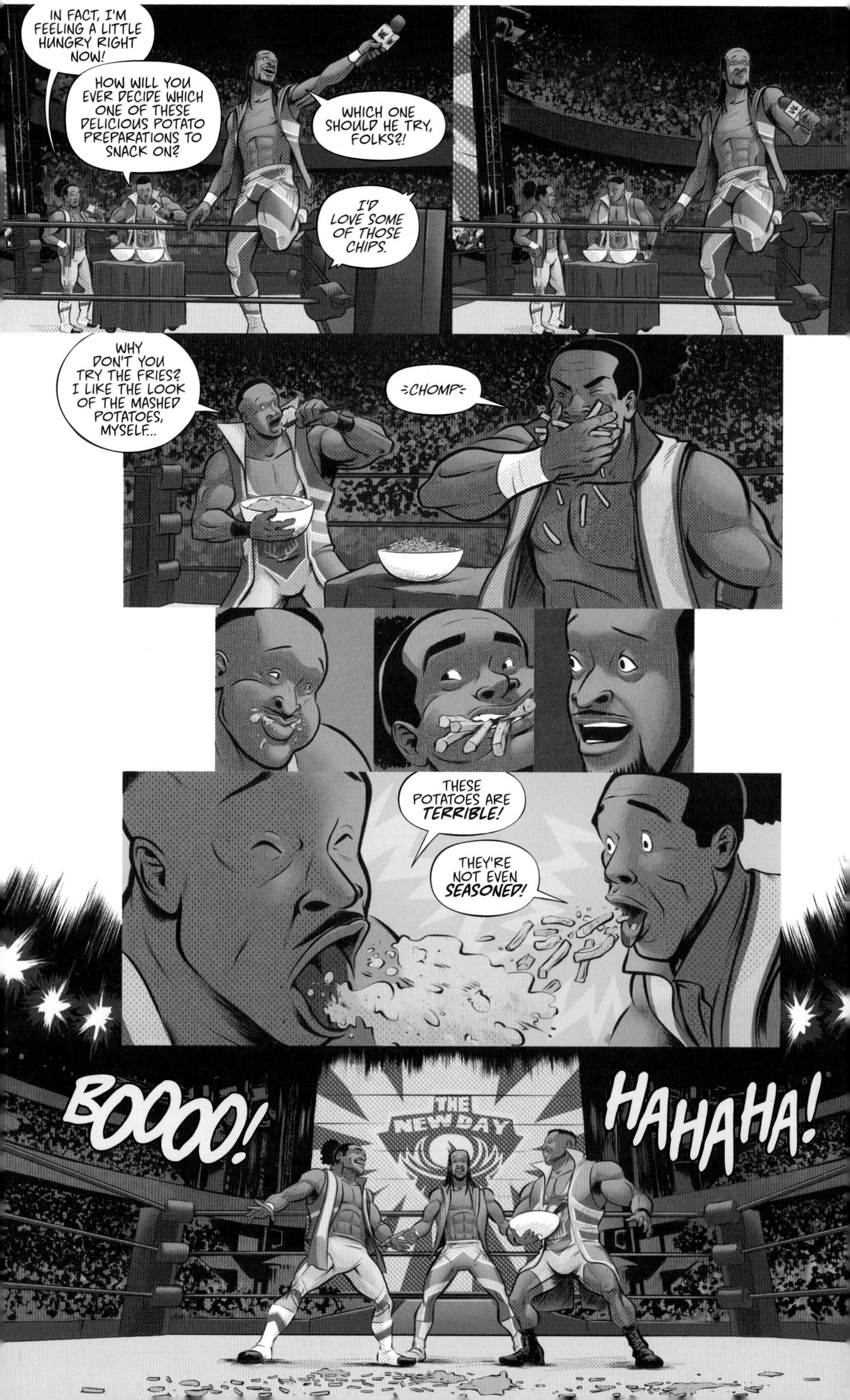
IN FACT, I'M FEELING A LITTLE HUNGRY RIGHT NOW!
HOW WILL YOU EVER DECIDE WHICH ONE OF THESE DELICIOUS POTATO PREPARATIONS TO SNACK ON?
WHICH ONE SHOULD HE TRY, FOLKS?!
I'D LOVE SOME OF THOSE CHIPS.
WHY DON'T YOU TRY THE FRIES? I LIKE THE LOOK OF THE MASHED POTATOES, MYSELF...
CHOMP
THESE POTATOES ARE TERRIBLE!
THEY'RE NOT EVEN SEASONED!
BOOOO!
THE NEW DAY
HAHAHA!

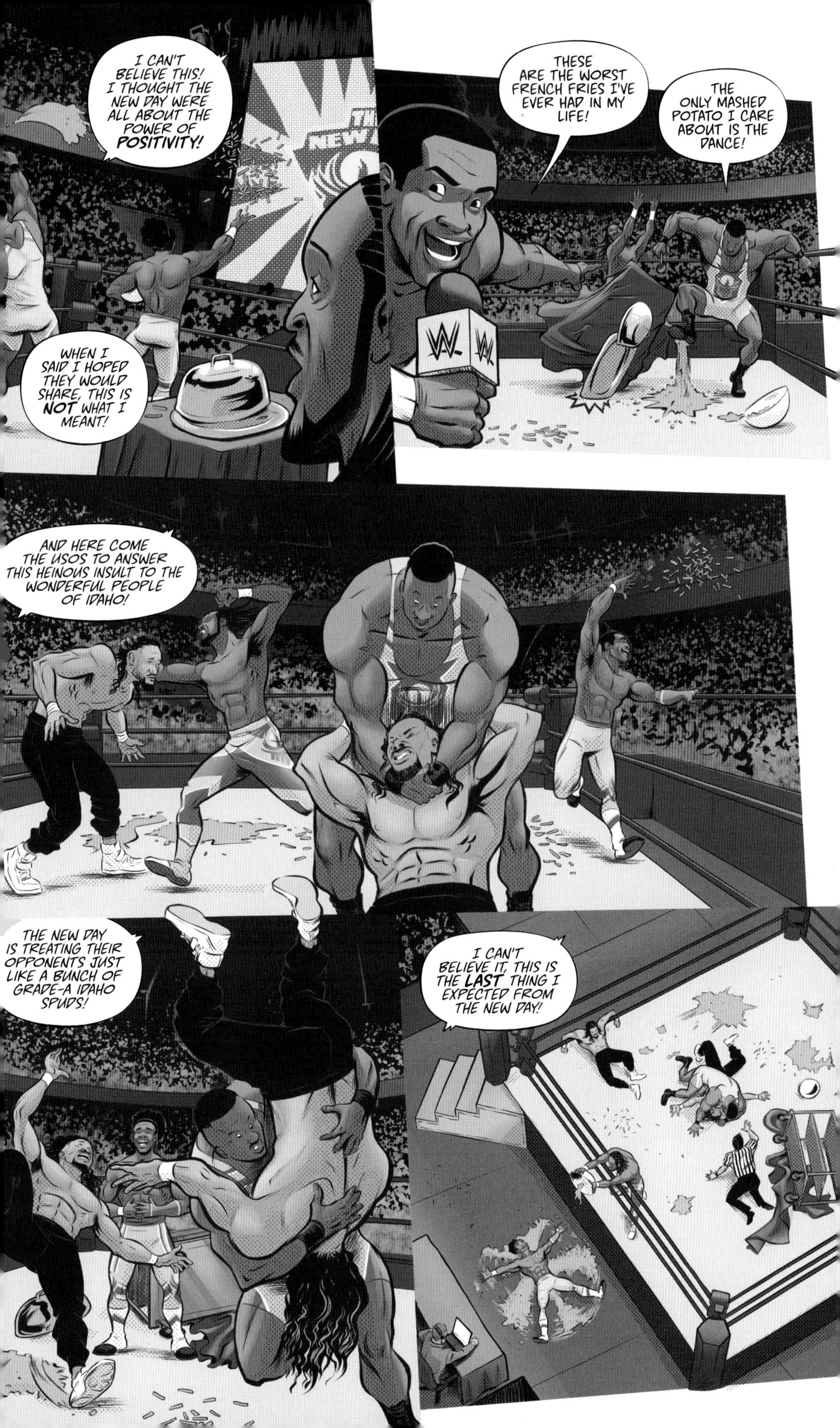
I CAN'T BELIEVE THIS! I THOUGHT THE NEW DAY WERE ALL ABOUT THE POWER OF **POSITIVITY!**
WHEN I SAID I HOPED THEY WOULD SHARE, THIS IS **NOT** WHAT I MEANT!
THESE ARE THE WORST FRENCH FRIES I'VE EVER HAD IN MY LIFE!
THE ONLY MASHED POTATO I CARE ABOUT IS THE DANCE!
AND HERE COME THE USOS TO ANSWER THIS HEINOUS INSULT TO THE WONDERFUL PEOPLE OF IDAHO!
THE NEW DAY IS TREATING THEIR OPPONENTS JUST LIKE A BUNCH OF GRADE-A IDAHO SPUDS!
I CAN'T BELIEVE IT, THIS IS THE **LAST** THING I EXPECTED FROM THE NEW DAY!

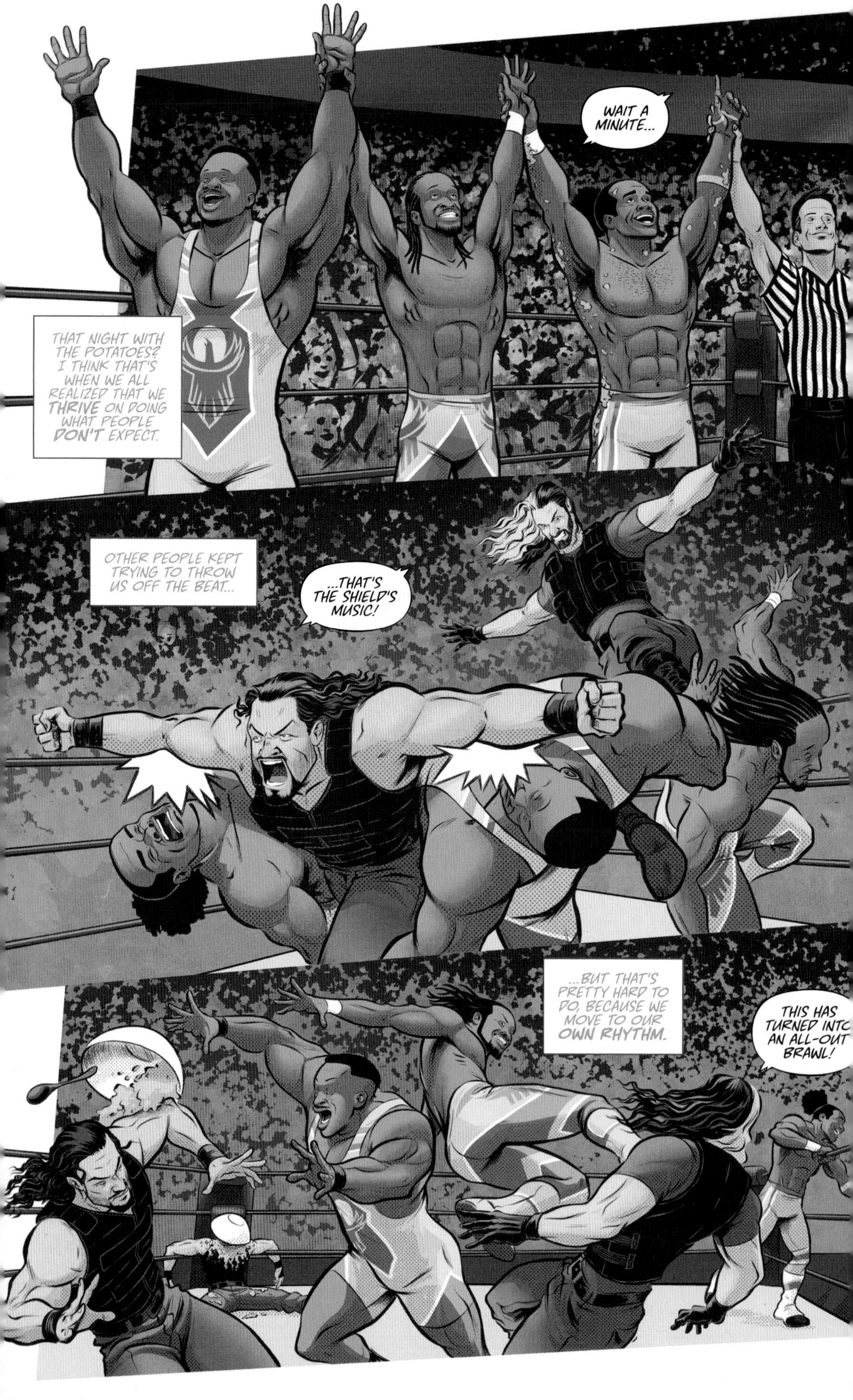
WAIT A MINUTE...
THAT NIGHT WITH THE POTATOES? I THINK THAT'S WHEN WE ALL REALIZED THAT WE THRIVE ON DOING WHAT PEOPLE DON'T EXPECT.
OTHER PEOPLE KEPT TRYING TO THROW US OFF THE BEAT...
...THAT'S THE SHIELD'S MUSIC!
...BUT THAT'S PRETTY HARD TO DO, BECAUSE WE MOVE TO OUR OWN RHYTHM.
THIS HAS TURNED INTO AN ALL-OUT BRAWL!

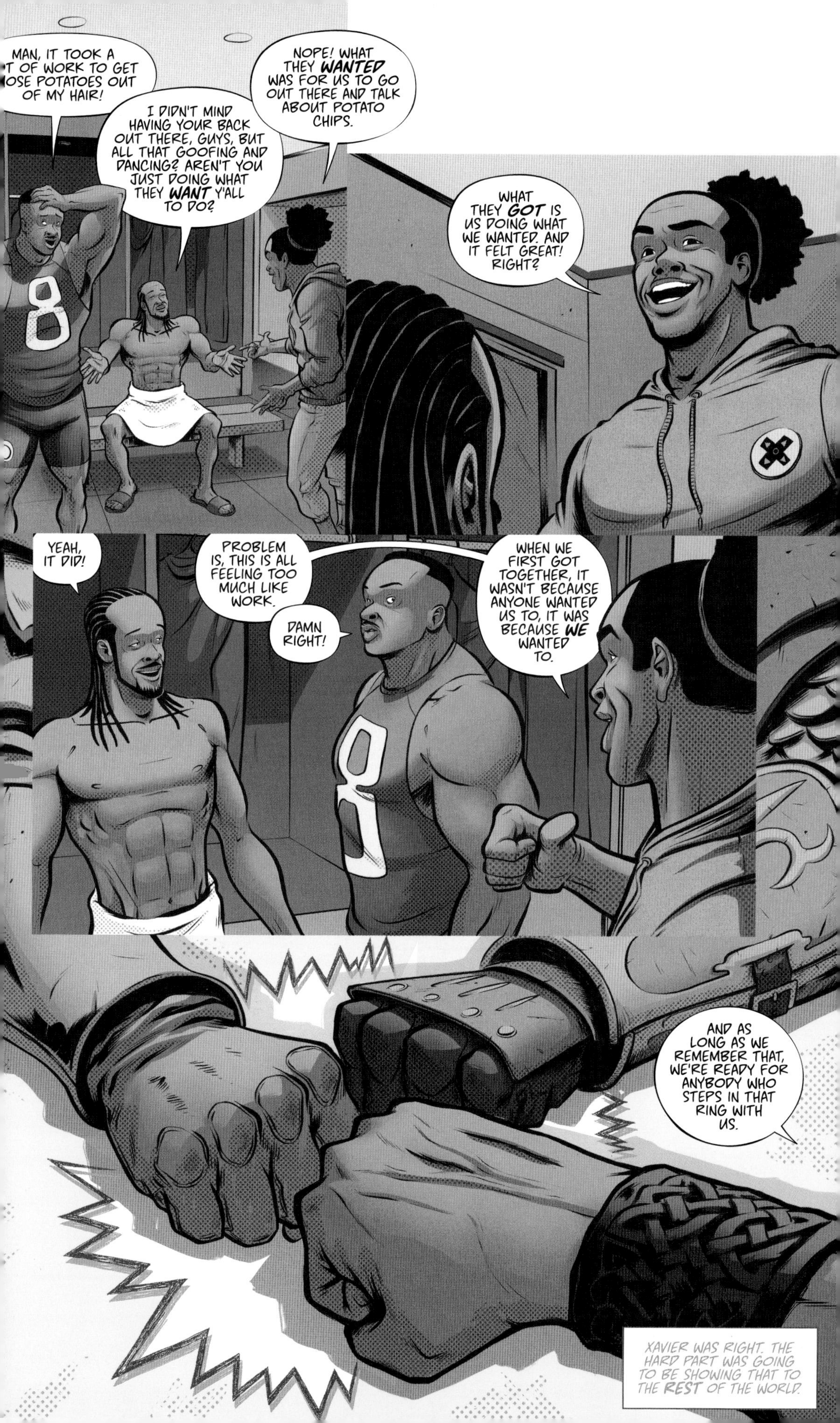
MAN, IT TOOK A
T OF WORK TO GET
OSE POTATOES OUT
OF MY HAIR!
I DIDN'T MIND HAVING YOUR BACK OUT THERE, GUYS, BUT ALL THAT GOOFING AND DANCING? AREN'T YOU JUST DOING WHAT THEY WANT Y'ALL TO DO?
NOPE! WHAT THEY WANTED WAS FOR US TO GO OUT THERE AND TALK ABOUT POTATO CHIPS.
WHAT THEY GOT IS US DOING WHAT WE WANTED. AND IT FELT GREAT! RIGHT?
YEAH, IT DID!
PROBLEM IS, THIS IS ALL FEELING TOO MUCH LIKE WORK.
DAMN RIGHT!
WHEN WE FIRST GOT TOGETHER, IT WASN'T BECAUSE ANYONE WANTED US TO, IT WAS BECAUSE WE WANTED TO.
AND AS LONG AS WE REMEMBER THAT, WE'RE READY FOR ANYBODY WHO STEPS IN THAT RING WITH US.
XAVIER WAS RIGHT. THE HARD PART WAS GOING TO BE SHOWING THAT TO THE REST OF THE WORLD.

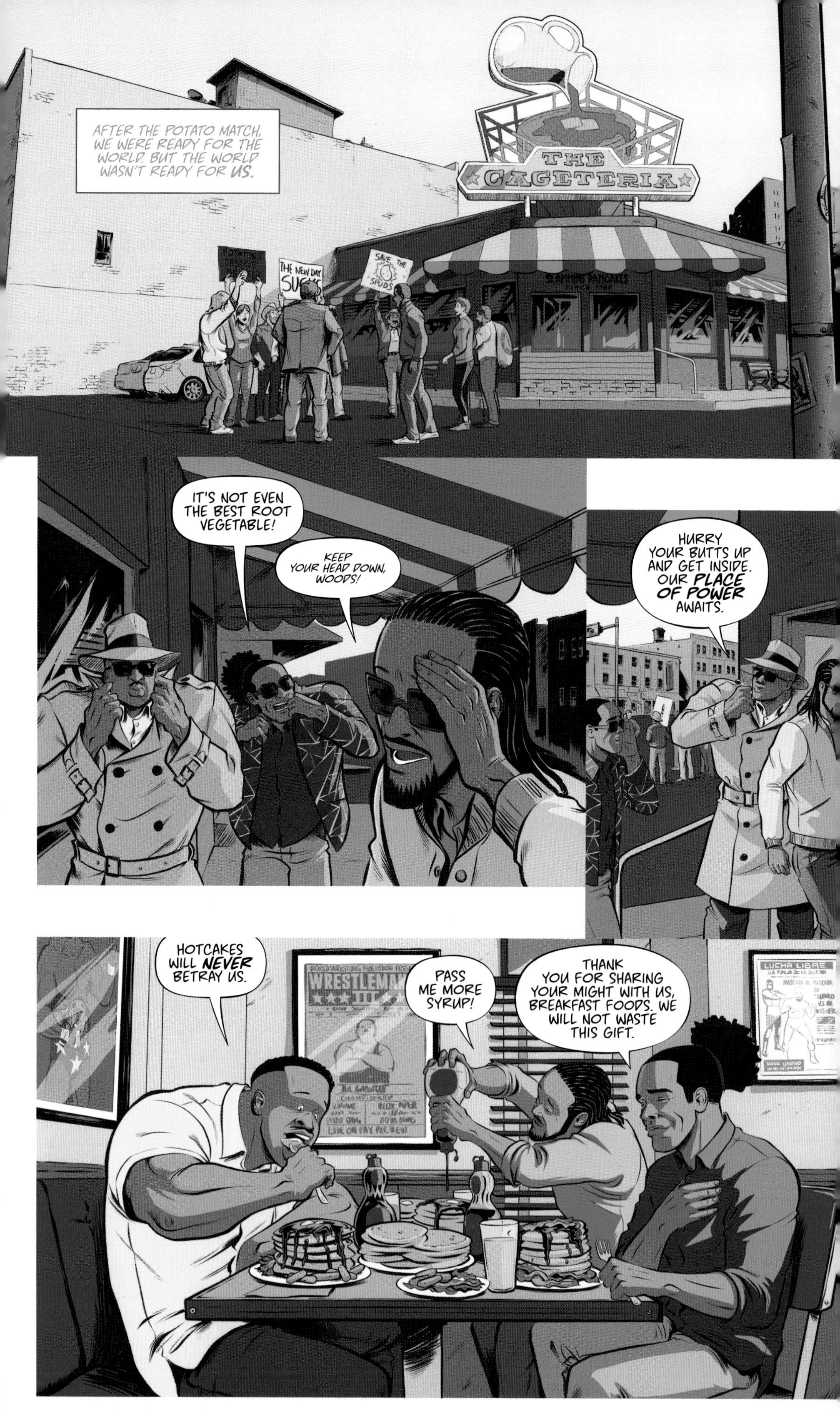
AFTER THE POTATO MATCH, WE WERE READY FOR THE WORLD. BUT THE WORLD WASN'T READY FOR US.
THE CAGETERIA
SAVE THE SPUDS
THE NEW DAY SUCKS
SLAMMING PANCAKES
IT'S NOT EVEN THE BEST ROOT VEGETABLE!
KEEP YOUR HEAD DOWN, WOODS!
HURRY YOUR BUTTS UP AND GET INSIDE. OUR PLACE OF POWER AWAITS.
HOTCAKES WILL NEVER BETRAY US.
PASS ME MORE SYRUP!
THANK YOU FOR SHARING YOUR MIGHT WITH US, BREAKFAST FOODS. WE WILL NOT WASTE THIS GIFT.
WRESTLEMANIA
LIVE ON PAY PER VIEW
LUCHA LIBRE

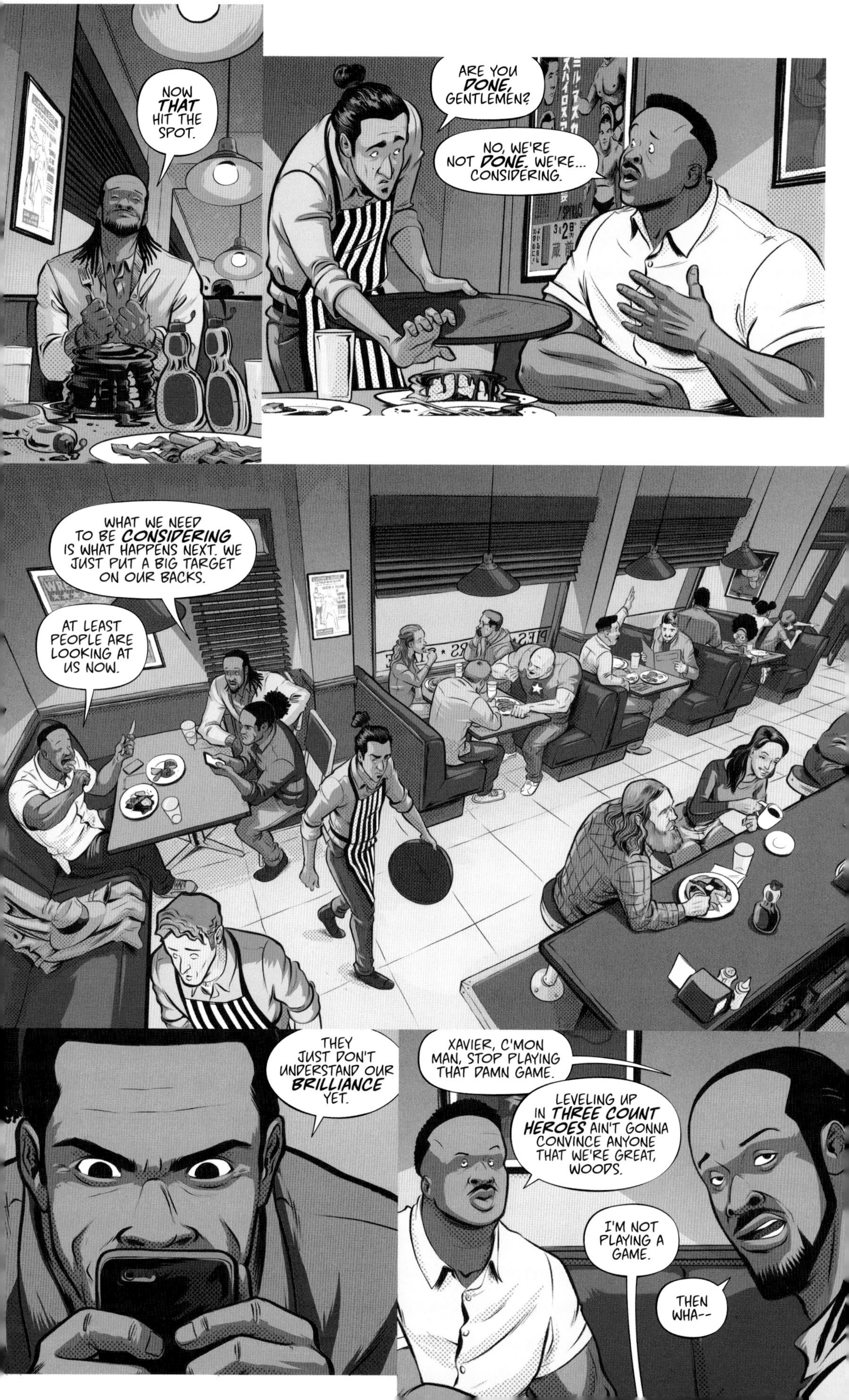
NOW *THAT* HIT THE SPOT.
ARE YOU *DONE,* GENTLEMEN?
NO, WE'RE NOT *DONE.* WE'RE... CONSIDERING.
WHAT WE NEED TO BE *CONSIDERING* IS WHAT HAPPENS NEXT. WE JUST PUT A BIG TARGET ON OUR BACKS.
AT LEAST PEOPLE ARE LOOKING AT US NOW.
THEY JUST DON'T UNDERSTAND OUR *BRILLIANCE* YET.
XAVIER, C'MON MAN, STOP PLAYING THAT DAMN GAME.
LEVELING UP IN *THREE COUNT HEROES* AIN'T GONNA CONVINCE ANYONE THAT WE'RE GREAT, WOODS.
I'M NOT PLAYING A GAME.
THEN WHA--

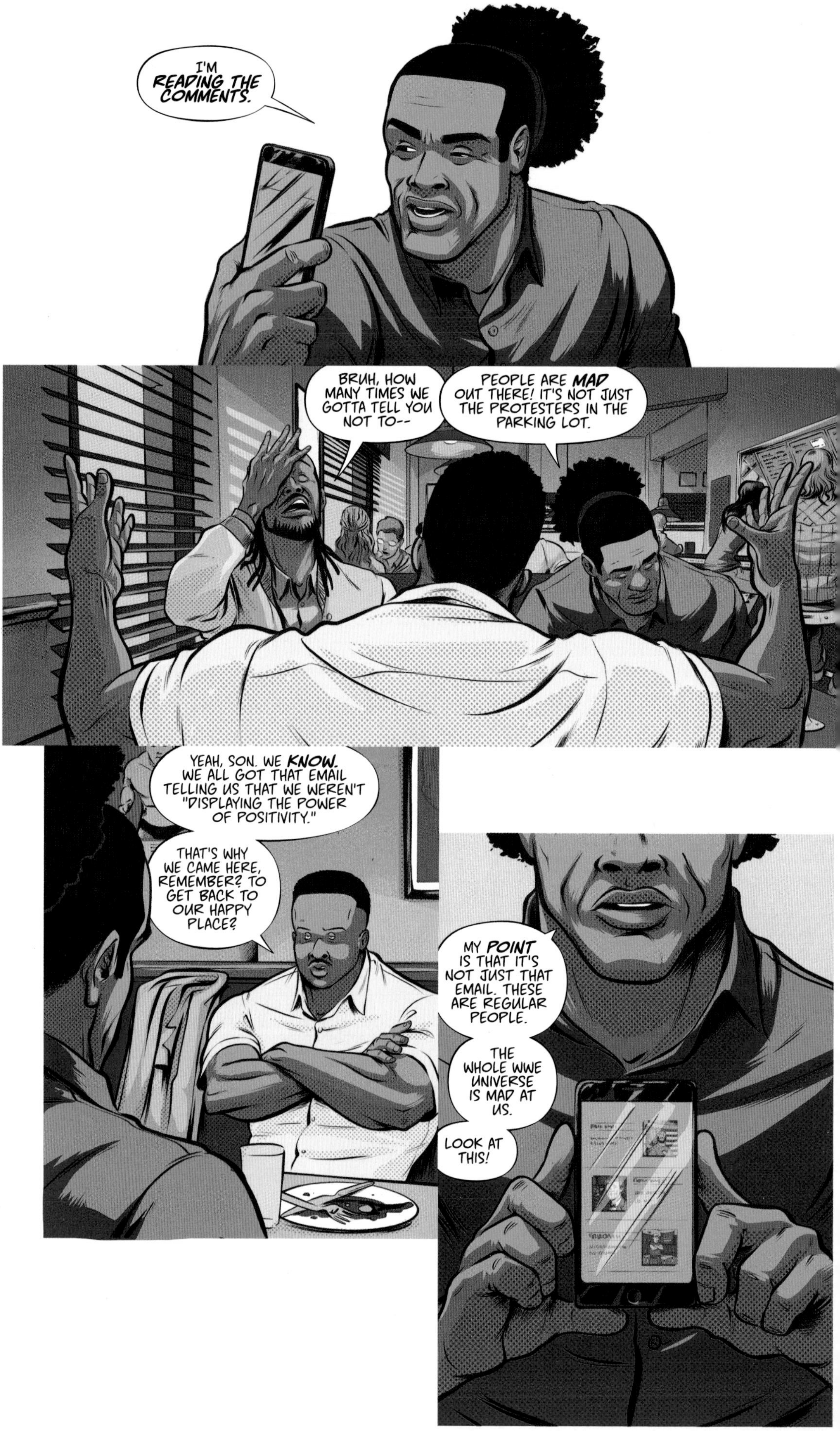
I'M READING THE COMMENTS.
BRUH, HOW MANY TIMES WE GOTTA TELL YOU NOT TO--
PEOPLE ARE MAD OUT THERE! IT'S NOT JUST THE PROTESTERS IN THE PARKING LOT.
YEAH, SON. WE KNOW. WE ALL GOT THAT EMAIL TELLING US THAT WE WEREN'T "DISPLAYING THE POWER OF POSITIVITY."
THAT'S WHY WE CAME HERE, REMEMBER? TO GET BACK TO OUR HAPPY PLACE?
MY POINT IS THAT IT'S NOT JUST THAT EMAIL. THESE ARE REGULAR PEOPLE.
THE WHOLE WWE UNIVERSE IS MAD AT US.
LOOK AT THIS!

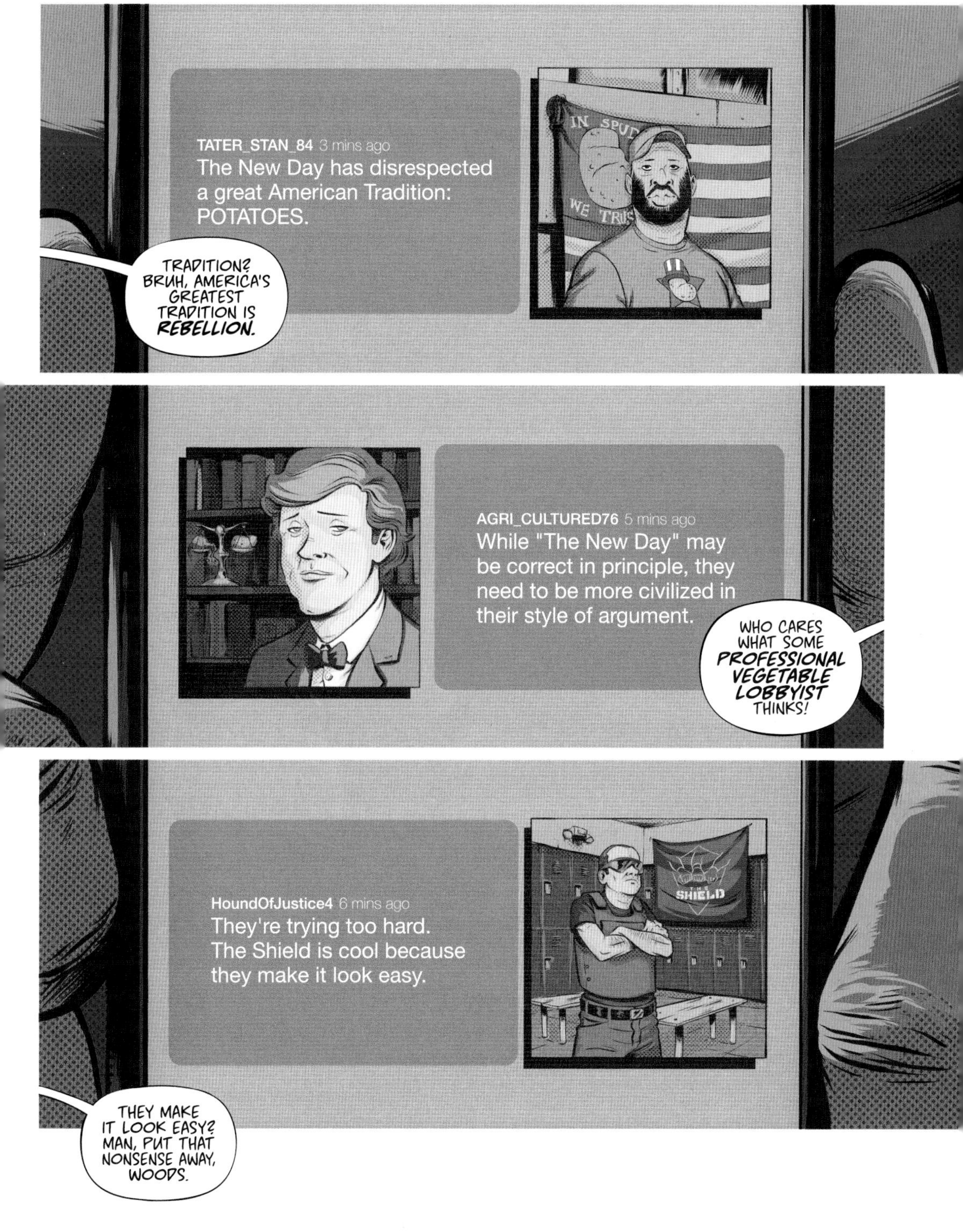
TATER_STAN_84 3 mins ago
The New Day has disrespected a great American Tradition: POTATOES.
IN SPUD WE TRUST
TRADITION? BRUH, AMERICA'S GREATEST TRADITION IS REBELLION.
AGRI_CULTURED76 5 mins ago
While "The New Day" may be correct in principle, they need to be more civilized in their style of argument.
WHO CARES WHAT SOME PROFESSIONAL VEGETABLE LOBBYIST THINKS!
HoundOfJustice4 6 mins ago
They're trying too hard. The Shield is cool because they make it look easy.
SHIELD
THEY MAKE IT LOOK EASY? MAN, PUT THAT NONSENSE AWAY, WOODS.

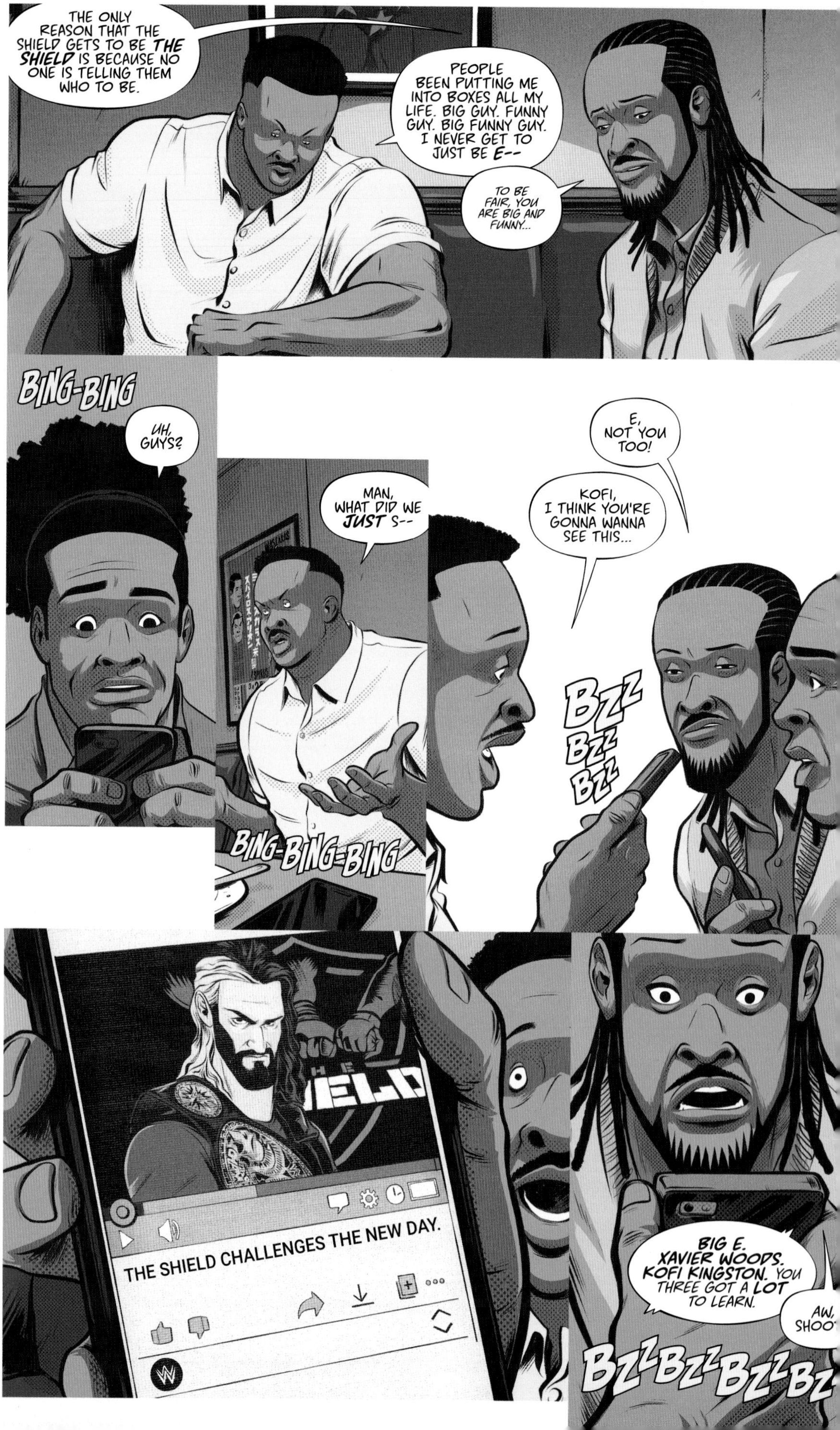
THE ONLY REASON THAT THE SHIELD GETS TO BE ***THE SHIELD*** IS BECAUSE NO ONE IS TELLING THEM WHO TO BE.
PEOPLE BEEN PUTTING ME INTO BOXES ALL MY LIFE. BIG GUY. FUNNY GUY. BIG FUNNY GUY. I NEVER GET TO JUST BE ***E--***
TO BE FAIR, YOU ARE BIG AND FUNNY...
BING-BING
UH, GUYS?
MAN, WHAT DID WE ***JUST*** S--
BING-BING-BING
KOFI, I THINK YOU'RE GONNA WANNA SEE THIS...
E, NOT YOU TOO!
BZZ BZZ BZZ
THE SHIELD CHALLENGES THE NEW DAY.
BIG E. XAVIER WOODS. KOFI KINGSTON. YOU THREE GOT A **LOT** TO LEARN.
AW, SHOO
BZZ BZZ BZZ BZ

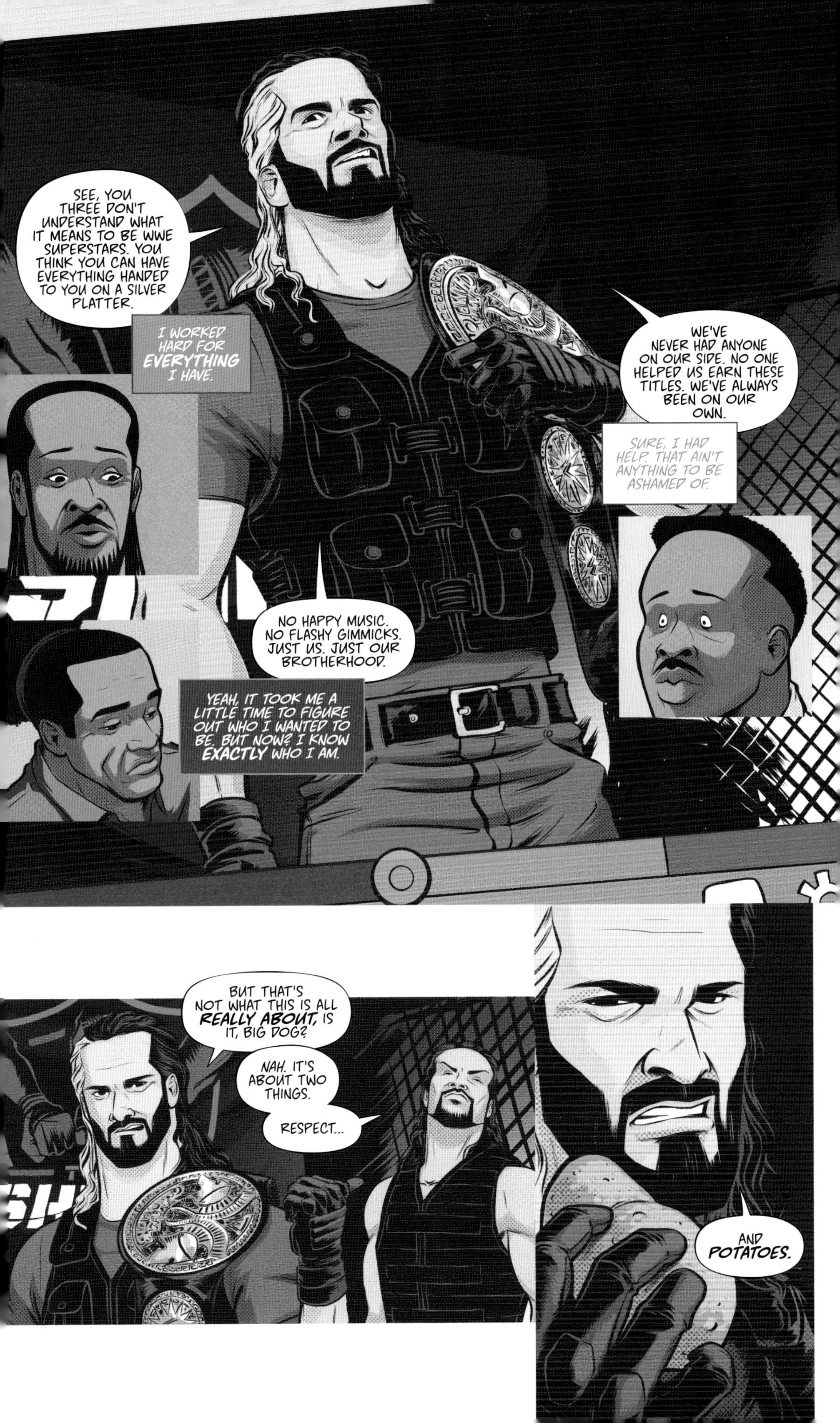
SEE, YOU THREE DON'T UNDERSTAND WHAT IT MEANS TO BE WWE SUPERSTARS. YOU THINK YOU CAN HAVE EVERYTHING HANDED TO YOU ON A SILVER PLATTER.
I WORKED HARD FOR EVERYTHING I HAVE.
WE'VE NEVER HAD ANYONE ON OUR SIDE. NO ONE HELPED US EARN THESE TITLES. WE'VE ALWAYS BEEN ON OUR OWN.
SURE, I HAD HELP. THAT AIN'T ANYTHING TO BE ASHAMED OF.
NO HAPPY MUSIC. NO FLASHY GIMMICKS. JUST US. JUST OUR BROTHERHOOD.
YEAH, IT TOOK ME A LITTLE TIME TO FIGURE OUT WHO I WANTED TO BE. BUT NOW? I KNOW EXACTLY WHO I AM.
BUT THAT'S NOT WHAT THIS IS ALL REALLY ABOUT, IS IT, BIG DOG?
NAH. IT'S ABOUT TWO THINGS.
RESPECT...
AND POTATOES.

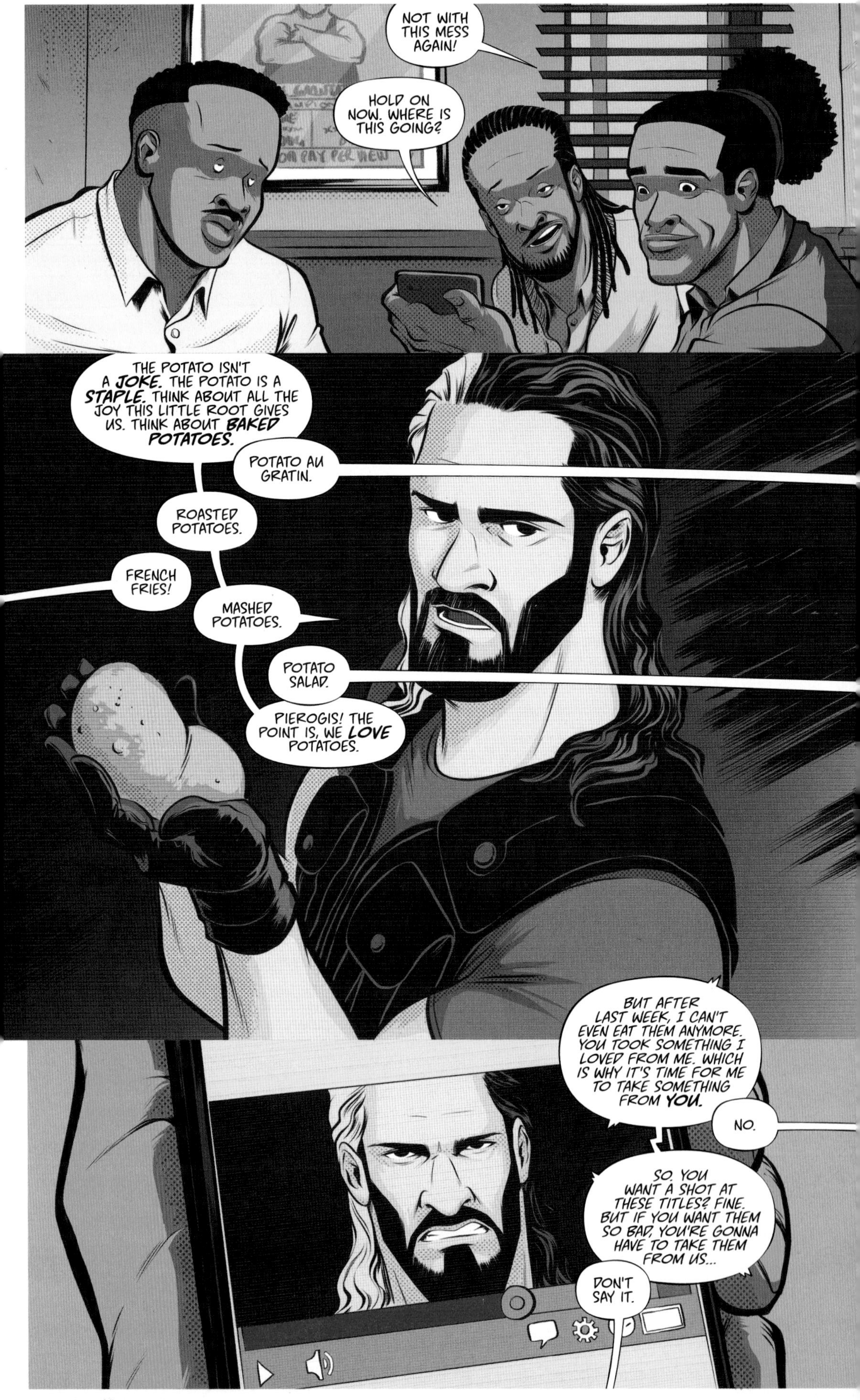
NOT WITH THIS MESS AGAIN!
HOLD ON NOW. WHERE IS THIS GOING?
THE POTATO ISN'T A JOKE. THE POTATO IS A STAPLE. THINK ABOUT ALL THE JOY THIS LITTLE ROOT GIVES US. THINK ABOUT BAKED POTATOES.
POTATO AU GRATIN.
ROASTED POTATOES.
FRENCH FRIES!
MASHED POTATOES.
POTATO SALAD.
PIEROGIS! THE POINT IS, WE LOVE POTATOES.
BUT AFTER LAST WEEK, I CAN'T EVEN EAT THEM ANYMORE. YOU TOOK SOMETHING I LOVED FROM ME. WHICH IS WHY IT'S TIME FOR ME TO TAKE SOMETHING FROM YOU.
NO.
SO. YOU WANT A SHOT AT THESE TITLES? FINE. BUT IF YOU WANT THEM SO BAD, YOU'RE GONNA HAVE TO TAKE THEM FROM US...
DON'T SAY IT.

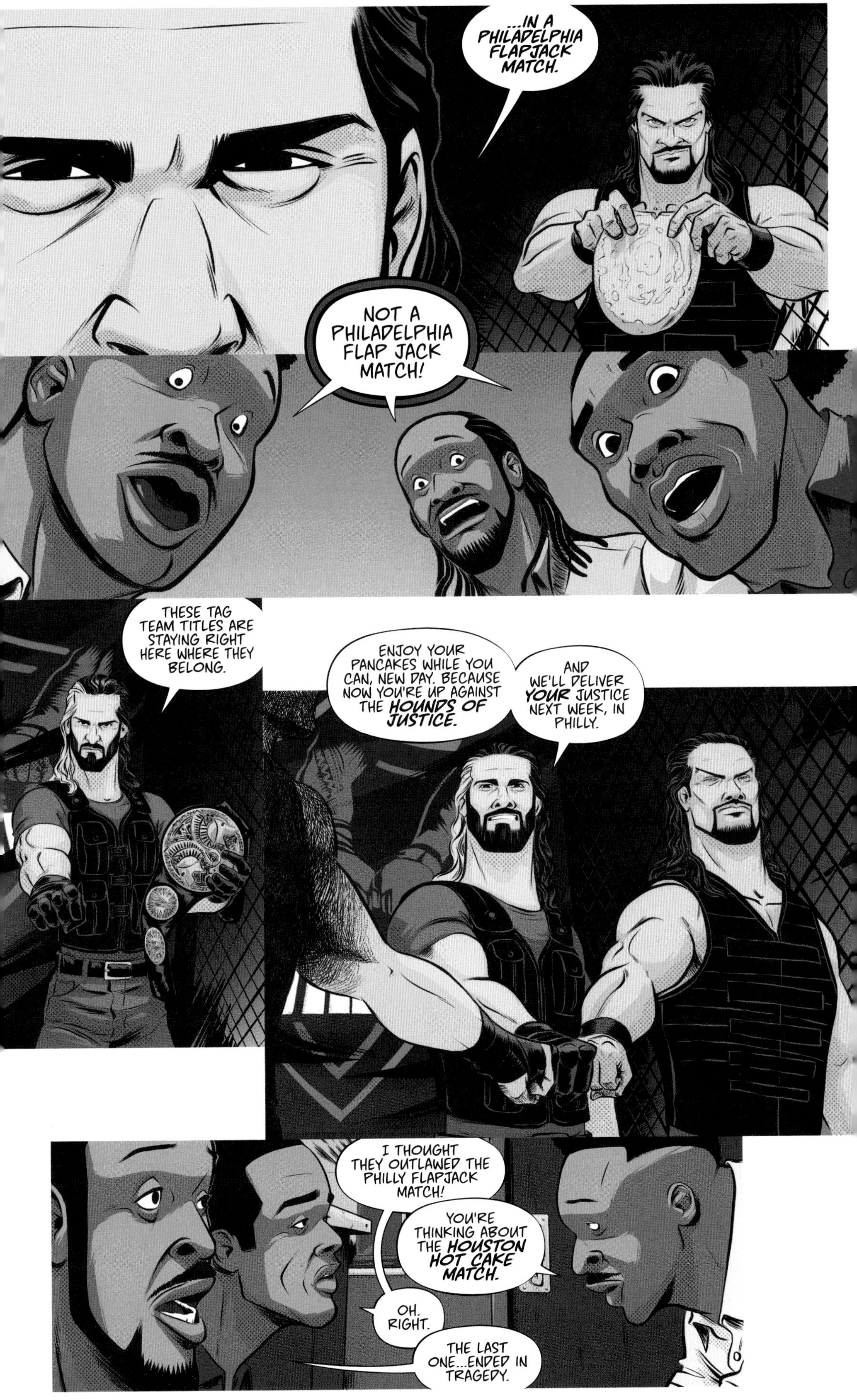
...IN A PHILADELPHIA FLAPJACK MATCH.
NOT A PHILADELPHIA FLAP JACK MATCH!
THESE TAG TEAM TITLES ARE STAYING RIGHT HERE WHERE THEY BELONG.
ENJOY YOUR PANCAKES WHILE YOU CAN, NEW DAY. BECAUSE NOW YOU'RE UP AGAINST THE HOUNDS OF JUSTICE.
AND WE'LL DELIVER YOUR JUSTICE NEXT WEEK, IN PHILLY.
I THOUGHT THEY OUTLAWED THE PHILLY FLAPJACK MATCH!
YOU'RE THINKING ABOUT THE HOUSTON HOT CAKE MATCH.
OH. RIGHT.
THE LAST ONE...ENDED IN TRAGEDY.

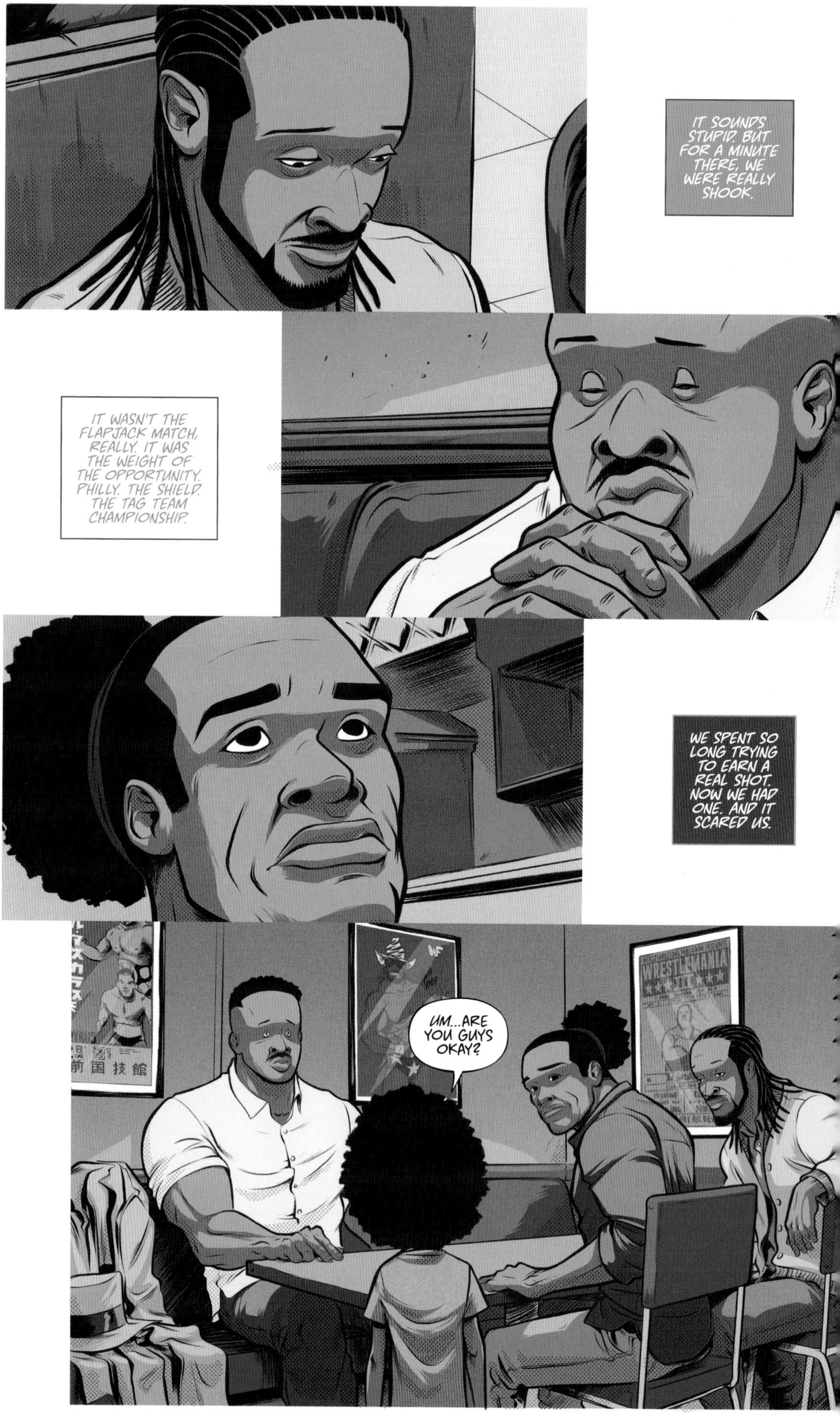
IT SOUNDS STUPID, BUT FOR A MINUTE THERE, WE WERE REALLY SHOOK.
IT WASN'T THE FLAPJACK MATCH, REALLY. IT WAS THE WEIGHT OF THE OPPORTUNITY. PHILLY. THE SHIELD. THE TAG TEAM CHAMPIONSHIP.
WE SPENT SO LONG TRYING TO EARN A REAL SHOT. NOW WE HAD ONE. AND IT SCARED US.
UM...ARE YOU GUYS OKAY?

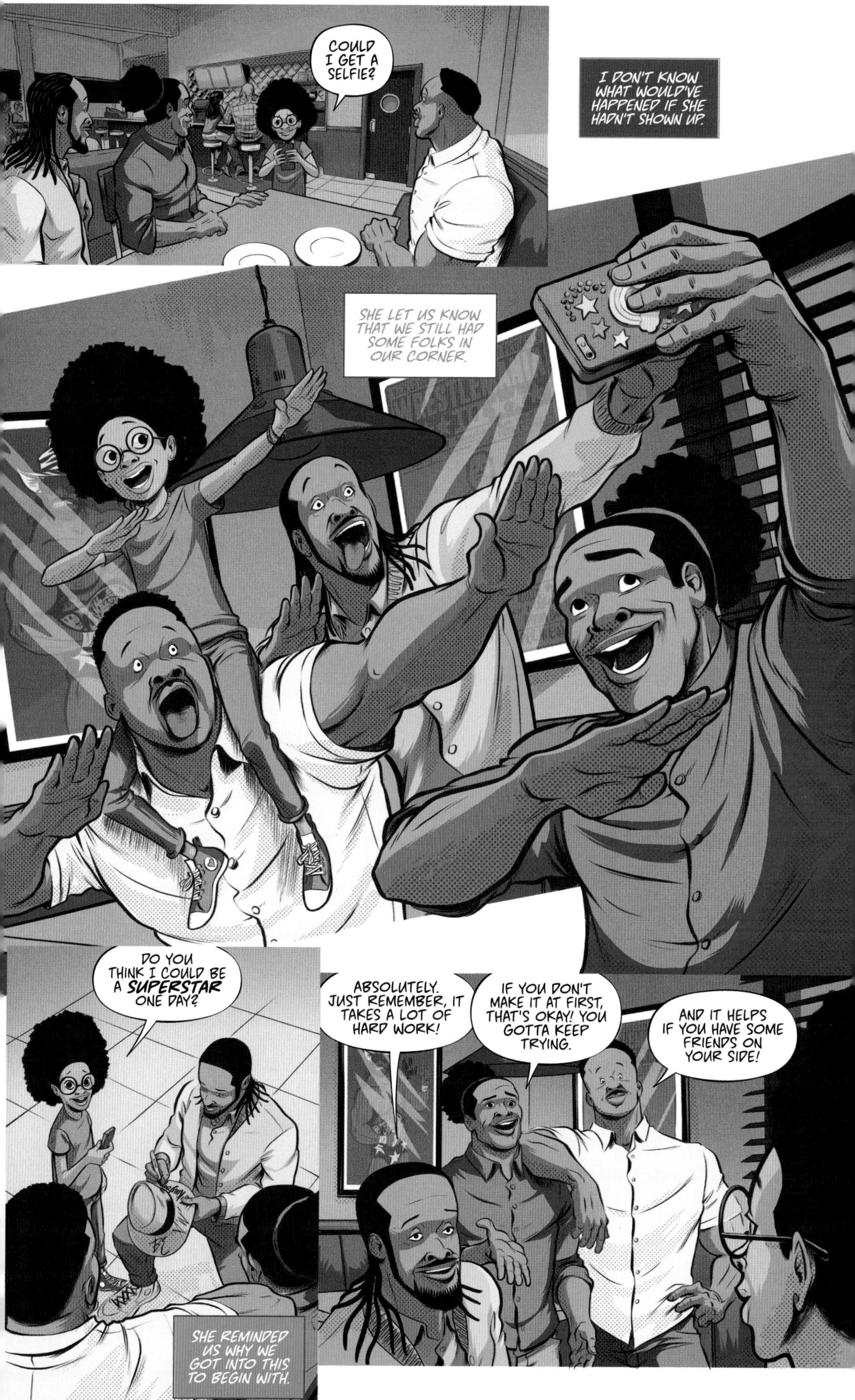
COULD I GET A SELFIE?
I DON'T KNOW WHAT WOULD'VE HAPPENED IF SHE HADN'T SHOWN UP.
SHE LET US KNOW THAT WE STILL HAD SOME FOLKS IN OUR CORNER.
DO YOU THINK I COULD BE A SUPERSTAR ONE DAY?
SHE REMINDED US WHY WE GOT INTO THIS TO BEGIN WITH.
ABSOLUTELY. JUST REMEMBER, IT TAKES A LOT OF HARD WORK!
IF YOU DON'T MAKE IT AT FIRST, THAT'S OKAY! YOU GOTTA KEEP TRYING.
AND IT HELPS IF YOU HAVE SOME FRIENDS ON YOUR SIDE!

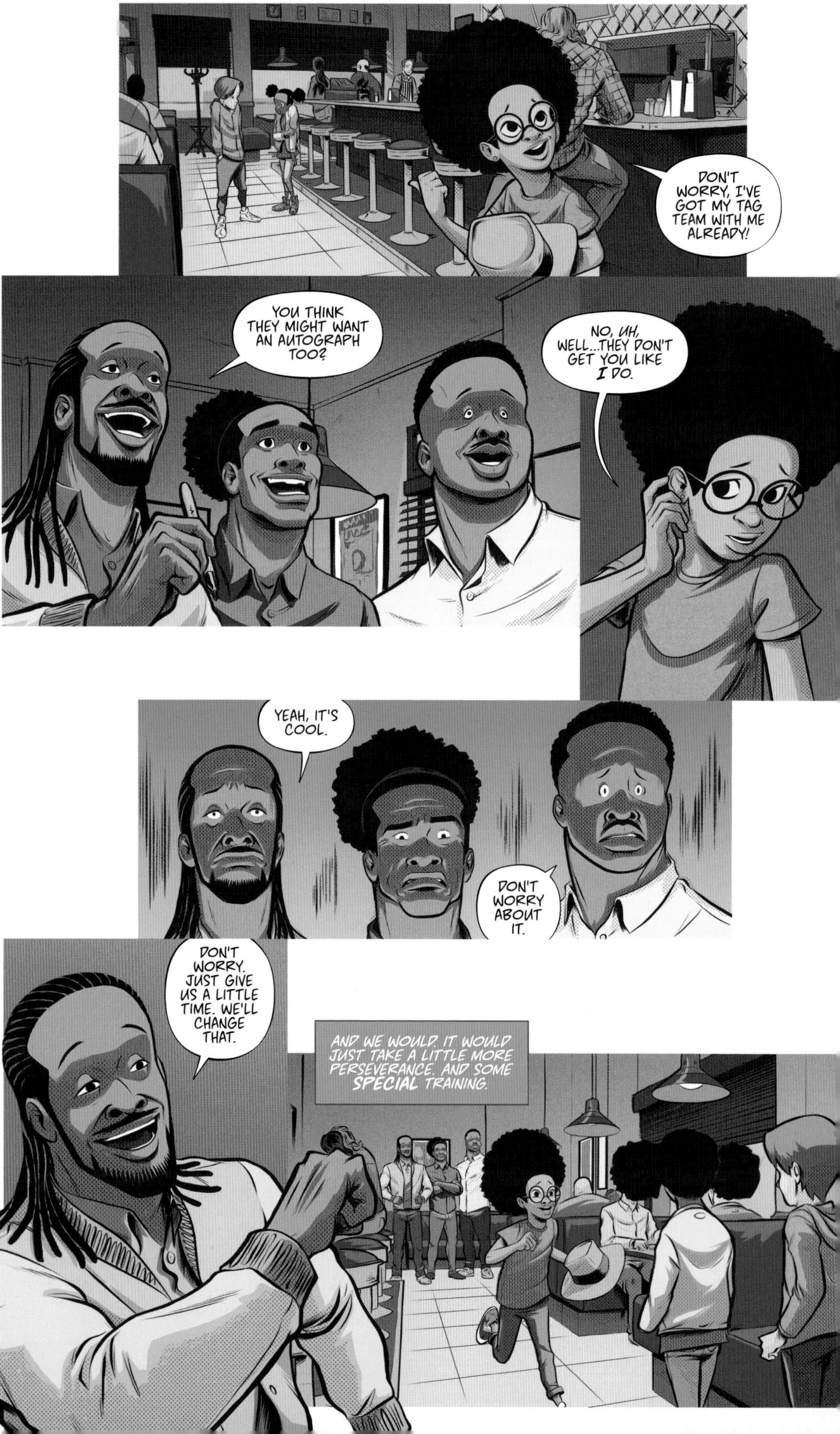
DON'T WORRY, I'VE GOT MY TAG TEAM WITH ME ALREADY!
YOU THINK THEY MIGHT WANT AN AUTOGRAPH TOO?
NO, UH, WELL...THEY DON'T GET YOU LIKE I DO.
YEAH, IT'S COOL.
DON'T WORRY ABOUT IT.
DON'T WORRY. JUST GIVE US A LITTLE TIME. WE'LL CHANGE THAT.
AND WE WOULD. IT WOULD JUST TAKE A LITTLE MORE PERSEVERANCE. AND SOME SPECIAL TRAINING.

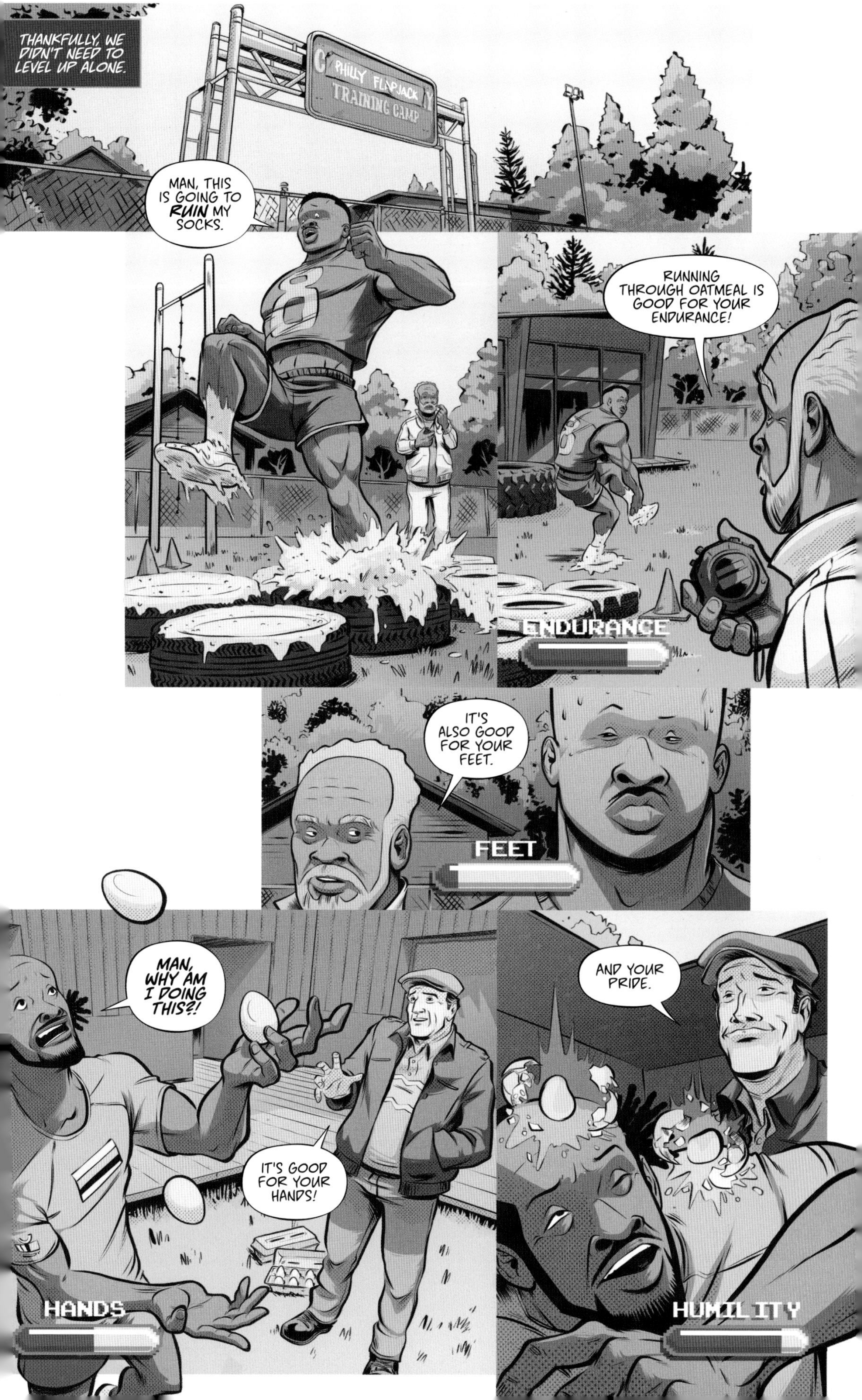

THANKFULLY, WE DIDN'T NEED TO LEVEL UP ALONE.
PHILLY FLAPJACK
TRAINING CAMP
MAN, THIS IS GOING TO RUIN MY SOCKS.
RUNNING THROUGH OATMEAL IS GOOD FOR YOUR ENDURANCE!
ENDURANCE
IT'S ALSO GOOD FOR YOUR FEET.
FEET
MAN, WHY AM I DOING THIS?!
IT'S GOOD FOR YOUR HANDS!
HANDS
AND YOUR PRIDE.
HUMILITY

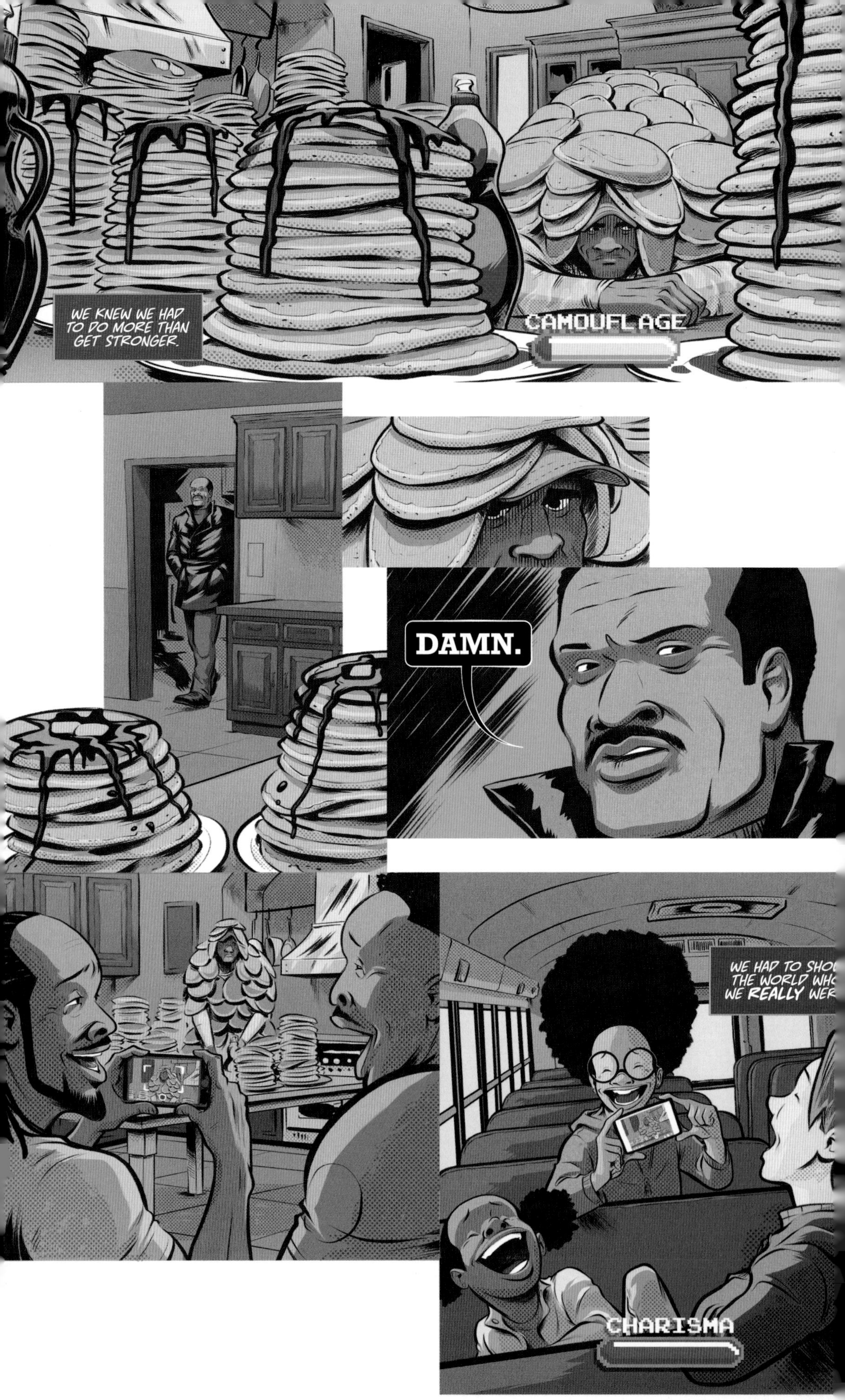
WE KNEW WE HAD TO DO MORE THAN GET STRONGER.
CAMOUFLAGE
DAMN.
WE HAD TO SHO THE WORLD WH WE REALLY WER
CHARISMA

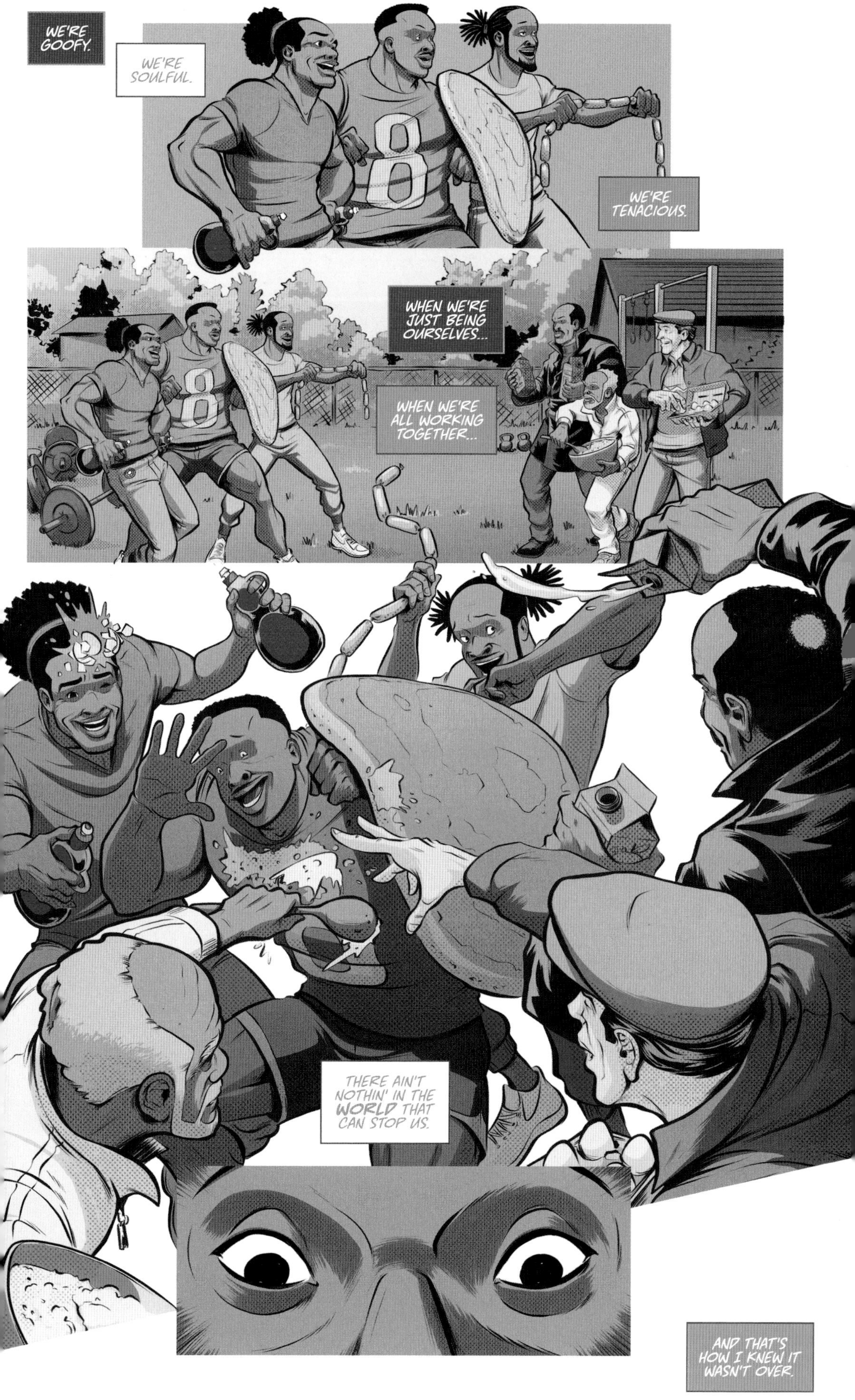
WE'RE GOOFY.
WE'RE SOULFUL.
WE'RE TENACIOUS.
WHEN WE'RE JUST BEING OURSELVES...
WHEN WE'RE ALL WORKING TOGETHER...
THERE AIN'T NOTHIN' IN THE WORLD THAT CAN STOP US.
AND THAT'S HOW I KNEW IT WASN'T OVER.

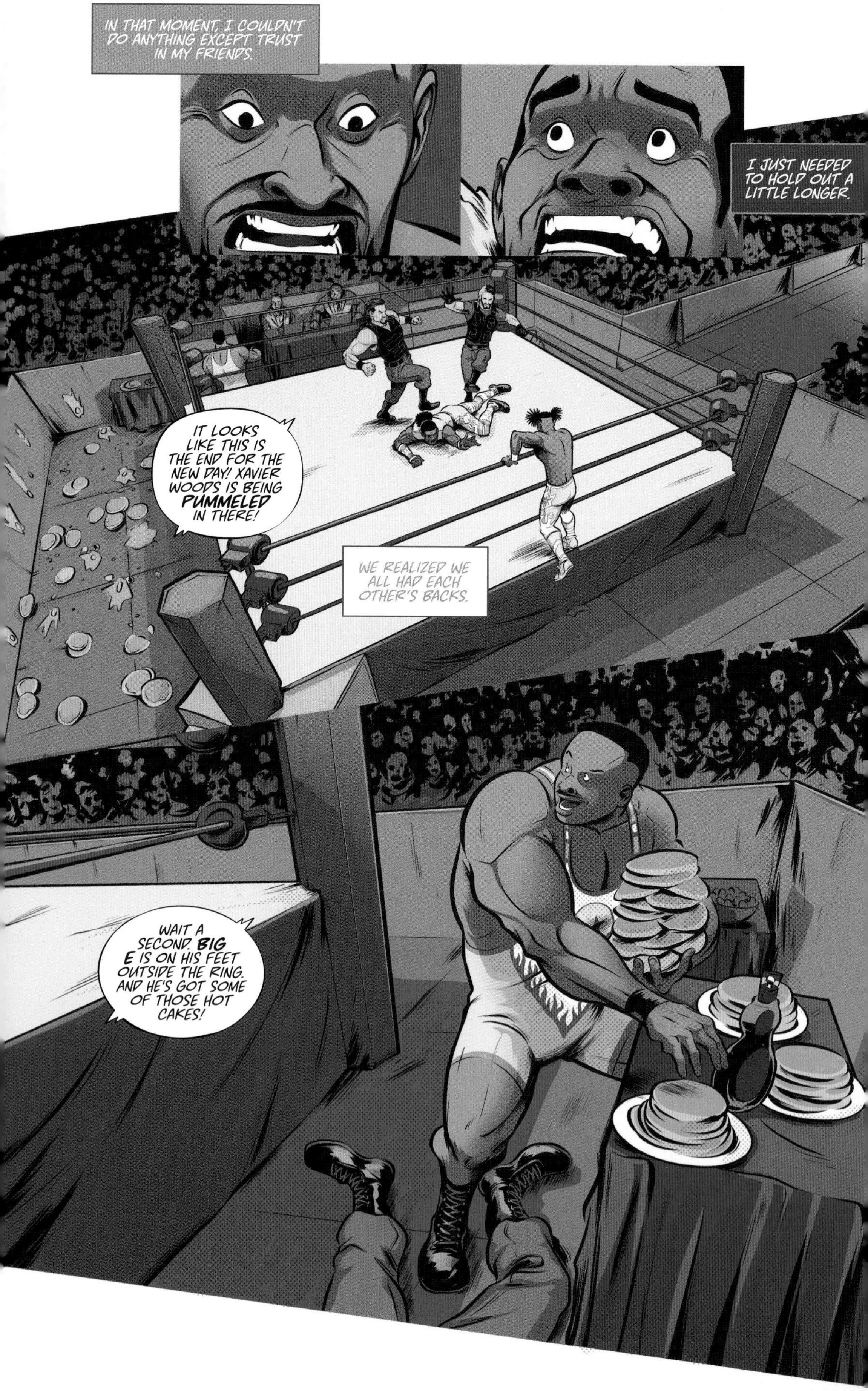
IN THAT MOMENT, I COULDN'T DO ANYTHING EXCEPT TRUST IN MY FRIENDS.
I JUST NEEDED TO HOLD OUT A LITTLE LONGER.
IT LOOKS LIKE THIS IS THE END FOR THE NEW DAY! XAVIER WOODS IS BEING PUMMELED IN THERE!
WE REALIZED WE ALL HAD EACH OTHER'S BACKS.
WAIT A SECOND. BIG E IS ON HIS FEET OUTSIDE THE RING. AND HE'S GOT SOME OF THOSE HOT CAKES!

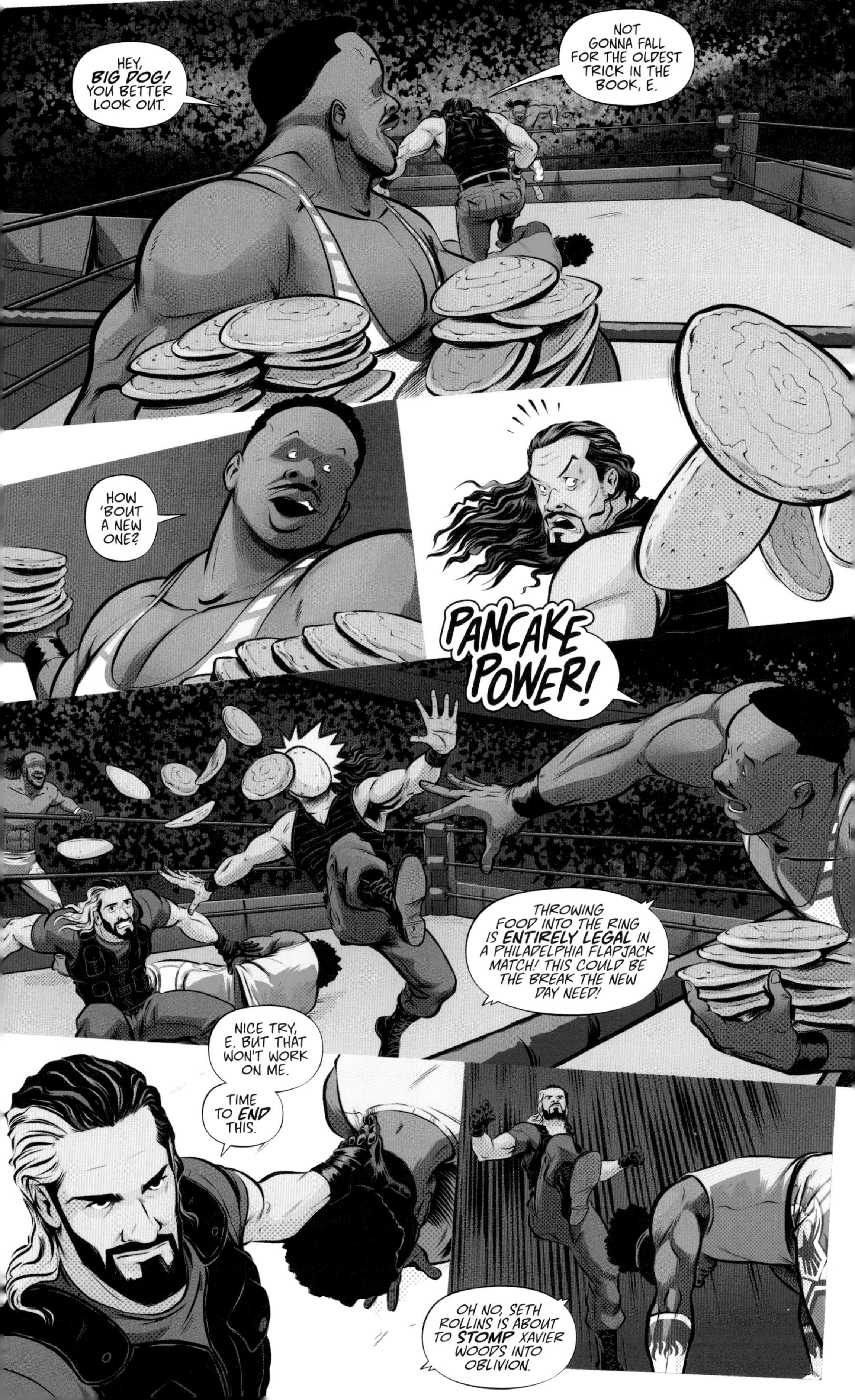

HEY, **BIG DOG!** YOU BETTER LOOK OUT.
NOT GONNA FALL FOR THE OLDEST TRICK IN THE BOOK, E.
HOW 'BOUT A NEW ONE?
PANCAKE POWER!
THROWING FOOD INTO THE RING IS **ENTIRELY LEGAL** IN A PHILADELPHIA FLAPJACK MATCH! THIS COULD BE THE BREAK THE NEW DAY NEED!
NICE TRY, E. BUT THAT WON'T WORK ON ME.
TIME TO **END** THIS.
OH NO, SETH ROLLINS IS ABOUT TO **STOMP** XAVIER WOODS INTO OBLIVION.

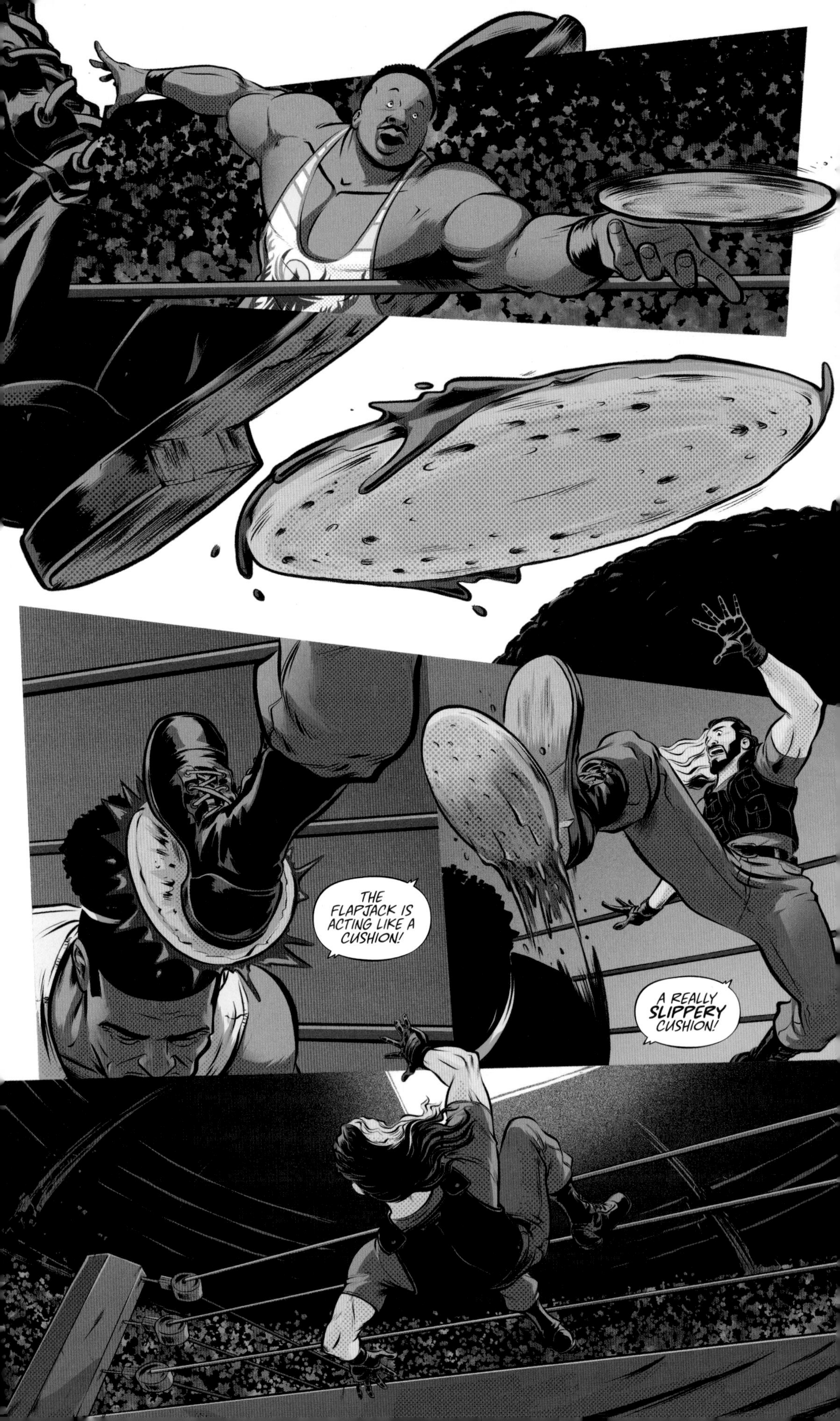
THE FLAPJACK IS ACTING LIKE A CUSHION!
A REALLY SLIPPERY CUSHION!

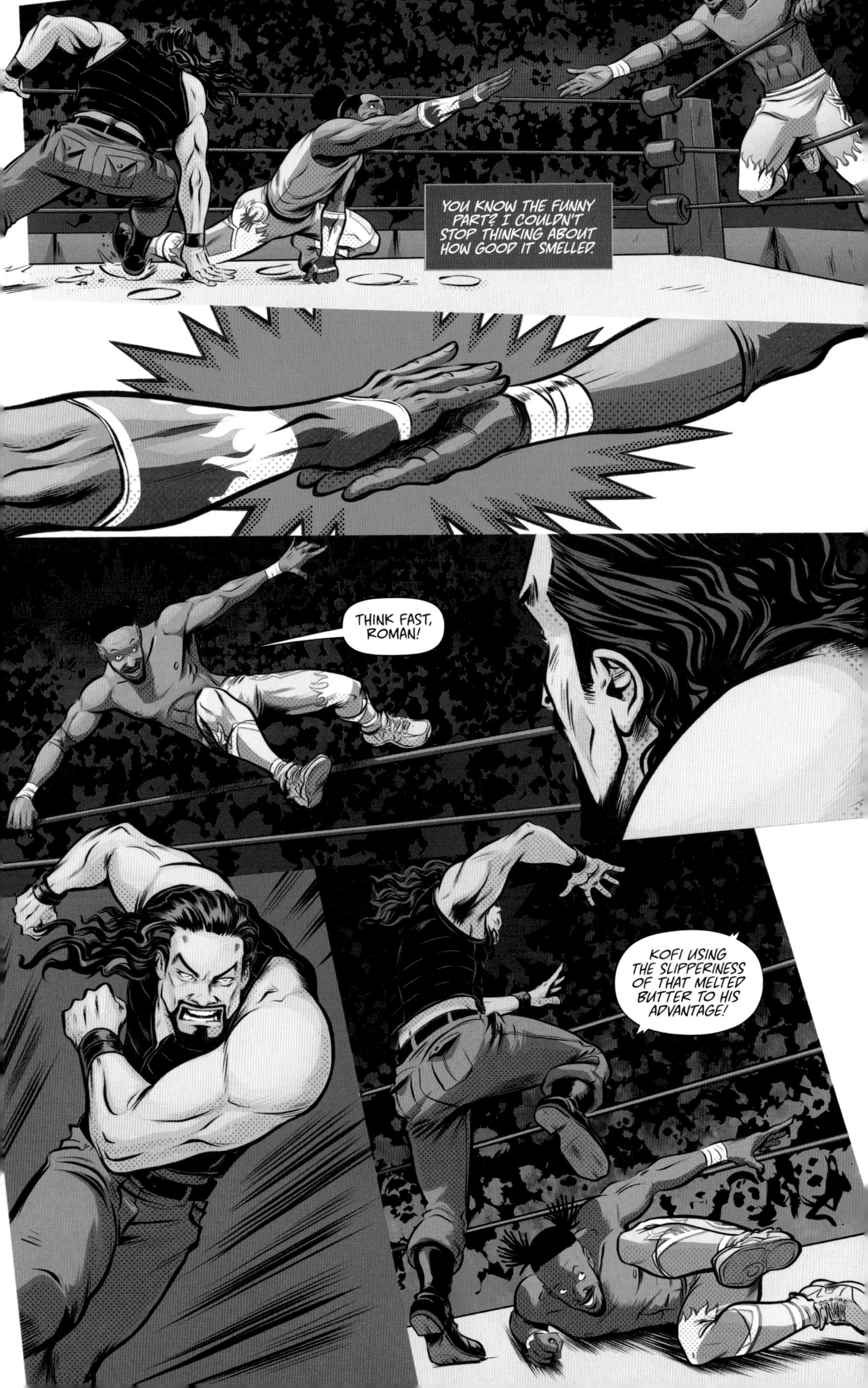
YOU KNOW THE FUNNY PART? I COULDN'T STOP THINKING ABOUT HOW GOOD IT SMELLED.
THINK FAST, ROMAN!
KOFI USING THE SLIPPERINESS OF THAT MELTED BUTTER TO HIS ADVANTAGE!

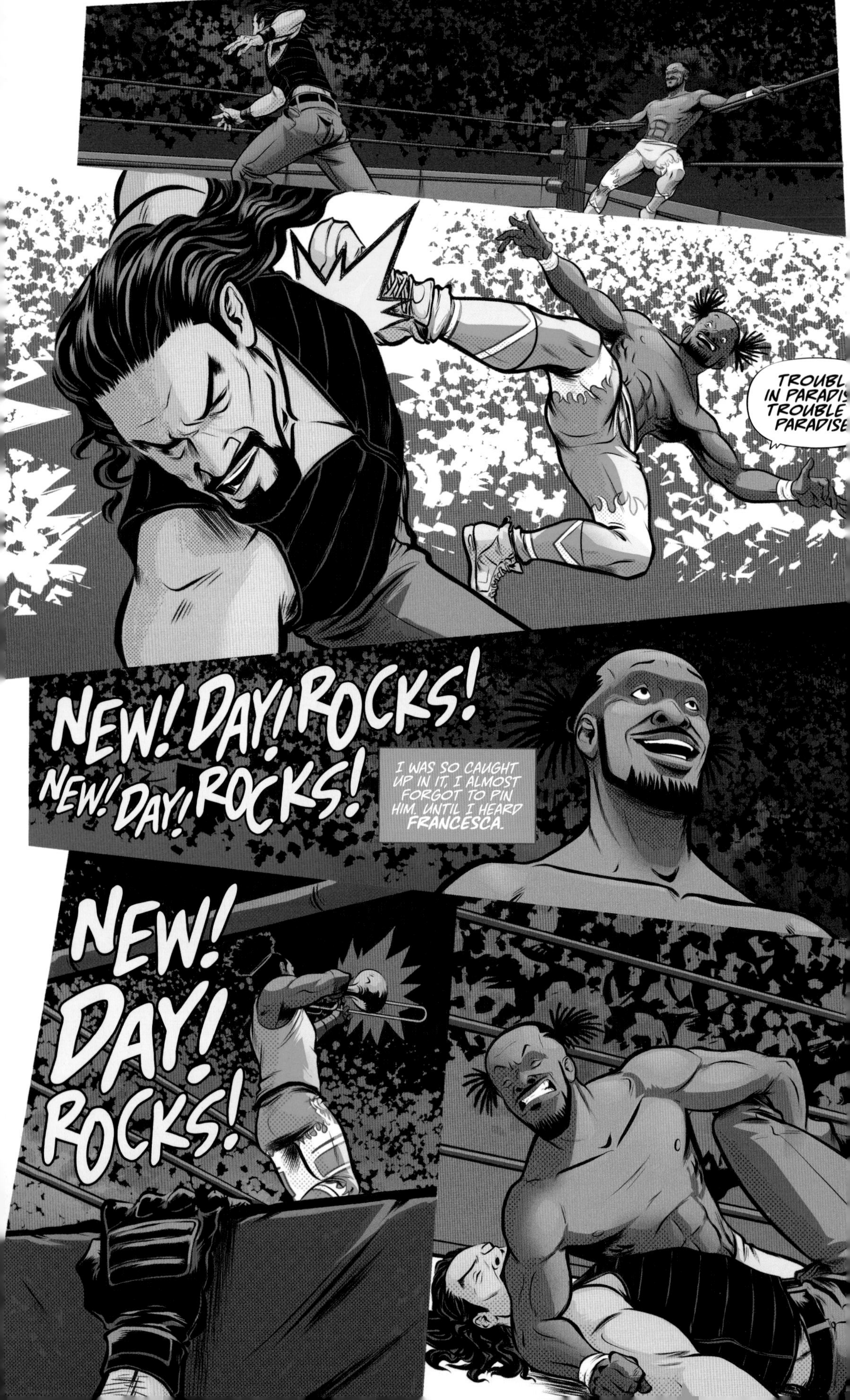
TROUBL
IN PARADIS
TROUBLE
PARADISE
NEW! DAY! ROCKS!
NEW! DAY! ROCKS!
I WAS SO CAUGHT UP IN IT, I ALMOST FORGOT TO PIN HIM. UNTIL I HEARD FRANCESCA.
NEW! DAY! ROCKS!

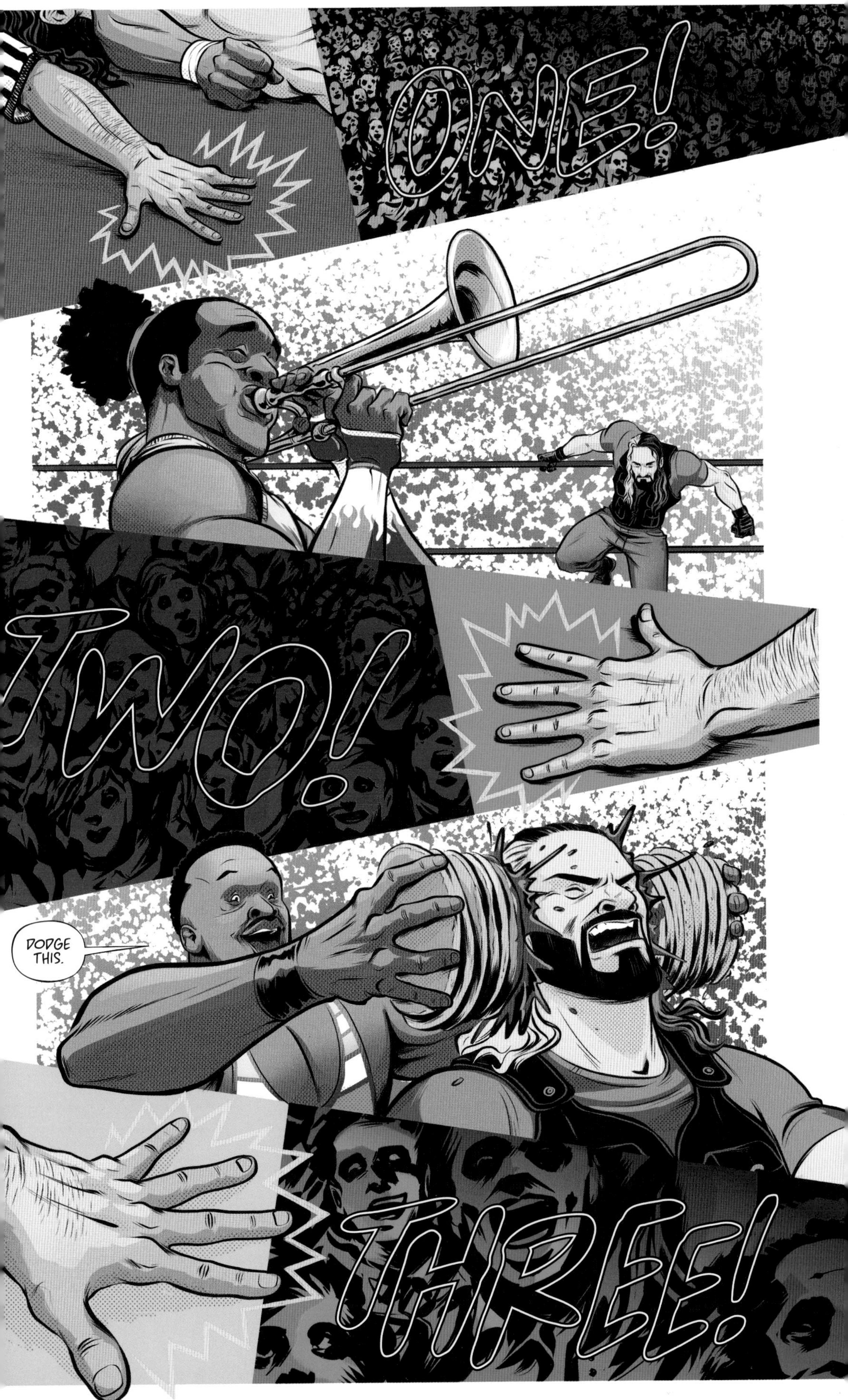
ONE!
TWO!
DODGE THIS.
THREE!

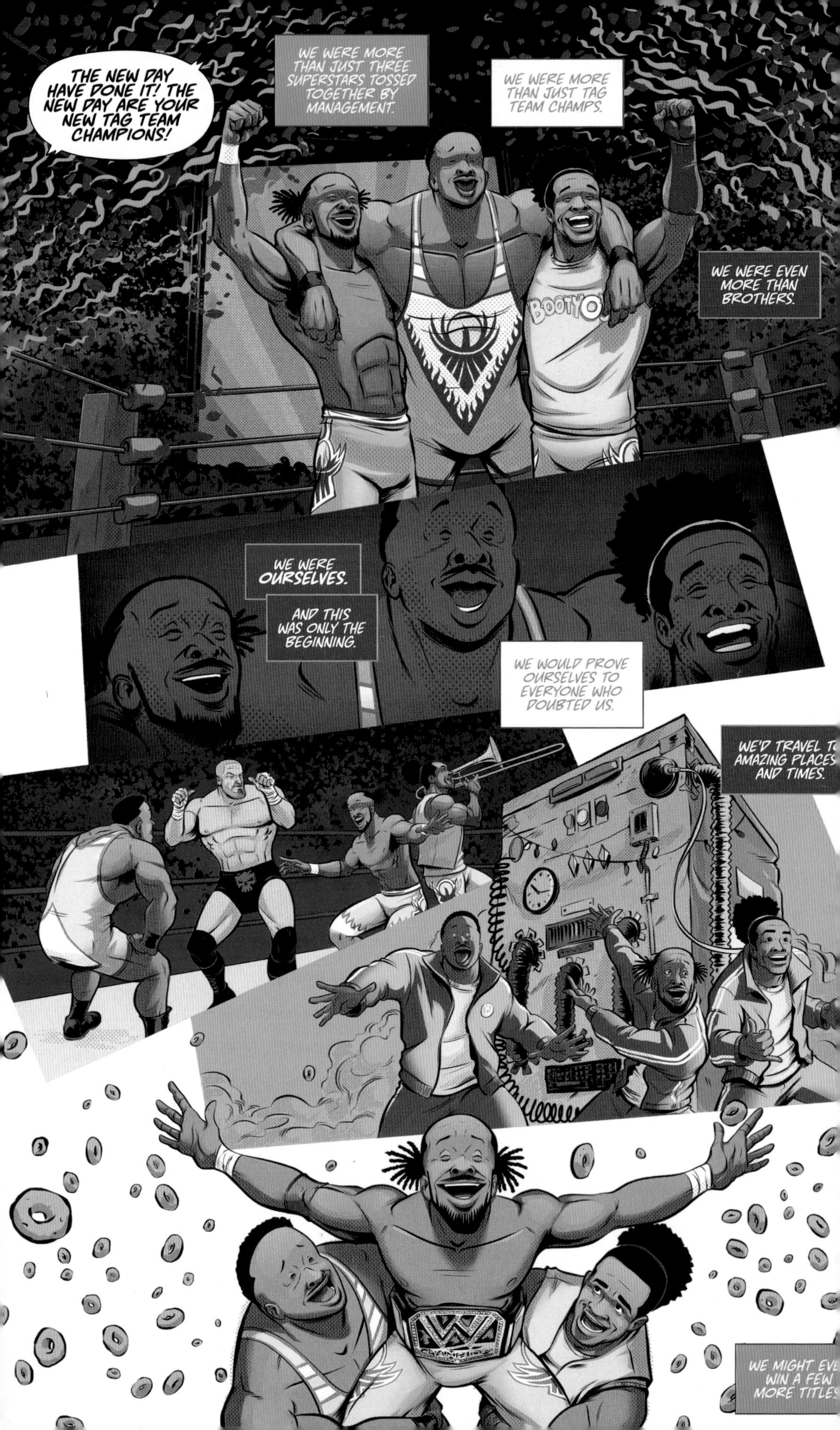

THE NEW DAY HAVE DONE IT! THE NEW DAY ARE YOUR NEW TAG TEAM CHAMPIONS!
WE WERE MORE THAN JUST THREE SUPERSTARS TOSSED TOGETHER BY MANAGEMENT.
WE WERE MORE THAN JUST TAG TEAM CHAMPS.
BOOTY O'S
WE WERE EVEN MORE THAN BROTHERS.
WE WERE OURSELVES.
AND THIS WAS ONLY THE BEGINNING.
WE WOULD PROVE OURSELVES TO EVERYONE WHO DOUBTED US.
WE'D TRAVEL T AMAZING PLACES AND TIMES.
WE MIGHT EV WIN A FEW MORE TITLE

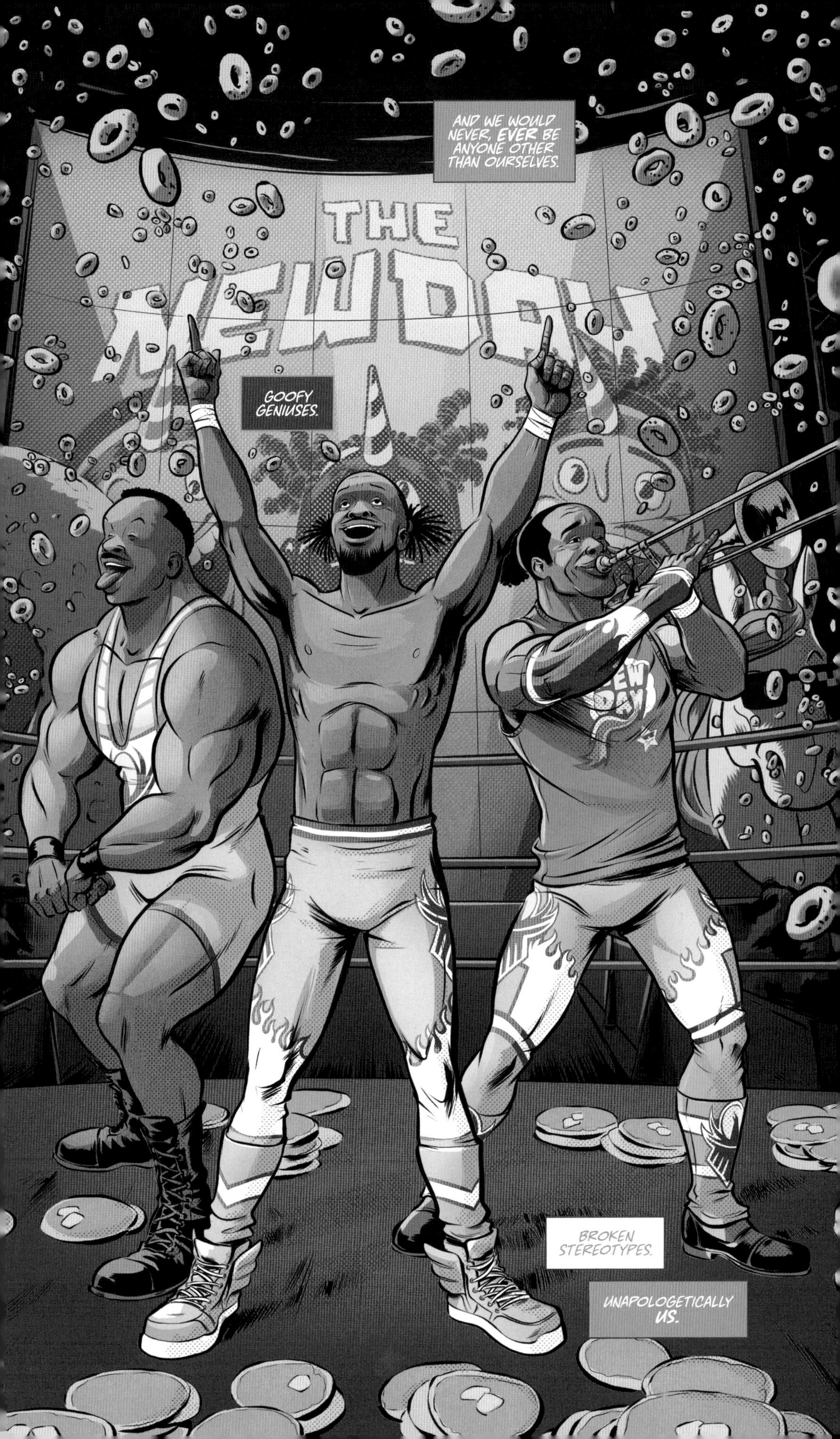
AND WE WOULD NEVER, **EVER** BE ANYONE OTHER THAN OURSELVES.
THE NEW DAY
GOOFY GENIUSES.
BROKEN STEREOTYPES.
UNAPOLOGETICALLY **US.**

COVER
GALLERY

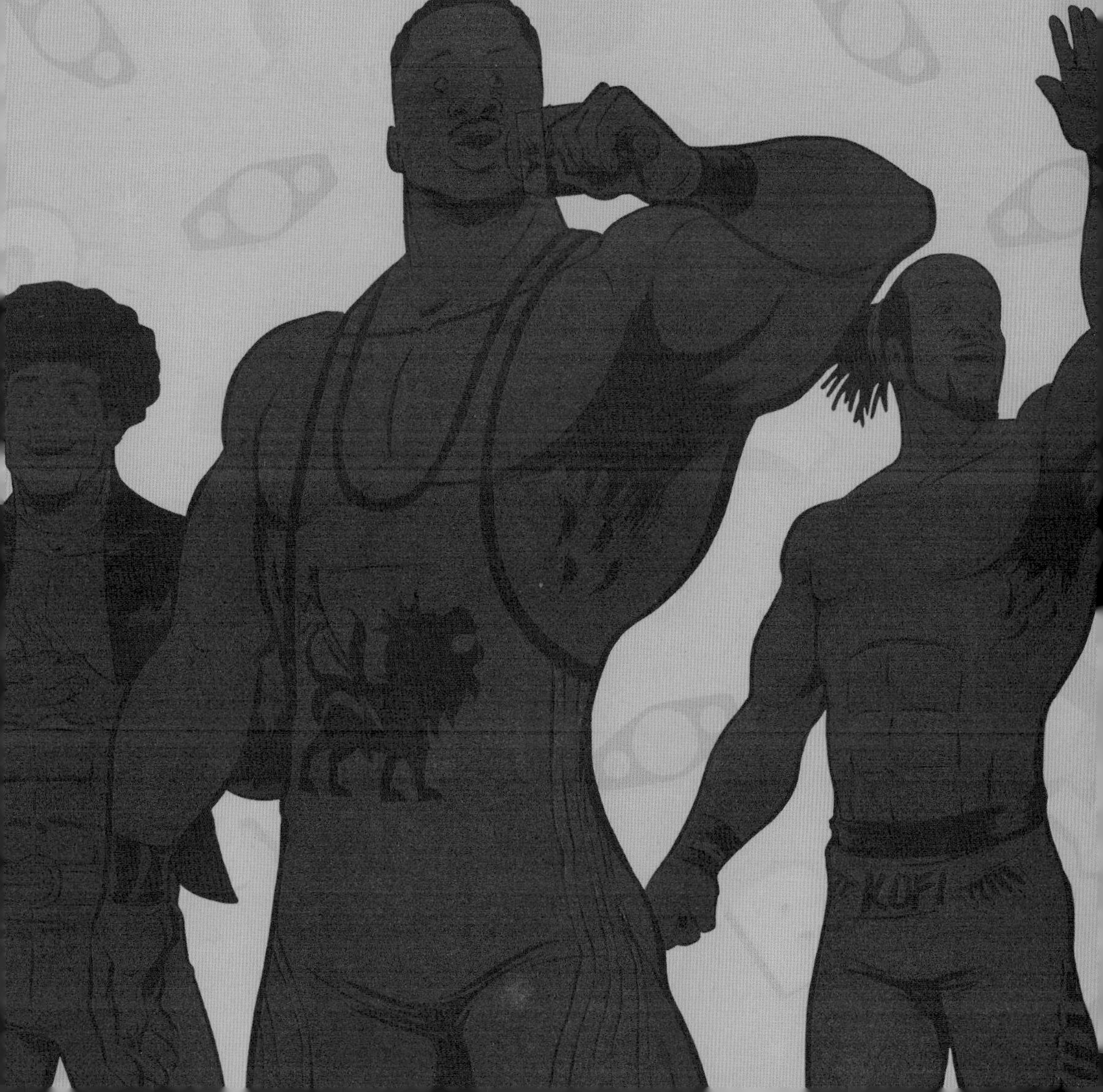
KOFI

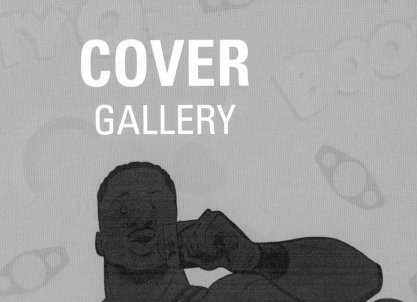

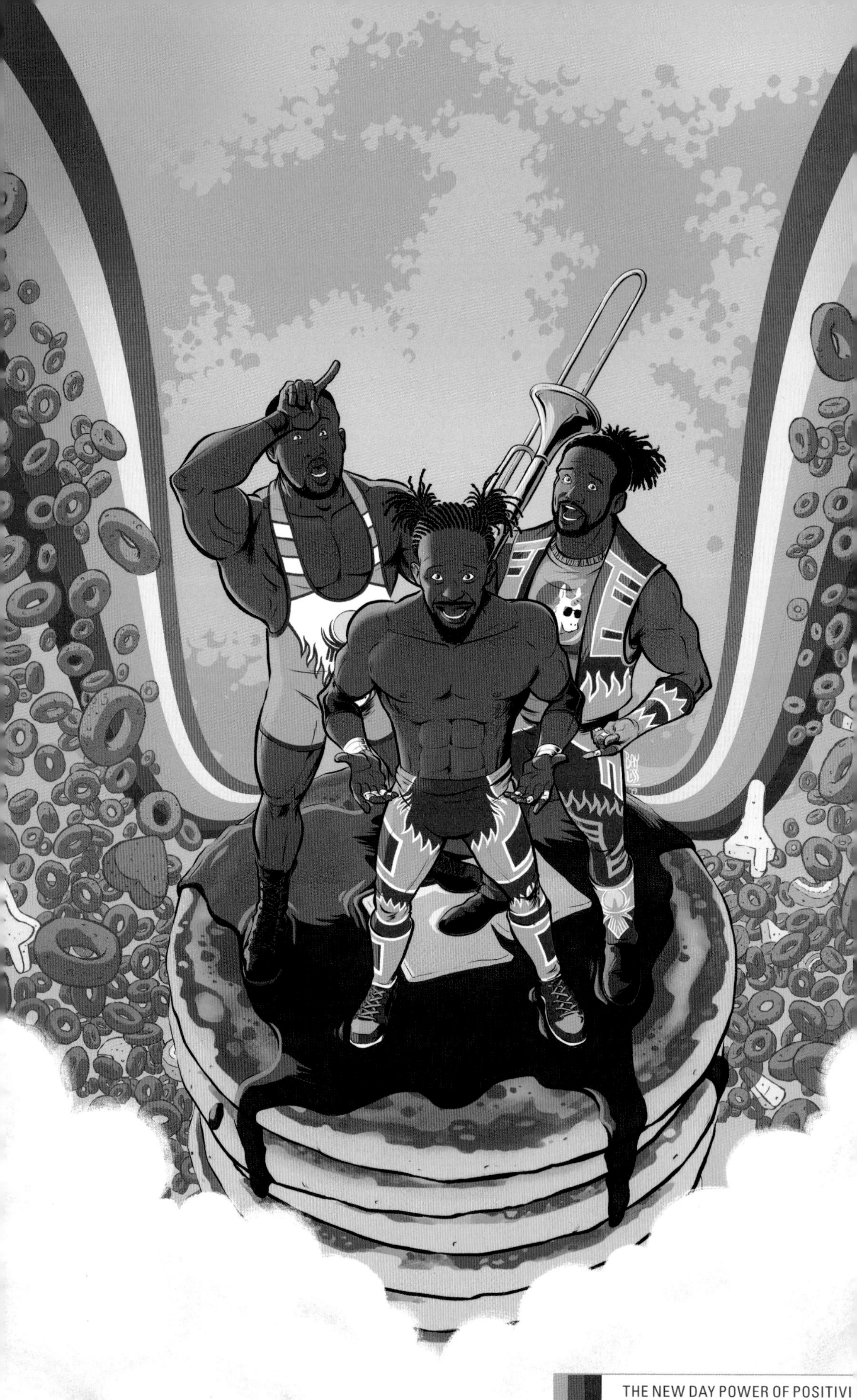

THE NEW DAY POWER OF POSITIVI
#1 MAIN COVER **DANIEL BAYLI**

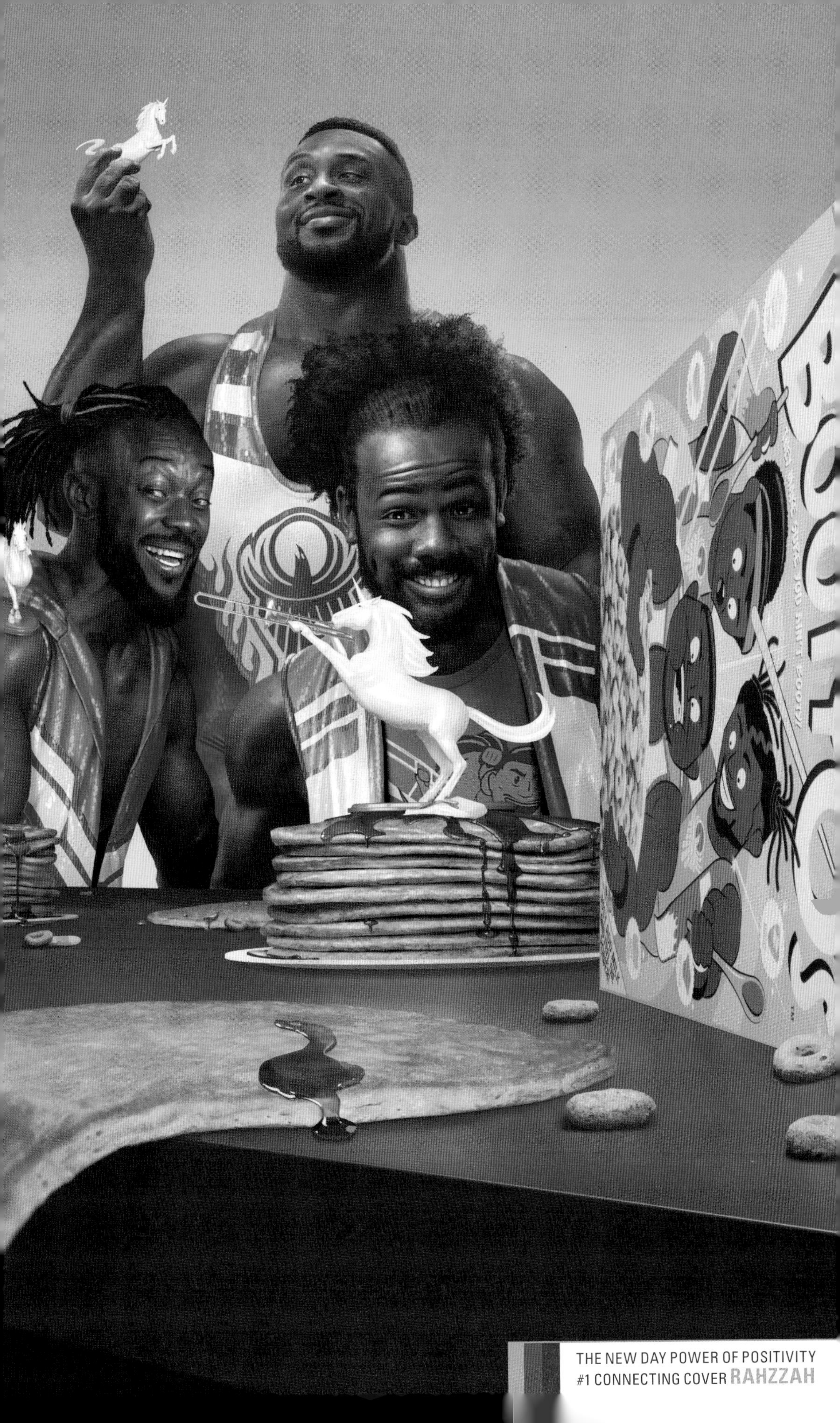

THE NEW DAY POWER OF POSITIVITY
#1 CONNECTING COVER **RAHZZAH**

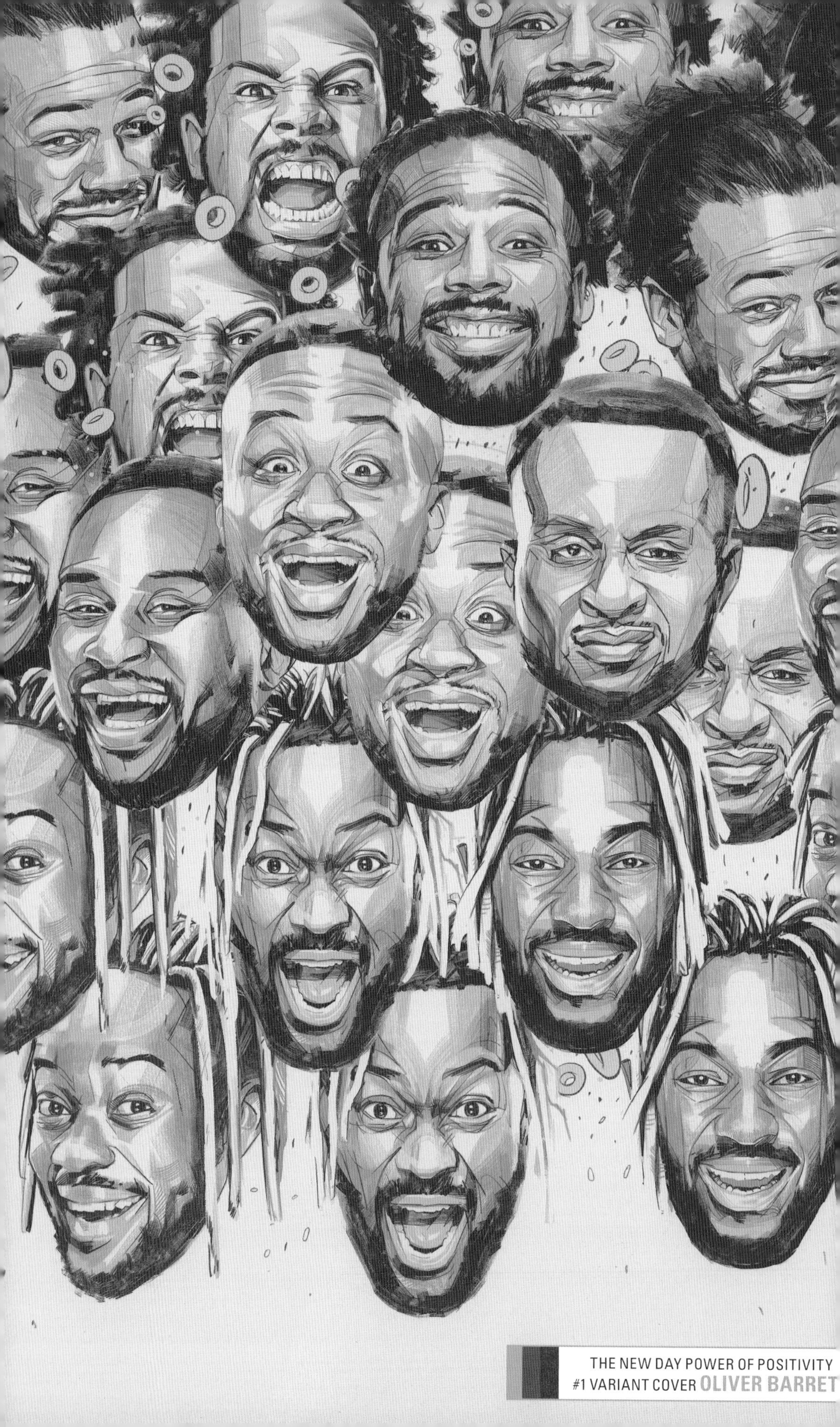

THE NEW DAY POWER OF POSITIVITY
#1 VARIANT COVER **OLIVER BARRETT**

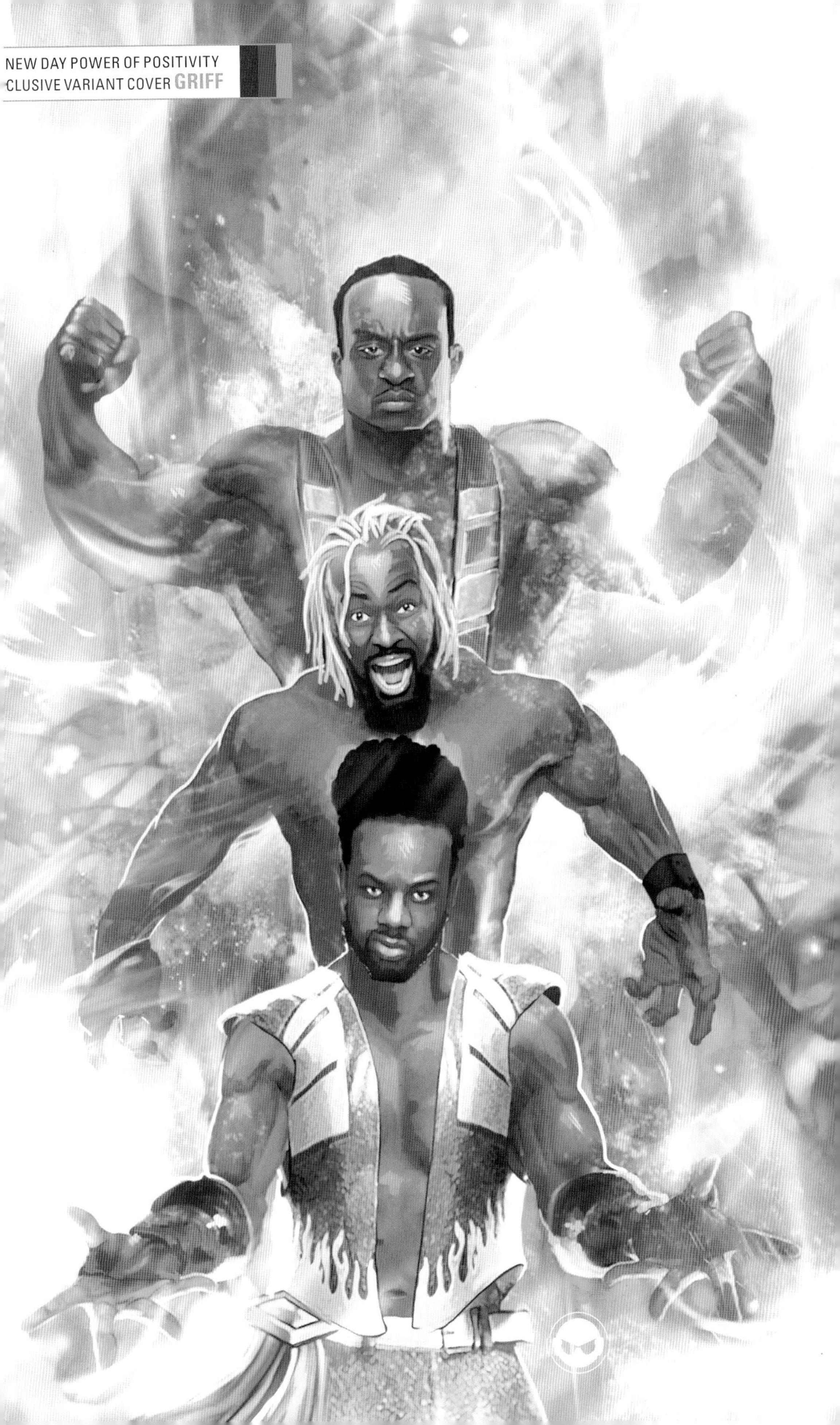
NEW DAY POWER OF POSITIVITY
CLUSIVE VARIANT COVER GRIFF

THE NEW DAY POWER OF POSITIVITY
#2 MAIN COVER **DANIEL BAYLISS**

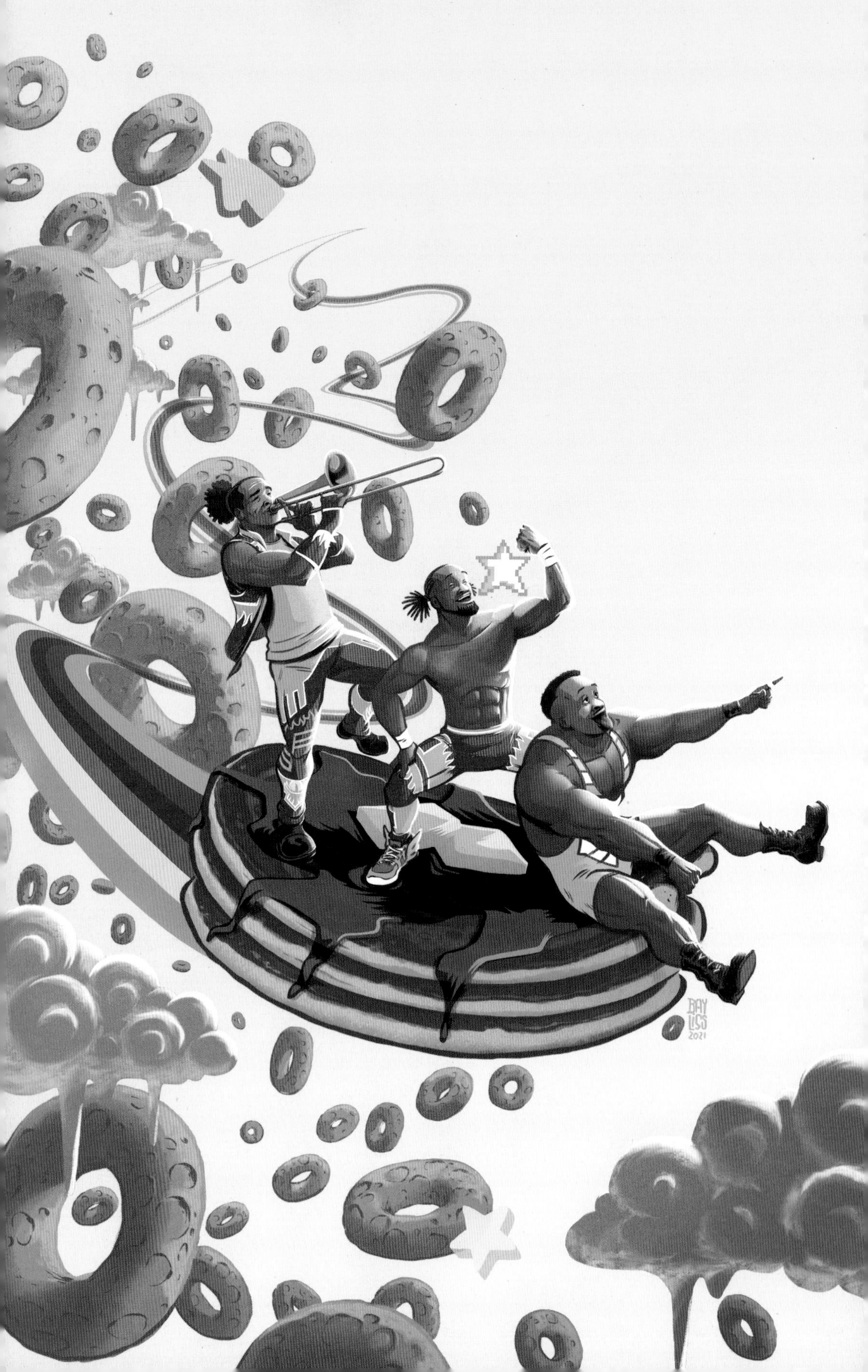
BAY LISS 2021

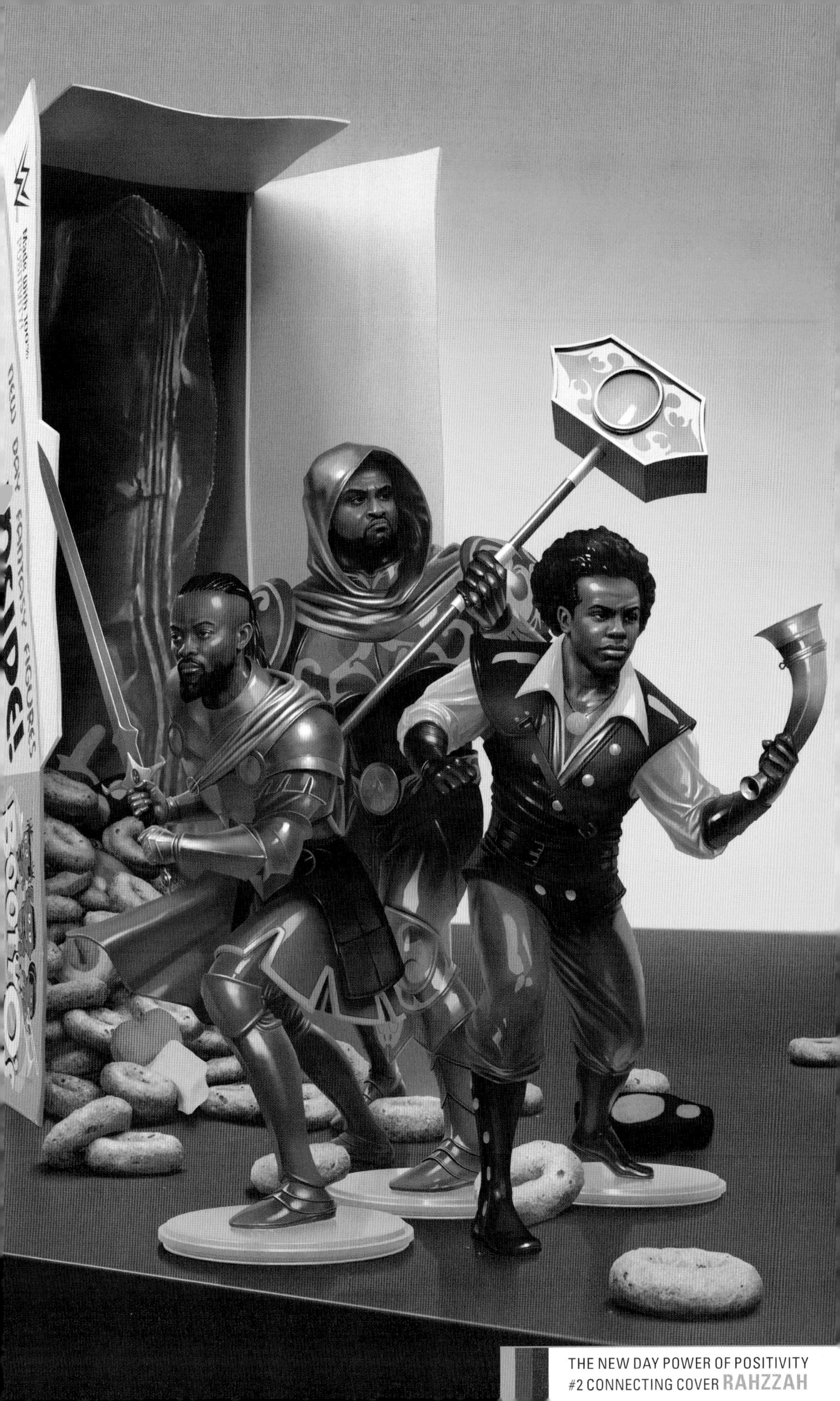
NEW DAY FANTASY FIGURES

THE NEW DAY POWER OF POSITIVITY
#2 CONNECTING COVER **RAHZZAH**

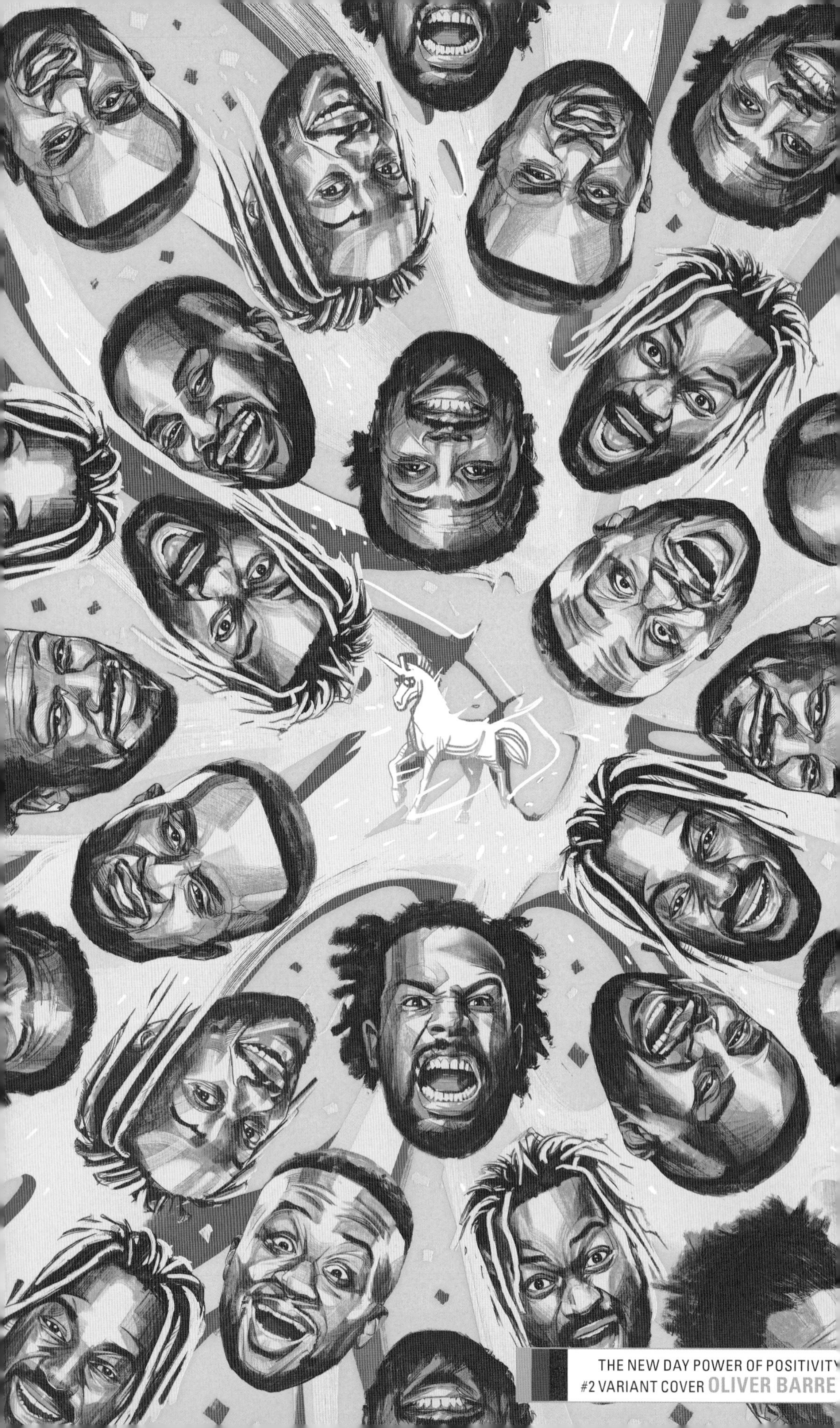

THE NEW DAY POWER OF POSITIVITY
#2 VARIANT COVER OLIVER BARRE

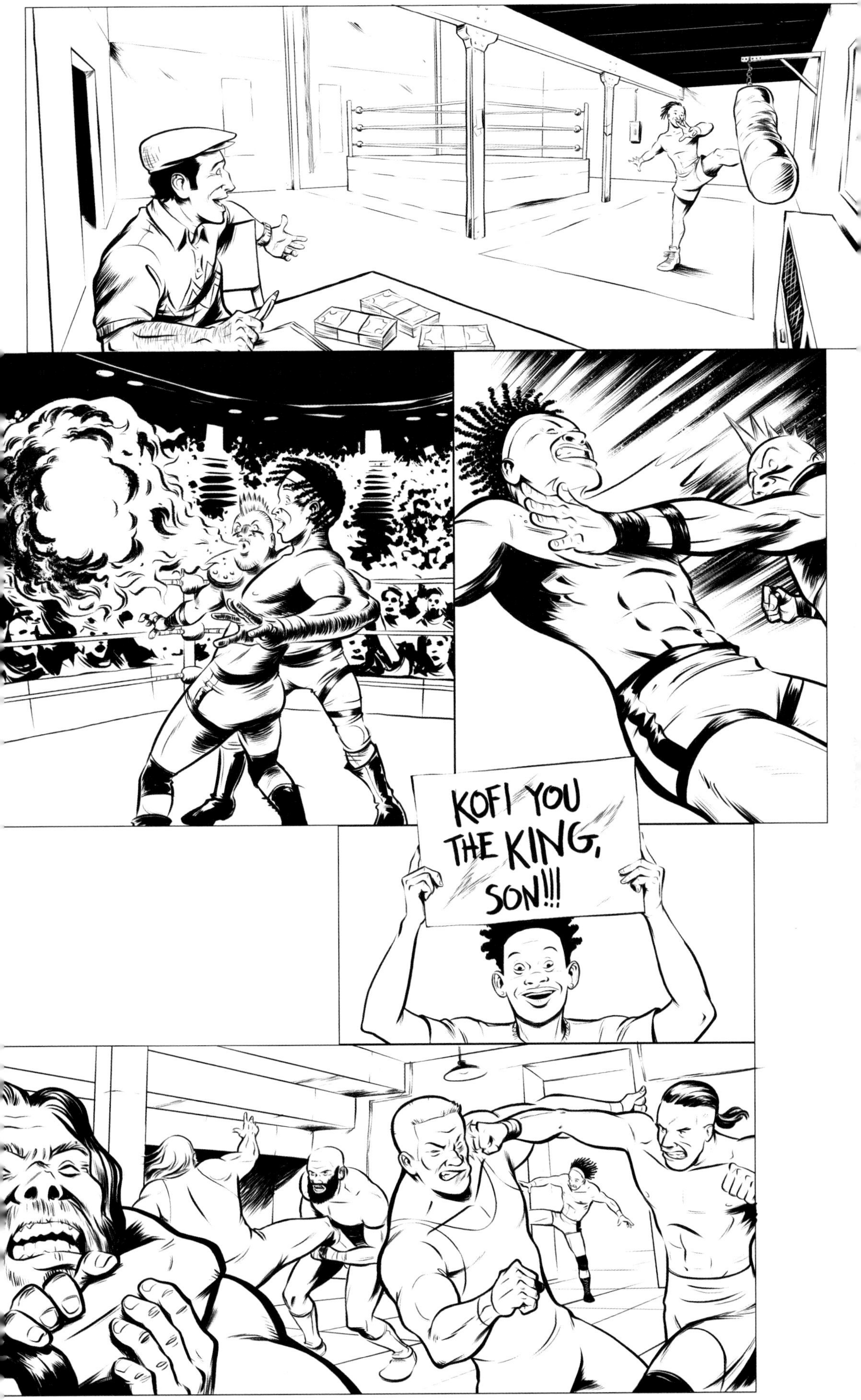
KOFI YOU THE KING, SON!!!

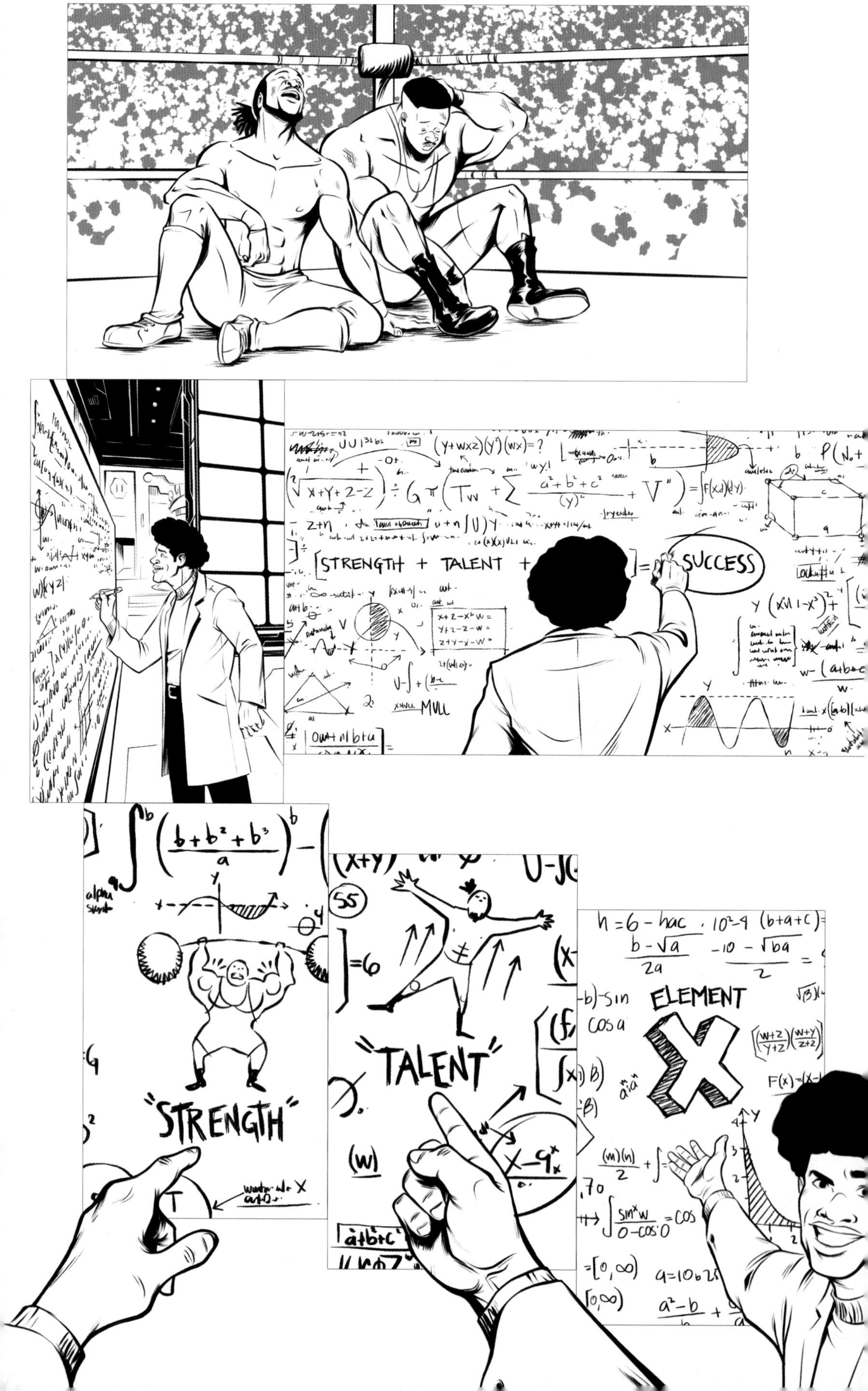

STRENGTH + TALENT +
= SUCCESS
"STRENGTH"
"TALENT"
ELEMENT X

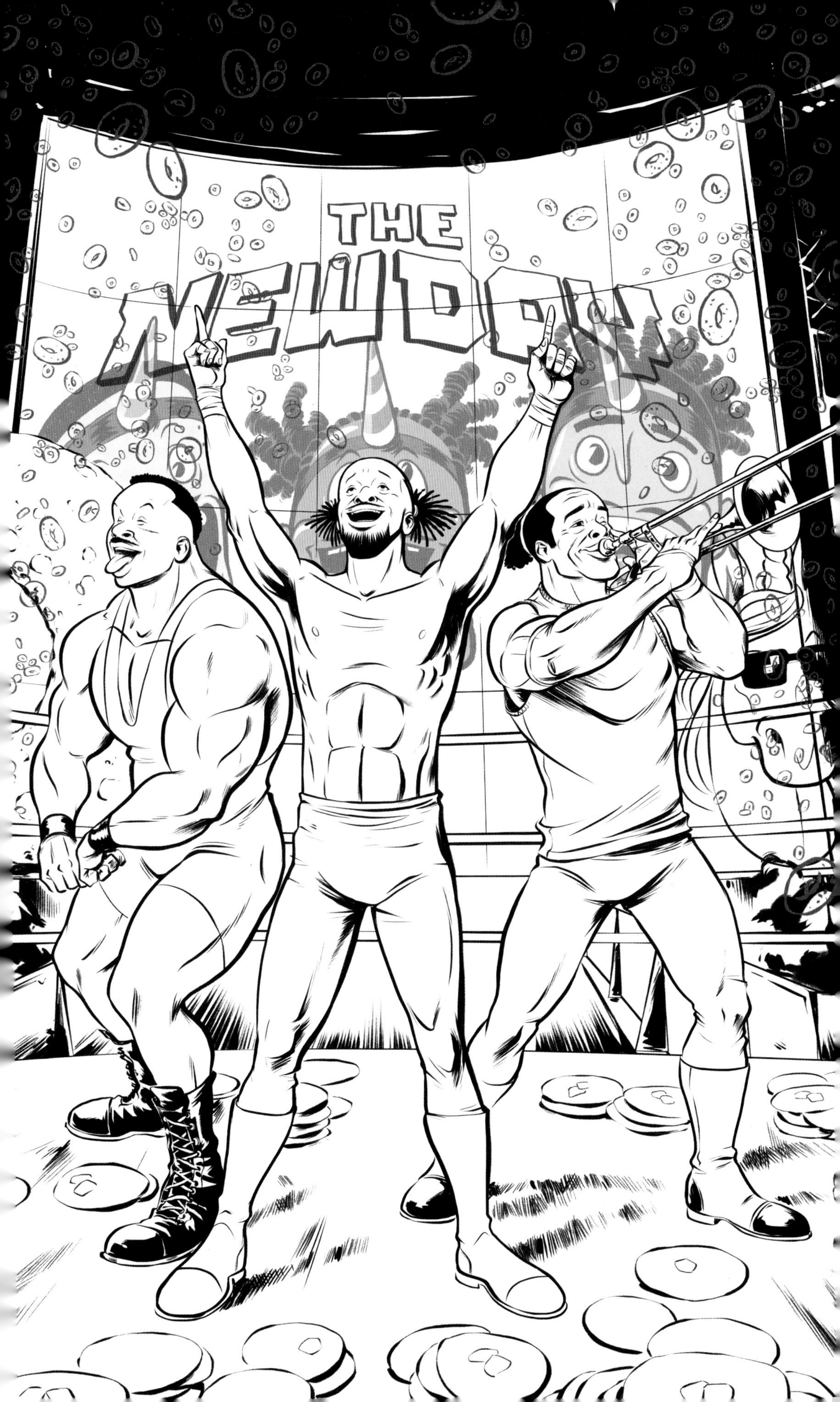
THE
NEW DAY

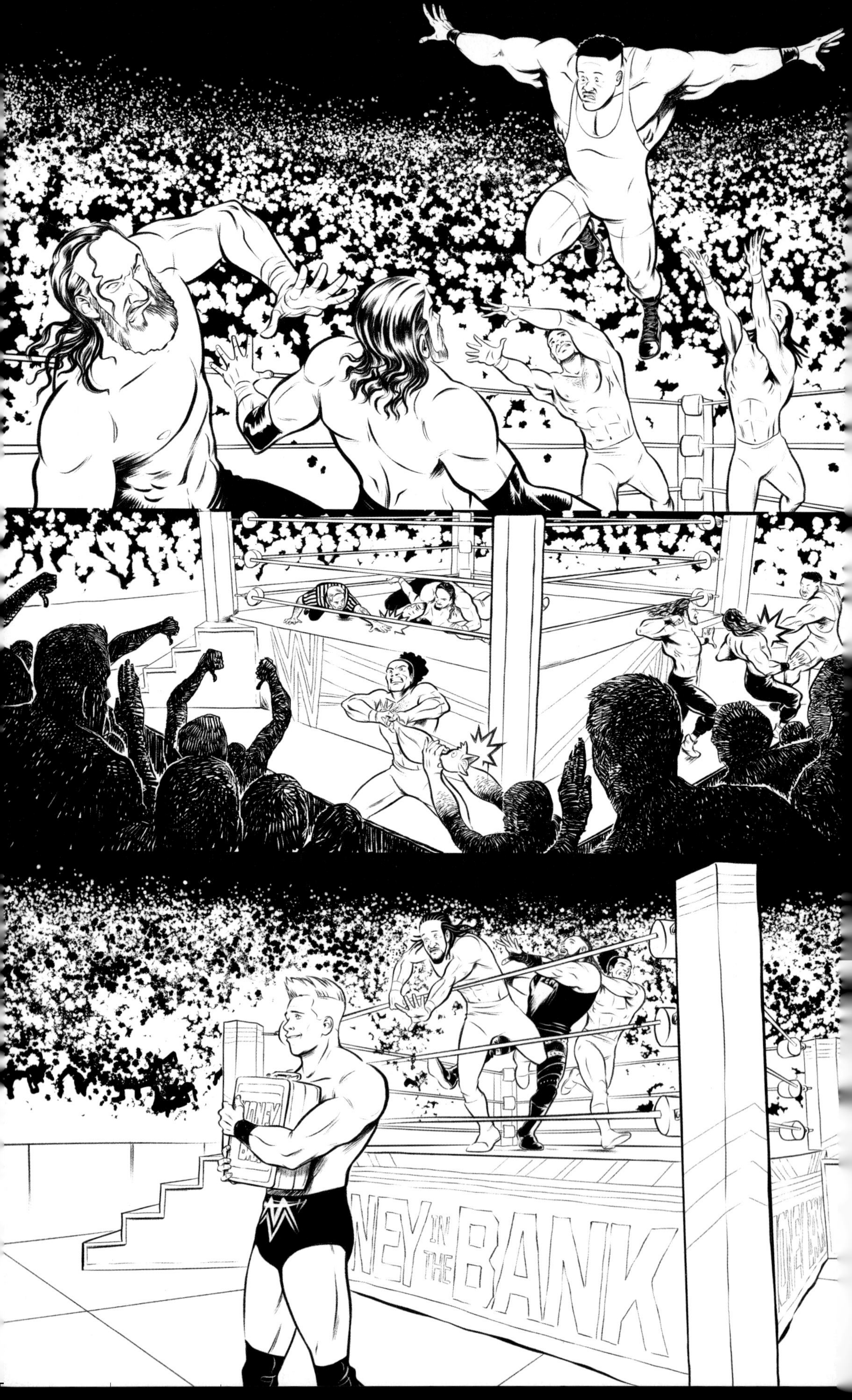
NEY IN THE BANK

DISCOVER
VISIONARY CREATORS

KIERON GILLEN DAN MORA
TAMRA BONVILLAIN
ONCE & FUTURE
VOLUME ONE
THE KING IS UNDEAD

JAMES TYNION IV
WERTHER DELL'EDERA
MIQUEL MUERTO
SOMETHING is KILLING the CHILDREN
VOLUME ONE
SCOTT SNYDER

Brian Azzarello · Maria Llovet
FAITHLESS

GRANT MORRISON DAN MORA
Klaus
How Santa Claus Began

SIMON SPURRIER × MATÍAS BERGARA
CODA
VOLUME ONE
"This one is really special!"
—JEFF LEMIRE
New York Times bestselling writer of Black Hammer

matt kindt tyler jenkins
GRASS KINGS

BOOM! STUDIOS

AVAILABLE AT YOUR LOCAL COMICS SHOP AND BOOKSTORE

To find a comics shop in your area, visit www.comicshoplocator.com

WWW.**BOOM-STUDIOS**.COM

Once & Future
Kieron Gillen, Dan Mora
Volume 1
ISBN: 978-1-68415-491-3 | $16.99 US

Something is Killing the Children
James Tynion IV, Werther Dell'Edera
Volume 1
ISBN: 978-1-68415-558-3 | $14.99 US

Faithless
Brian Azzarello, Maria Llovet
ISBN: 978-1-68415-432-6 | $17.99 US

Klaus
Grant Morrison, Dan Mora
Klaus: How Santa Claus Began SC
ISBN: 978-1-68415-393-0 | $15.99 US
Klaus: The New Adventures of Santa Claus HC
ISBN: 978-1-68415-666-5 | $17.99 US

Coda
Simon Spurrier, Matias Bergara
Volume 1
ISBN: 978-1-68415-321-3 | $14.99 US
Volume 2
ISBN: 978-1-68415-369-5 | $14.99 US
Volume 3
ISBN: 978-1-68415-429-6 | $14.99 US

Grass Kings
Matt Kindt, Tyler Jenkins
Volume 1
ISBN: 978-1-64144-362-3 | $17.99 US
Volume 2
ISBN: 978-1-64144-557-3 | $17.99 US
Volume 3
ISBN: 978-1-64144-650-1 | $17.99 US

Bone Parish
Cullen Bunn, Jonas Scharf
Volume 1
ISBN: 978-1-64144-337-1 | $14.99 US
Volume 2
ISBN: 978-1-64144-542-9 | $14.99 US
Volume 3
ISBN: 978-1-64144-543-6 | $14.99 US

Ronin Island
Greg Pak, Giannis Milonogiannis
Volume 1
ISBN: 978-1-64144-576-4 | $14.99 US
Volume 2
ISBN: 978-1-64144-723-2 | $14.99 US
Volume 3
ISBN: 978-1-64668-035-1 | $14.99 US

Victor LaValle's Destroyer
Victor LaValle, Dietrich Smith
ISBN: 978-1-61398-732-2 | $19.99 US

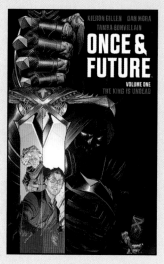

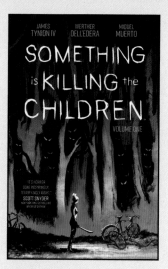

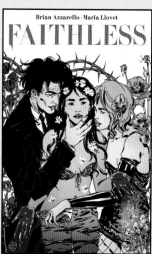

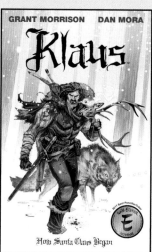

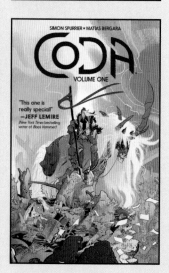

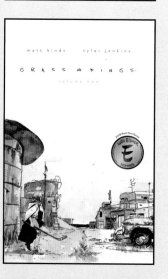

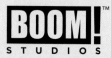